3rd EDITION

Entrepreneur
MAGAZINE'S

ULTIMATE

GUIDE TO

Google

AdWords

FREE!
GOOGLE
SUCCESS TOOLKIT
— $85 VALUE —
PLUS MARKETING
SOFTWARE
Details inside!

How To Access 100 Million People in 10 Minutes

PERRY MARSHALL AND BRYAN TODD

EP
Entrepreneur
PRESS®

Entrepreneur Press, Publisher
Cover design: Beth Hansen-Winter
Composition and production: Eliot House Productions

This publication is designed to provide accurate and authoritative information in regard to the subject matter covered. It is sold with the understanding that the publisher is not engaged in rendering
legal, accounting, or other professional services. If legal advice or other expert assistance is required,
the services of a competent professional person should be sought.

Library of Congress Cataloging-in-Publication Data
Marshall, Perry S.
    Ultimate guide to Google AdWords advertising: how to access 100 million people in 10
minutes/by Perry Marshall and Bryan Todd.
    p. cm.
    Rev. ed. of: Entrepreneur magazine's ultimate guide to Google AdWords: how to access 100
million people in 10 minutes. 2nd ed. ©2010
    ISBN-10: 1-59918-441-9 (alk. paper)
    ISBN-13: 978-1-59918-441-8 (alk. paper)
    1. Internet advertising. 2. Google. 3. Web search engines. I. Todd, Bryan. II. Marshall, Perry S.
Entrepreneur magazine's ultimate guide to Google AdWords. III. Title.
HF6146.I58M36 2012
659.14'4—dc23   2012011323

Printed in the United States of America

16 15 14 13 12   10 9 8 7 6 5 4 3 2 1

Contents

Preface: Wait! Before You Read This Book xi

CHAPTER 1

How to Force Prospects to Choose Your Site
and Buy from You, Not Your Competition 1

Here's How to Make Sure They Find *You* and Buy from *You*. Not Someone Else. 4

CHAPTER 2

How to Build Your Own Autopilot Marketing Machine 9

It All Starts When People Search for Something. 10

The Search Process. 12

A Few Tools You Need If You're Just Getting Started 13

CHAPTER 3

How to Build a Google Campaign from Scratch—The *Right* Way 15

The Best Way to Research Your Market. 16

How to Set up Your Campaign 20

Things You Can Tweak Right Now. 24

CHAPTER 4

Organizing Your Campaign: How to Pay Less and Get More Clicks 27

What Google Doesn't Tell You: The Wrong Way to Organize
an AdWords Campaign. 28

The Right Way to Organize an AdWords Campaign 29

Split Test Your Ads! 32

The "Peel & Stick" Strategy: Get a Higher CTR Just by Moving
Your Keywords into New Ad Groups 35

CHAPTER 5

Develop High-Quality Keyword Lists to Craft Killer Headlines 41

More Tools for Your Toolbox: Google's Free Keyword Tool 43

Your Ultimate Keyword List 45

Second-Guessing Your Customers 48

More on the Psychology of Keywords 49

More Markets, More Cash: How to Get Beyond the "Obvious" Keywords 50

Expanding Your Control over Your Keywords: Uncover Keyword Niches,
Save Money . . . and Keep Your Sanity 55

The Killer Keyword Secrets 57

Headlines and Killer Copy from *Cosmopolitan* Magazine 58

CHAPTER 6

How to Write Google Ads That Attract Eyeballs, Get Clicks, and Earn You Money 61

Great Headlines: Riveting to Your Customer, Dead Boring to Anyone Else 62

Your Ad Text: Where Your Inner Salesman Comes Alive 64

The "Goldilocks Theory": Why the Best AdWords Ads Are Never Over-the-Top . . . 66

Focusing Your Ads to Save $$$ on Clicks 68

If the Guys at the Bar Will Buy It, You've Got a Winning Ad 70

CHAPTER 7

Knowing Your Numbers = Money in the Bank: How Google's Conversion Tracking Tells You What's Working 71

Bloated Corporate Advertising Budgets vs. Your Lean, Mean Traffic Machine . . . 72

How to Set Up Google to Track Your Conversions and Grow Your Business 73

Counterintuitive Bidding Strategies 77

The Savvy Marketer: How to Track Your Sales Numbers and Go on Autopilot . . 80

CHAPTER 8

How to Triple Your CTR (and Cut Your Bid Prices by Two-Thirds, if You Want)—No Genius Required 83

How to Set Up a Split Test: It's a No-Brainer 85

The Split-Tester Tool and How to Use It 86

CHAPTER 9

The Winning Method the World's Smartest Marketers Stole from the Wright Brothers 89

How the Wright Brothers' Savvy Testing Method Made Them "First In Flight"... 90
People Who Test, Fly. People Who Rely on Brute Force, Die. 92
Marketing Misery Is *Not* Necessary 93

CHAPTER 10
Triple Your Traffic with Google's Display Network 95
How Is This Different from Regular Google Searches? 97
How to Turn It On and Off. 97
Rolling Out a Successful Display Network Campaign. 99
Google Wants "Themes" 99
There's More than One Way to Target Traffic on the Display Network 100
How Do I Find Out Where Google is Showing My Ads?. 101
How Does Google Decide Where to Show My Ads?. 102
The Wild Phenomenon We Call the "Jet Stream" 103
What Are Managed Placements? 104
Keys to Making Managed Placements Work. 106
The Third Way to Find Your Audience: Topic Targeting 106
How Google's Bots Find You New Customers. 107

CHAPTER 11
Google Image Ads: Banner Advertising Is Here to Stay 109
Are Display Ads on Google a Huge Deal? Yup. 110
How to Set It Up 112
Getting Ads Made 114
Rare Find: A Newbie AdWords Advertiser
Ready to Do Image Ads 116

CHAPTER 12
Local Advertising on Google: Mostly Virgin Territory
How Retailers, Restaurants, and Service Businesses Can Beat the Yellow Pages..... 119
You're Reaching Two Kinds of People, Not Just One. 121
How to Reach the First Person. 121
How to Reach the Second Person 122
Hone Your Chops on a Local Test Campaign Before You Go National 124
Something Called "Google Places" 124
How to Be Sure People Find You on Their Mobile Devices 127

CHAPTER 13
Slashing Your Bid Prices: Quality Score and How Google
Rewards You for Relevance "Which One Do You Think Will
Get Us to the Martinis Faster?" 129
It Ain't His Neck Under the Guillotine Blade. 130
Here's How Google Rewards You for Relevance 130

The Quality Score Story 131

There's Low Quality Score, and Then There's Being "Suspended" 132

Quality Score: What It Is, How It's Measured, When It Matters,

and When It Doesn't 133

Quality Score Is a Trailing Indicator, Not a Leading Indicator 133

Acting All Uppity Won't Earn You a Penny More 136

CHAPTER 14

The Dark Side of Google **139**

The Most Dangerous Number in Any Business Is: **"ONE"** **140**

"My Site Is Suspended. What Do I Do?" 146

Is Google "Evil"? 147

How to Diversify in a World Where Google Is King 148

Build a Site That Converts *All* Forms of Qualified Traffic 148

CHAPTER 15

Google, Vegas, and Those Who Live by Gaming the System **149**

Everyone's Been Talking About the Google Bans—As If It's Something New . . . 150

Dear Reader, I Hope You Read That Twice 152

A Warning Against "Game the System" Mentality 153

CHAPTER 16

The Butt-Ugly Truth About Social Media, and the Beautiful

Untold Story: How to Convert the World's Number-One Time-Suck

into a Treasure Trove of Customer Insights **155**

How to Use Social Media to Do Market Research and Get Great Copy Bullets . . . 159

CHAPTER 17

How to Harness the Psychic Power of Social Media

in Your Google Campaigns **163**

Right-Angle Targeting 164

How We Used Facebook Right-Angle Targeting to Improve

Google Campaigns by 11 Percent Overnight 165

The Revolutionary "One Sentence" Principle 166

Why Facebook Data and Google AdWords Are a Super-Powerful Combo 167

How to Glean Right-Angle Insights from Facebook 167

The "Handshake" Tool 168

CHAPTER 18

How to Get Customers to Eat Out of Your Hand: Get the Biggest

Money from Your Market When You Give Your Customers

Exactly What They Want to Buy **173**

How We Used Google AdWords to Pick a Title for a Seminar. 174

How to Be Sure There's a More Profitable Market for Your Idea, By
     Developing a Product *After* Your Customers Tell You What They Want 176

What You Learn When This Doesn't Work the First Time Out 177

CHAPTER 19

The Most-Ignored Secret Behind the Most
Profitable Marketing Campaigns in the World........................ 183

What Is a USP?. 184

How to Identify Your USP. 184

Say It in Just One Sentence: Your Elevator Speech 186

Your USP Makes a Great Google Ad. 187

Big Ass. Big Ass Fans. How to Build an Unforgettable Personality
     Around Your USP. 187

Why a Good USP May Save Your Life, Literally. 189

The Number-One Symptom of a Bad USP Is 190

A Great USP Is Always a Work in Progress 191

CHAPTER 20

How Email Transforms Those Expensive Clicks into
Long-Term, Profitable Customers................................. 193

How to Put Personality and Pizzazz into Your Email Marketing. 194

Power in the Personal: Six Keys to Email Marketing Success. 196

A Medium That Will Never Go Away 202

Opt-Ins: More Than Just an Email Address?. 202

They Can Knock Off Your Product, But They Can't Knock Off *You* 203

CHAPTER 21

The One Magic Number That Defines
the Power of Your Website 205

Dollars Mean More Than Percentages 206

How to Use Split Testing to Boost Your Visitor Value 207

CHAPTER 22

Maintaining Your Edge: How to Consistently Stay Ahead of
Your Competition in Google AdWords 213

Custom Geo Targeting 214

Other Ways to Precision Target 216

Reality Check. 218

Why I Love AdWords!. 219

CHAPTER 23

Persuasive Ad Copy: The Ultimate Silver Bullet:
How to Mint Money with the Printed Word 221
Your First Rookie Lesson in Classic Salesmanship 222

CHAPTER 24

So You Have a Killer Sales Machine. Now What?:
The New Army of Generation-X Marketers 233
The Improvements Don't Just Add Up, They Multiply! 234
Expanding into Other Media: Profiting from the Winner-Take-All Phenomenon .. 236
Affiliates: The Momentum Kicks In 237
How to Grind Down Your Competition: A Google Lesson from Han Solo 237
Nouveaux Skin Care Company Gets an Unexpected Turn in Advertising 240
America's Second Harvest Wins by Attrition and We Donate to
   Hurricane Katrina Victims 241

CHAPTER 25

How to Get High Rankings in Google's Organic
(Non-PPC) Search Results 243
Search Engine Optimization 244
How to Get Started with SEO 245
Be Realistic in Your Time-Frame Expectations 246
Keyword Selection for Organic Search Ranking Success 247
Keyword Placement for Organic Search Ranking Success 247
How to Get Natural Looking Links from Important Pages 248
Choose Your Links Wisely 249
Get Links from Trusted Pages That Match Your Topic 250
Count the Number of Links on the Referring Page 250
Avoid Getting Involved with Run-of-the-Site Links 250
Maintain Consistency in the Format of Your Incoming Link URLs 250
Get Your Keywords into Your Anchor Text 251
Go for Deep Links 251
Beware of the "Nofollow" Tag 251
Be Careful Who You Link To! 252
Train Your Eye on the Primary Goal—Profits! 252
The Best Place to Start Getting Links 253
Link Outside the Box 254
The Problem with Reciprocal Links 255
Creating and Promoting *Buzz* to Turbo-Charge Your Website Rankings! 256
Don't Sweat the Small Stuff 256
Catching the Local Search Tidal Wave 257

What Really Smart Online Marketers Do 257

CHAPTER 26

Introduction to Remarketing: By Jeff Martyka, Neckties Inc. 259

Terminology 261
How Do I Know if My Remarketing is Working? 261
What Remarketing Indicators Do I Need to Pay Attention To? 262
What Are Some Google Analytics Remarketing Indicators? 264
Enough Talk! Let's Create Some Audiences 265
Creating Remarketing Campaigns in AdWords 268
How Should I Bid on Remarketing Campaigns? 268
Add Ads 270

CHAPTER 27

Place Pages: Google's Gold Mine for Local Business By Dave Jabas 273

Ranking on Page One of Google Used to Be Tough for Local Businesses 274
But That's All Changed 274
Here's Your Free Key to the Front Page of Google 275
How to Optimize Your Place Page for High Rankings 276
Reviews Are Your Most Powerful Online Credibility Tool 277
Reach for the Stars 277
How to Handle a Negative Review 278
Here's Your Secret Weapon for Collecting Steady Online Reviews 279
Dominate Your Local Market Starting Today 280
Google Maps 281

CHAPTER 28

17 Things Yo Momma Never Told You About Google 283

1. Ten Thousand Hours 283
2. The "Before" Circle and the "After" Circle 284
3. The Pie Chart of Desires 284
4. Telltale Signs of Markets 286
5. Impression Share 287
6. Doing AdWords for Clients 288
7. Hyper-Responsive Customers 289
8. Innovation and the Hyper-Responsive Buyer 290
9. Google Lackeys vs. Real Google Reps 290
10. "Would I Send Grandma to this Site?" 291
11. Every Market Has a Hole 291
12. Bootstrapping vs. Venture Capital 292
13. Just Buy the Stuff and Ship It 293
14. Artificially High Bids in a Ferociously Competitive Market 294

15. Personality vs. Transactional Marketing.................................. 295
16. What I Learned from Infomercials 295
17. "Pick the Chicken Clean" 296

CHAPTER 29

That Last Winner-Take-All Edge: Google's Tools for Smarter AdWords Results...................................... 299

The Best AdWords Advertisers Live and Die by AdWords Editor 300
For Broad- and Phrase-Matched Keywords, Know Precisely
  What Your Visitors Typed in to Find You 301
More Thorough and Specific Information in Your Ad Results in More
  Qualified Clicks, More Conversions, More Phone Calls, and
  More Customers in the Door 302
Cut Costs and Earn a Better Quality Score by Slicing Up Your Data
  in New Dimensions 306
What Percentage of the Time are Your Ads Actually Showing?.............. 309
Google Conversion Optimizer 311
Imagine You're 15 Years Old Again............................. 312
Sharpening Your Edge 314

CHAPTER 30

FAQ: Answers to All Your Frequently Asked Questions........................... 317

Organizing and Getting the Most from Your Keywords and Ads.............. 320
The Peel & Stick Method 324
Getting a Better Click-Through Rate 324
Better Landing Pages....................................... 326
Getting Your Customer to Talk to You 327
Testing and Converting Your Traffic 328
Using Special Tools 329
Where and When to Show Your Ads............................. 331
Working in Specialized Markets 333
Google's Regular Search Engine................................ 335
How to Become an Affiliate................................... 335

CHAPTER 31

Signature Victories... 337

Mega-Victories 340

About the Authors 343

Index 345

Wait! Before You Read This Book . . .

f you're brand-new to Google AdWords and you're just getting started, you MUST read this short section first.

■ ■ ■

And:

The first thing you need to do is register for AdWords updates and get the $85.00 of bonuses that come with this book. Get it at www.perrymarshall.com/supplement. Enter your contact information. Inside the members' area you'll find a collection of immediately applicable tools and resources.

Go to www.perrymarshall.com/supplement. Enter your contact information. Once inside the member's area you'll find a collection of supplemental material I consider vital to this book.

OK, now that you've done that, let me tell you how to go about learning AdWords. Please pay attention.

If you're a rank beginner . . .

There's an old saying, "You can't learn to ride a bicycle at a seminar," and it definitely applies to AdWords. AdWords and really everything you ever do in direct marketing is hands-on. It's not theory. It's real-world. It's school-of-hard-knocks.

About the school-of-hard-knocks part: When AdWords was brand new, there were lots of inexpensive clicks and you could find your way by making lots of cheap mistakes.

Those days are over. Today that strategy will get you killed.

When you open a Google AdWords account, go ahead and enter your keywords, write some ads, and set some bid prices. It's OK if you don't really know what you're doing, you'll learn. The first couple of chapters of this book will show you exactly how to do it. But here's the most important thing of all:

Set a low daily budget, say $5.00 or $10.00 per day, to make absolutely sure that your first experience with AdWords is a GOOD one, not a painful one.

Because . . .

The worst thing you can do in your new career as a Google advertiser is accidentally run up $2,500.00 of clicks that you have no idea how you're going to pay for. Most advertisers have to go through some trial-and-error before things really come together. There are many assumptions Google will make about how to set up your account that are wrong, and if you blindly follow its menus, you'll make some costly mistakes.

The best thing you can do is *enjoy the process of watching those clicks come in and see your handiwork produce results.*

One of the most important AdWords strategies we teach is called "Peel & Stick." Make sure you know this. Read about it in Chapter 4.

So yes, go ahead and get started. Roll up your sleeves and jump in. As you go from one chapter to the next, make changes to your Google account. You'll literally be able to see the performance difference in a few hours.

Before you've even spent $10.00 on Google clicks, please make sure you're using this book as your guide. If you don't, you'll make a slew of common mistakes and blow a lot of cash that you could have used to grow your business.

Also, make sure you access the Fanalytix™ software, read the special reports, and see the audios and videos in the Book Bonus members' area. They're at www.perrymarshall.com/supplement.

If You're a Veteran Pay-Per-Click Marketer . . .

This is the 3rd edition of the *Ultimate Guide to Google AdWords*. We've added a bunch of new chapters and segments for those who are already experienced Google advertisers. Here are some of our favorites:

- *Harnessing Social Media.* This is not about "liking" and "Tweeting" and "bookmarking" and being chatty. It will make your Google ads work better but not how you think. What is it? It's very unique. Page 163.
- *The Dark Side of Google.* You must understand the perils, lest you get blindsided. Page 139. And on page 149 my colleague Phil Alexander reveals lessons you can learn about Google from the Vegas casinos.
- *Image Ads.* Compared to the old "banner ads" of the 1990s, Image Ads are an entirely new game on Google. Fewer than 10 percent of all Google advertisers use them. So if the content network is important to you, you can achieve a significant advantage. See page 109.
- *Remarketing (Tracking Potential Customers).* Chapter 26 covers remarketing, or retargeting: ads that draw in people who've already visited your website but haven't bought.
- *Google Place Pages.* Chapter 27 shows you how to skyrocket the effectiveness of local listings. In the age of smartphones and last-minute decisions, doing this is critical for every local business.
- *A Guide to Must-Have Software Tools.* We've added new, advanced material at www. perrymarshall.com/supplement/ for savvy advertisers, including a guide to Google Conversion Optimizer, and software tools that give you keen insights on your customers' eccentricities.

One last thing:

I mince no words: Google is THE benchmark for advertisers and information providers worldwide. In fact from the standpoint of ordinary people getting things done every single day in the world, Google is the most trusted brand in business. If you're up to Google's standards, you're world class.

I'm not saying that's easy. But I do promise—it IS rewarding. Make no mistake about that.

Follow the guidelines in this book and you'll be a world-class promoter in your market, your niche, your chosen profession. I wish you the very, very best of success.

—Perry Marshall
Chicago, Illinois

How to Force Prospects to Choose Your Site and Buy from You, Not Your Competition

Google gets searched more than 1 billion times every day. That's 720,000 searches a minute.

Google can bring thousands of visitors to your website 24 hours a day, 7 days a week, 365 days a year . . . whether you're taking a shower, eating breakfast, driving to work, picking up your kids at school, taking a phone call, sleeping, sitting on the commode, daydreaming, busting your butt to beat a deadline, chasing some customer, typing an email message . . .

■ ■ ■

And it can all happen on autopilot: 100 percent predictable and completely consistent, like clockwork.

Ten or 15 years ago, an impossible dream . . . today, a reality.

Just think of the lengths to which we entrepreneurs, business owners, and salespeople go just to get a company off the ground, just to get a sale.

I could recount in agonizing detail the *years* of my life I spent pounding the phone, pounding the pavement, making cold calls. Renting trade show booths, going to no-show appointments, booking meetings that were a total waste of time.

But not anymore. I don't go to them anymore; customers come to me. It's been that way so long, I'm very much used to it now.

They'll come to you, too.

Getting new customers is a real grind for a lot of people. It's the number-one obstacle to starting a new business. But all that can be a thing of the past. Instead of your chasing customers, they can now come to you, all day and all night.

History has proved Google AdWords is the most important development in advertising in the 25 years. Never before had it been possible to spend five bucks, open an account, and have brand-new, precisely targeted customers coming to your website within minutes.

There are a lot of things you might want from Google. Maybe you're adding an online component to your retail operation, giving you steadier cash flow and deeper discounts from your suppliers. Maybe payroll is going to get easier. Maybe your consulting business will be positioned better.

Maybe you're already getting traffic but free listings are too unreliable. Maybe you've been successful selling on eBay, and now you want to play with the big boys. Maybe you've been futzing around with "social media," and you've finally decided it's time to make some money instead. Maybe you're a working mom, and you want to finally be able to come home.

If you're privy to the secrets of online marketing, all those opportunities open up to you. You'll have fresh hot sales leads waiting for you in your email box every morning when you sit down at your desk. You'll have customers buying from you 24/7/365.

Instead of your chasing customers, they come to you. Instead of trying to guess whether your next product launch will work, you can *know*.

Why is this even possible? Because in the last five years the very direction of business itself has reversed.

In the old days (remember the 1990s?), entrepreneurs and salespeople chased customers with phone calls, letters, and ads in newspapers. Now customers chase businesses on the web.

Back then you had a list of prospects you tried to get to buy. Now the buyers— millions of them—are trolling the web every second of the day, looking for businesses that can scratch their itch.

Ever heard Woody Allen's saying, "90 percent of success is showing up"? The phrase takes on a whole new meaning in the 21st century. If you just *show up* on Google and its search partners, when people type in the right phrase, a starving crowd will bust your doors down to eat at your restaurant.

They'll fill every table and book the kitchen with orders. If they like the daily special and the dessert, they'll come back and eat again.

There's a big feast going on, *if* you show up.

Here you'll discover the secrets of showing up. Not just somewhere, but the right places and times. In front of the right people. And if you're already advertising on Google, you'll learn how to cut your bid prices 20 percent, 50 percent, maybe even 70 percent or more.

This book is for . . .

- Online catalog and "mail order" marketers
- Local retail stores and service businesses
- Niche product marketers
- Home businesses run from spare bedrooms or basement offices
- Authors, speakers, consultants, and publishers
- Business-to-business marketers collecting sales leads
- Nonprofits, churches, and charities
- Resellers, repair services, parts suppliers
- Online communities and membership sites

Google AdWords can help your business whether you're the little old lady selling quilts in Eastern Kentucky or the multinational corporation. You don't have to be a geek to do this; many of the best online marketers are nontechnical people who succeed simply because they understand their customers.

A lot of these success stories are from "invisible entrepreneurs." By invisible, I mean that their next-door neighbors have no idea what they do and probably just assume they're unemployed or something.

Google gets searched more than 1 billion times every day.

Every one of them is typed in by a person who has an itch they want to scratch.

*Source: *The New York Times*, March 5, 2011, "Google Schools Its Algorithm"

But they're running micro-empires from their spare bedroom. And they're in hundreds of industries, ranging from the mundane to the ridiculous to the outrageously specialized.

Some of these guys and gals are making *serious cash*. Tens, even hundreds of thousands of dollars a month. And they're not in "sleazy" businesses, either.

In this book I'm going to show you exactly how they do it.

HERE'S HOW TO MAKE SURE THEY FIND *YOU* AND BUY FROM *YOU*. NOT SOMEONE ELSE.

Got a watch with a second hand?

Tick. 12,000 people just searched Google for something and went to somebody's website.

Tick. 12,000 more.

Tick. 12,000 more.

720,000 people a minute. Every minute, all day long.

All night long.

Here they come. Every second. Every minute. Every hour.

Are they finding your website?

Are they buying from you?

Or are they finding someone *else's* website and buying from them instead?

They could be finding you. They *should* be finding you. They can find you and buy from you. Many of them will come to your site, buy from you, and come back again and again, *if* you follow the simple instructions in this book.

Google AdWords can be the traffic monster that feeds your autopilot marketing machine and churns out a profit for you every day and every night, hitting the entire world up for customers while you sleep. Not just bringing you tire kickers but highly qualified buyers who are proactively looking for exactly what you sell right this very minute.

Buying from *you*. Not somebody else.

If the internet matters to your business, then no book you've ever bought has more potential to make or save you money than this one.

This book is written so you can blow through it, fast, and get going immediately on your course to make serious money with Google insider marketing tactics. That's the fun part: quickly implementing killer tactics that will flood your business with prospects and profit.

But there's a serious side, too. I've held nothing back here. So not only will you know how to play the Google AdWords game, you'll discover how to craft powerful marketing messages and hooks, bond with your customers, and dominate your market.

In this book you'll discover:

- Tragic, costly mistakes that almost all Google advertisers and online entrepreneurs make—and how to easily avoid them (including techniques Google itself *should* teach you, but doesn't).
- How to disaster-proof business startups and product launches, and pound the risk out of new ventures. (Most times you've only got one or two shots to nail it—why would you want to leave anything to chance?)
- Profiles of successful online businesses. Having coached hundreds of online entrepreneurs to success, I've accumulated a list of vital characteristics that separate winners from the losers—many of which defy normal "business school wisdom."
- How to create ultra-persuasive Google ads and web pages that not only convert visitors to buyers, but automatically improve with time, making it impossible for your rivals to catch up to you.
- The advanced (but simple) shortcut secrets of getting deep into your customer's head . . . so you know exactly where his hot buttons are, and how to punch them at will. Result: Customer loyalty that reaches fanatical levels, and a rabid customer base that eagerly buys almost everything you ask them to buy.

And if you're already advertising on Google, you'll get 30 percent to 300 percent more visitors, for less money than you're paying right now.

While many hard-core "let's get after it" types will mark up and dog-ear this book, you can really start seeing results *while* you're reading it. There are shortcuts you can get after tonight, and see results before you go to bed an hour later.

Your business can literally be better by tomorrow morning.

So strap on your crash helmet because you're in for a wild ride. Onward! Stick with me and my partner Bryan as we show you the secrets to online business success.

—Perry Marshall

P.S.: I've created an online supplement to this book with more than $85.00 worth of extended book chapters, audio interviews, information on specialized topics, and ongoing updates on Google's ever-changing rules. You can access it at www.perrymarshall.com/supplement.

P.P.S.: Here are some cool success stories I've gotten from my customers:

"I first purchased Perry's AdWords Guide about five years ago and just recently purchased the newest version.

"That's about five years of Perry Marshall information and I've never once been offered a dream. I don't do AdWords advertising because I can't afford it.

"But Perry never promised me that I could get rich using AdWords, i.e., he never tried to sell me a dream. I really appreciate that. Like he said, AdWords is not a business. It's a tool you can use to advertise your business, and I don't know anyone that's more qualified than Perry Marshall that can teach you how to benefit from AdWords.

"I can promise you this. The Perry Marshall information will save you a lot of money and possibly even an arm and a leg . . . it all depends on what kind of fish you're swimming with."

—ROGER KELLEY, DECATUR, AL

"Since your last coaching call, we made the keyword matching changes as you recommended, and have the following to show you. Our overall CTR is 4.4 percent—our best ad is 12.4 percent and the worst one is a very respectable 3.1 percent!"

—SIMON CHEN, THE EIGHTBLACK GROUP, MELBOURNE, AUSTRALIA

"I've been a faithful Perry fan since I met him at a Dan Kennedy event about five years ago. I own most of Perry's products, I've been through the Bobsled run twice, and I attended a four-man intensive at his house last year.

"Perry always tells it like it is. He's not like most of the 'gurus' out there always trying to sell you their next product or coaching program. Perry gives us rock solid advice on how to grow our business or how to sell more products. He repeats his solid advice over and over with no sales hype. That's why we love and trust Perry. That's why I've been a longtime customer and I buy everything he offers.

"Recently I took a real job after being on my own for 10 years. I'm now an Online Marketing/SEO Analyst for a local software company. I'm managing their AdWords campaigns, which are over $20k/month worldwide.

"Using what Perry taught me, I increased their CTR from just over 1 percent to over 6 percent in just one day. They're running three times more ads on the same budget and they're getting better qualified leads.

"Think about using your knowledge managing AdWords campaigns as a consultant or for a company. There are tons of online marketing jobs out there right now and most pay over six figures a year. I never thought I could go back to a real job but I love getting that steady paycheck and going home at five every day not worrying about keeping my business going. Plus I'm consulting on the side still so I'm making more than I ever have."

—Ted Prodromou, San Anselmo, CA

"So far I've found your least expensive material to be your most valuable. Your $49 AdWords guide is worth hundreds of times its cost. And the free advice in your marketing emails—one story in particular about the Wright brothers and Samuel Langley—has been absolutely priceless."

—Paul Del Piero, Austin, TX

"I was getting about 2,830 clicks per month with Google AdWords at $1.06 per click. I've spent about eight hours total reading your stuff and implementing it. Based on the results of my last few days I am on track to get 7,815 clicks in the next month and spend the same $3,000 a month . . . a savings of $23,400 per year, or $2,925 per hour for the eight hours I have invested. This is without doubt one of the absolute best investments I've ever made and I haven't even started! And yes, I have done most of this while sitting at home in my underwear."

—Keith Lee, TMS, Kent, WA

"I'm telling everyone that your book is 'required reading' if they want to market online. I actually read your 'Definitive Guide' in one day, and that evening started my first AdWords campaign. I now have four of them running, and the average click-through rate for all campaigns is above 2 percent. I also get well over a 3 percent CTR (some as high as 15 percent) on my more targeted keywords. This has increased the traffic to my sites tenfold in some cases, and has made my monthly revenues much more consistent (which is always nice). Best of all, I've never had a keyword shut down by Google for low CTR, and I've only done one round of 'peel and stick' with my ads. I give all the credit to my recent AdWords success to you and your book."

—Ryan Deiss, Austin, TX

"I had spent almost 100k on wasted SEO firms and websites with no real reward. I discovered Perry on another podcast I was listening to and have learned so much in only a year. I have just started employing his processes to Google AdWords and am reaping the benefits already. I appreciate your delivery of information and the lack of BS in your sales tactics to everyone.

"You bring great info to the table so we do not have to sort through to find what is useful. It's simply amazing watching my click-through rate go from 0.3 percent up to 48.0 percent in less than 30 minutes.

"The most important part is, I AM BEATING THE COMPETITION in cost, and better yet finding areas of 'no competition.' Thanks for such awesome marketing advice, your material is by far the most valuable I have purchased. Your concepts are working for me, and I intend on running this as a service for a lot of my web hosting clientele."

—EDDIE SYMONDS, UPPER MARLBORO, MD

"WOW! I got a 500 percent increase in response . . . with just a quick 'Band-Aid' fix. Can't wait to see what happens when I follow all of your suggestions."

—JENNY HAMBY, COPYWRITER AND SEMINAR MARKETING CONSULTANT,
SEMINARMARKETINGPRO.COM, PLAINFIELD, IL

Chapter 2

How to Build Your Own Autopilot Marketing Machine

We're not going to just teach you a handful of Google tricks. We're going to show you how to make the internet your slave. (Plus you'll find out why selling on the internet is way simpler than most people think, because . . . only a handful of things really matter anyway.)

If you're at a party and tell folks you're starting an online business, they won't spare a bit of advice. They'll give you an endless list of things they think you need—dedicated servers, security certificates, iPhone apps, Facebook apps, pop-up windows, blogs, Meta tags, streaming video, WordPress, SEO plug-ins, Cascading Style Sheets, RSS feeds . . . all kinds of stuff.

(Are your eyes glazing over yet?)

Some of the things on that list will certainly come into play for you at some point. But people way smarter than you or me have blown hundreds of thousands of dollars before the first visitor even showed up and bought anything.

Big mistake.

Techno-wizardry is, for the most part, a distraction and a waste of time. So in this short chapter we're going to show you the moving parts you need and just how simple a thriving, profitable website can be.

IT ALL STARTS WHEN PEOPLE SEARCH FOR SOMETHING

Karli types in "homeschooling" at her computer and here's what shows up on Google:

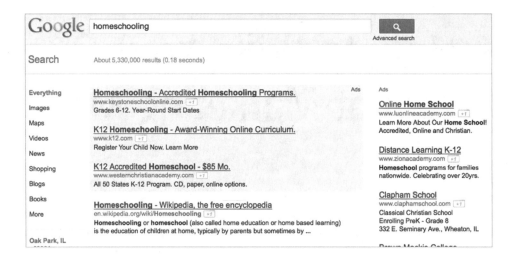

On the top and right are the AdWords ads, which are paid. Running down the left are the free "organic" search listings.

She clicks on the ad near the top that says

> K12 Homeschooling—Award-Winning Online Curriculum.
> www.k12.com
> Register Your Child Now. Learn More

Or . . .

Karli is trolling the web and she's at www.JustEnoughBlog.com reading the latest news on the topic:

And she sees the ad over on the right that says

> K12 Homeschool Online
> Give Your Kids An Academic Edge. K12
> Online Curriculum. Learn More!
> www.K12.com

This ad is also served by Google through the *AdSense* program for website owners, to dozens, hundreds, possibly thousands of websites.

The ad sounds interesting. She clicks on the ad and is taken to this page:

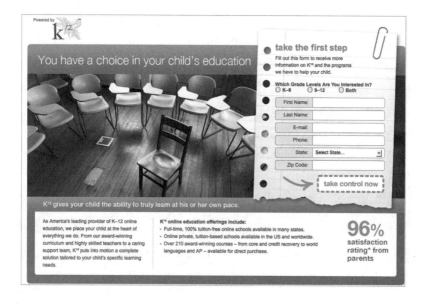

That's the first step. Now Karli has a choice: She can ask for more information, or she can leave. On other sites she may be given the option to buy.

There's a number of sites where the best thing to offer is information instead of a product upfront. The way Karli gets the information is by entering her address to get a gift, sample, download, white paper, report, or guide. This offer is especially important if the problem Karli wants to solve is an ongoing area of interest, as opposed to a one-time impulse buy.

If this were a product for people with diabetes, for example, it would be a very good idea to collect Karli's email address, because if Karli is a diabetic, she's going to have diabetes next week and next year, not just today. Could be a valuable email list! Plus this gives you a chance to talk to all the Karlies on your list and get to know them better.

THE SEARCH PROCESS

In the course of Karli's search process, one of three actions will occur:

1. *She will buy something* (like a guide to homeschooling or a report with the latest on diabetes).
2. *She will leave.*
3. *She will ask for more information.*

If you have obtained her email address (by having her opt-in and sign up), you can invite her to come back to learn more about your information, products, or services.

That's what this is all about.

Anything that gets this done is good. Anything that complicates it or gets in the way is bad.

See, this is really simple. Futzing around with Flash presentations and 19 different ways to build a web page—all that stuff is beside the point. The point is: *Scratch Karli's itch and move the stuff from your shelf to hers, as quickly, easily, and simply as possible.*

Your Mission, Should You Choose to Accept It

Your mission is to buy clicks for $1.00 and make $2.00 while Karli is on your website. Your mission is to make more money from your clicks than your competitors make from theirs. And if that means making 50 cents while Karli is on your website, going negative initially but then earning $1.50 back during the next three months, you've succeeded.

That's it.

The rest of this book is all about how to do this.

Most people don't realize how powerful this one-dollar-in, two-dollars-out mindset is in the grand scheme of things—and why Google AdWords is usually the best place to make this happen.

If You Do This Right, It Can Literally Make You Rich. Here's Why . . .

My friend and legendary marketer Jonathan Mizel says, "Internet traffic goes where it's rewarded, respected, and paid for." If you reward and respect your visitors—and if you're able to pay more for them than everyone else advertising in your category—*then you can have as much traffic as you want*. The traffic will literally *seek you out*.

This is not an exaggeration. It's completely true. But traffic will only seek you out when it's profitable.

So you develop your Google campaigns, send traffic to your site, collect information requests, make sales, follow up with your customers, and . . . do whatever you need to do, to make the whole process flow like water running downhill.

Only when your Google campaign is working do you focus on other marketing strategies. Then (and only then) do you go to all of the *other* traffic sources available to you, like Bing, banner ads, email lists, and affiliates.

As we'll discuss in other chapters, affiliates (people who send you traffic in exchange for commission on sales) can be a *huge* source of traffic. If your website doesn't pay, affiliates won't send you anything. But good affiliates can turn the tide in your favor, making you the dominant force in your market.

By following the steps in this book, you'll set yourself up to get massive amounts of traffic and your business will grow exponentially.

A FEW TOOLS YOU NEED IF YOU'RE JUST GETTING STARTED

Whether you're selling skin cream or e-books or computer games or imported wood carvings, you need a handful of tools to be in business:

- A domain name
- A website with web pages
- An email broadcast/auto-responder service
- A shopping cart service
- A product to sell
- A Google AdWords account

The online supplement to this book (www.perrymarshall.com/supplement) has links to dozens of resources for getting these things done, plus additional tutorials and MP3 files. But here's a quick rundown of the most important stuff:

You can register a domain name at www.BulkRegister.com. You can host your website at www.hostgator.com.

You can create your site with an online content management platform like WordPress.

An excellent email system is Aweber. You can queue up automatic messages that go out when people request information or buy. You can send email newsletters and announcements to your customers and prospects. Aweber also does a good job of getting your messages through the spam filters.

If you're just getting started, *do not* futz around with installing payment software on your server, etc. Go to a third party like 1ShoppingCart—it has a great service that allows you to quickly set up order forms, take orders, process credit card transactions, follow up with emails, and manage your customer list.

If you're a more mature marketer, InfusionSoft is a complete e-commerce platform with customer and email management, autoresponders, and a shopping cart.

The product is up to you. You can use your Google ads and your website to learn about any market you want and decide if you want to stay in it.

The next chapter shows you how to quickly set up a Google account. Let's get it started, shall we?

Chapter 3

How to Build a Google Campaign from Scratch—The *Right* Way

Ten minutes from right now you can have a Google campaign up and running, sending visitors to your website. The speed at which you can do new things and make changes in Google's system is stunning.

■ ■ ■

But speed can also be a trap. Sometimes people do rash things when they're in a hurry.

This is not a long chapter, but it contains some seriously important concepts. Many have skipped these steps and landed on the pay-per-click slagheap. So take a little extra time to go carefully through these steps. It'll save you a lot of money. And you'll still have your Google campaign up and running in an hour or two—and it'll be set up better than 95 percent of Google campaigns on the web.

THE BEST WAY TO RESEARCH YOUR MARKET

What keywords are you going to use to reach your market? Answering that question the right way can spell the difference between success and failure. Ultimately you're out to hunt down the top *one or two keywords* that will bring you the most paying customers, and tweak your entire sales process around that. That's what the most successful AdWords advertisers we know are doing now.

To find that bull's-eye keyword, or "keyword center," we're going to use Google's Keyword Tool and Traffic Estimator, both of which you find under "Reporting and Tools" in your AdWords account:

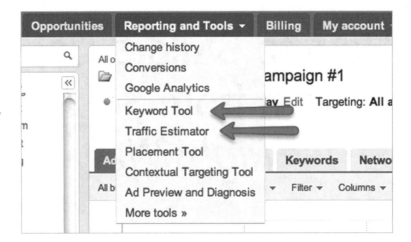

One of the huge advantages of AdWords is that it links you with people who are already "sold" on the concept that you are promoting. You don't have to talk them into anything—they're already on Google looking for what you've got. You just need to figure out the keywords they use to describe *what you offer*, so you can connect with them.

To answer this question, you need to describe what you're promoting as clearly as possible—and identify who wants to buy it. This is your ideal customer.

1. Define the Perfect Customer.

We recommend that you stop right now, pull out a piece of paper, and physically write down a one-sentence description of your ultimate money-in-hand-and-ready-to-buy paying customer.

Those are the people who already know something about the type of product (or information) you sell or the service you offer. These people probably don't know about you, but they do know about your product. Often they have an immediate problem and have decided to go online looking for a solution. They may have already made up their mind about how they want to solve the problem. Now they're searching Google, trying to locate the product that fits their solution, and then buy it.

Your description may look like one of these, which we borrow from our friend Glenn Livingston, who teaches this bull's eye concept in powerful depth (at www.PerrySentMe. com):

· "My best prospect is someone who already believes in nonpharmaceutical and natural remedies for migraines and is actively searching for the best one to purchase."
· "My best prospect is someone who has already made up his or her mind to buy pottery via the web."
· "My best prospect already knows pay-per-click management services exist and is proactively searching to hire one."

Have this description physically written out and keep it there in front of you as you go through the keyword search process.

2. What Are the Keywords Your Potential Customers Are Using to Search for Your Product or Services?

Head over to Google's keyword tool (do a quick Google search to find it) and enter some phrases that you think reflect customers who are in that mind-set. Let's take the migraine example. A starter idea would be "natural migraine remedies," because that would seem to specify people who are looking for a *natural* solution, something for *migraines* as opposed to more general issues, and *remedies* as opposed to facts or data or information.

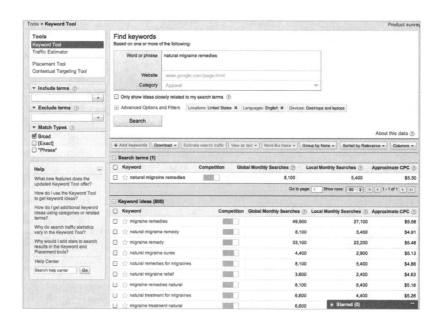

Google gives a decent-sized list here. We can now go through the list keyword by keyword and compare each to our written customer description, choose the keywords we feel are a fit, and ignore the ones that aren't.

Yes, this is a subjective judgment, which is fine; you can make an educated guess as to its relevance on a 0–10 scale. Is it a 1? a 5? a 9? If you feel it's less than 3, skip it as a keyword, for now.

You may collect a total list of no more than one to two dozen keywords. That's perfectly fine.

3. How Many People Are Searching on this Keyword?

We're aiming to find the ultimate bull's-eye keyword here. We don't have to nail it down today, but this search narrows the playing field and makes the job easier.

For your one to two dozen keywords you can go with what Google's keyword tool already told you. Or you can take each one and do a further keyword tool search on it and add in totals from other variations that you believe would *fully match your written customer description*.

Note how many searches some of the variations get:

Keyword ideas (800)				
Keyword	Competition	Global Monthly Searches ⑦	Local Monthly Searches ⑦	Approximate CPC ⑦
☆ migraine remedies		49,500	27,100	$5.58
☆ natural migraine remedy		8,100	5,400	$4.91
☆ migraine remedy		33,100	22,200	$5.48
☆ natural migraine cures		4,400	2,900	$5.13
☆ natural remedies for migraines		8,100	5,400	$4.86
☆ natural migraine relief		3,600	2,400	$4.63
☆ migraine remedies natural		8,100	5,400	$5.18
☆ natural treatment for migraines		6,600	4,400	$5.28
☆ migraine treatment natural		6,600	4,400	$5.45
☆ all natural migraine remedies		110	91	$5.77
☆ migraine herbal remedies		5,400	2,900	$5.49
☆ natural migraine treatments		6,600	4,400	$5.11
☆ natural remedies for migraine headaches		1,300	880	$5.32
☆ natural remedies migraines		8,100	5,400	$5.46
☆ migraine natural remedies		8,100	5,400	$4.82
☆ natural migraine headache remedies		1,900	1,300	$5.18
☆ migraine home remedies		12,100	8,100	$5.57
☆ natural migraine treatment		6,600	4,400	$5.07
☆ migraine surgery		2,900	1,900	$4.24
☆ migraine headache remedies		8,100	5,400	$5.21

You'll want to consider search volume when choosing your top keyword(s).

4. How Much Money Are Advertisers Making off this Keyword?

(You can judge this by how much the keyword costs.)

We're looking for the keywords where the money is. The market has its own way of answering this. The maximum cost per click that people pay represents the upper limit of the money available in that market.

Head over to Google's Traffic Estimator to find this out (you can access this handy tool with another Google search). When I ran the Traffic Estimator for "natural migraine remedies" and other variations (in the United States), I got this:

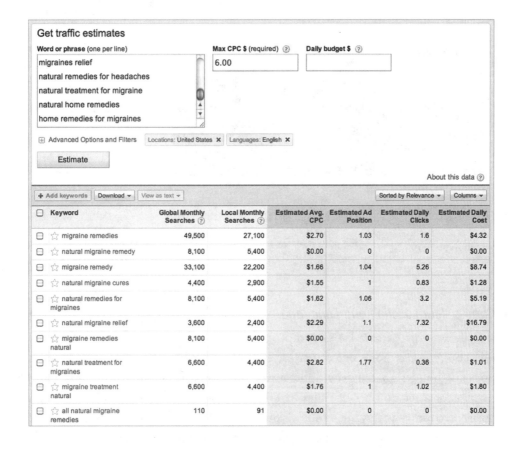

. . . which of course is just the beginning. I can collect as many relevant keywords like this as I want, and then make an educated comparison among them to find the best fit for my profile. You're off to the best start when you've got 6 to 12 *tightly matched groups* of keywords.

And ultimately you're best off with that one single bull's-eye keyword. Glenn Livingston goes through this issue thoroughly at www.PerrySentMe.com.

HOW TO SET UP YOUR CAMPAIGN

To start your campaign, go to https://adwords.google.com, find the "Start now" button, and sign up for an AdWords account.

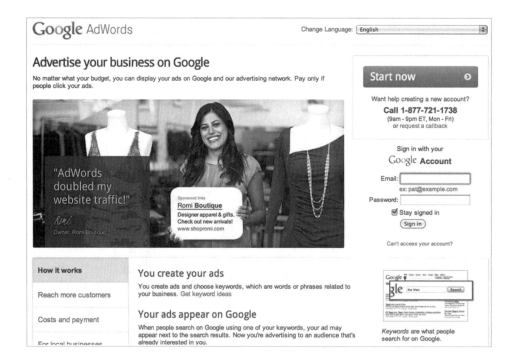

1. Choose Your Location and Language

Decide how large or small a geographic area you want to target. You can choose whole countries, regions of countries, states or provinces, or cities. You can also choose custom-designated geographic areas, such as latitude-longitude coordinates or the radius of a set number of miles or kilometers around a specific address. You can choose the country you want to show your ads in, followed by your state/province or even a city or group of cities. Choose from the list Google gives you automatically, or click on "Select one or more other locations":

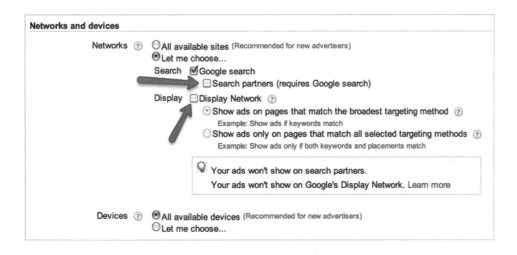

2. Select Your Setting Under Networks and Devices

There's one hidden setting you'd better tweak now: Under "Networks and devices," click the "Let me choose. . ." button. We strongly recommend that you uncheck the buttons next to Search partners and the Display Network (both accessed under Networks):

3. Choose Your Currency, and Set Your Daily Budget

Your daily budget is the maximum that Google is authorized to charge you per day. Chances are that you will hit that maximum most days. Google offers several payment options: "You can make payments *before* your ads show (manual payments) or make payments *after* your ads show, and have those payments made automatically (automatic payments). Some businesses are also eligible for a Google credit line (monthly invoicing)."

Bidding and budget

Bidding option ⑦ Basic options | Advanced options

⦿ Manual bidding for clicks

💡 You'll set your maximum CPC bids in the next step.

○ Automatic bidding to try to maximize clicks for your target budget

Budget ⑦ $ [_____] per day

Actual daily spend may vary. ⑦

Set your daily budget such that if you screw up big-time, your checking account won't be emptied out. You can always come back and bump it up, but it's important to have a safety net. That's how you should use the daily budget tool.

4. Create Your First Ad Group and Write Your First Ad

We'll enter the "CRM Software" ad that we've written:

✓ Select campaign settings ▶ Create ad group

Create ad group

Name this ad group

An ad group contains one or more ads and a set of related keywords. For best results, try to focus all the ads and keywords in t service. Learn more about how to structure your account.

Ad group name: [CRM Software]

Create an ad

⦿ Text ad ○ Image ad ○ Display ad builder ○ WAP mobile ad

To get started, just write your first ad below. Remember, you can always create more ads later. Help me write a great text ad.

Headline	CRM Software
Description line 1	1-to-1 Marketing for Every Prospect
Description line 2	30-Day Free Trial & 24/7 Support
Display URL ⑦	www.crm1to1.com/FreeTrial
Destination URL ⑦	http:// ⬍ www.crm1to1.com/google/freetrial

Ad preview: The following ad previews may be formatted slightly differently from what is shown to users. Learn more

Side ad
CRM Software
1-to-1 Marketing for Every Prospect
30-Day Free Trial & 24/7 Support
www.crm1to1.com/FreeTrial

Top ad
CRM Software
1-to-1 Marketing for Every Prospect 30-Day Free Trial & 24/7 Support
www.crm1to1.com/FreeTrial

Now let's explain what we just did, and why.

More people click on ads when the *headline* includes the keyword they're searching on. So use your keywords in your headline when you can. You're limited to 25 characters here, so for some search terms you'll need to use abbreviations or shorter synonyms.

The *second and third lines* allow for 35 characters of text each. In most markets you'll be more successful if you describe a *benefit* on the second line, followed by a *feature* or *offer* on the third line. Later on you can test which order converts better.

Even though Google places the field for your *display URL*—the web address people see in your ad—below your main ad copy here, when your ad displays on the search results page, its URL will actually show up right below your headline. The display URL has to be the same domain as your site, though the URL itself doesn't necessarily have to be the specific landing page that you take people to.

The last line is your actual *destination URL*, or your specific chosen landing page. You can also use a tracking link here.

Here's the short version of your ad template:

Headline—up to 25 characters of text
2nd line—up to 35 characters
3rd line—up to 35 characters
4th line—your destination URL

5. Insert Your Keywords Into the Keyword Field in Your Account

Paste in your keywords. We'll start with just one set, and we'll add plus signs (+) and put them in brackets ([ ]) and quotes (" ") to see precisely how many searches of each type we'll get. More on this in Chapter 5.

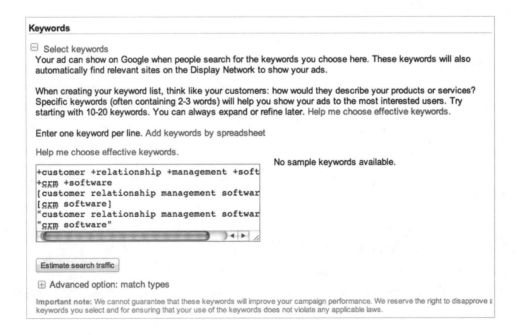

Note: When you're getting started, it's *not* a good idea to dump hundreds or thousands of keywords in. Start with a tiny handful of important ones and work from there.

6. Set Your Maximum Cost-Per-Click

Set your maximum price-per-click now (called your "default bid"), but realize this: Every keyword is theoretically a different market, which means that each major one will need a bid price of its own. Google will let you set individual bids for each keyword later. Don't set a bid for your Google Display Network (GDN) ad here: Run that traffic through a different campaign.

If you can only afford $50 per day instead of $170, it's better to bid on low-cost keywords so that your ad can be seen by as many people as possible. Due to the limitations of any budget, if you're going after high-priced keywords, you'll exhaust your budget quickly and your ads will only be seen part of the day, rather than a full 24 hours.

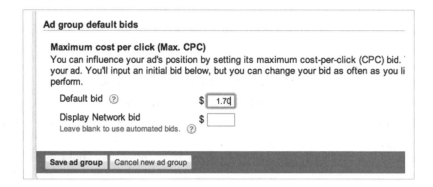

7. Review Everything

Double-check your ad, your keywords, your cost-per-click, and your daily budget to be sure you start your campaign off the right way.

8. Enter Your Billing Information

Your ads will start showing as soon as you confirm your payment information. Now you're set.

THINGS YOU CAN TWEAK RIGHT NOW

You can almost always improve on the number of clicks you'll get from the ad you've just written. As you'll see later, it's almost impossible to guess what is going to make people click; you need to let the visitors vote. So write a second ad you think can beat it, and go back into your ad group to post it:

CRM Software
www.crm1to1.com/FreeTrial
Manage 1000 to 10,000 Customers
30-Day Free Trial & 24/7 Support

Google will rotate this automatically against your first ad. After a few days or weeks, you can pick the winner and delete the loser. Results will come in faster if you test just two at a time.

You can also add more keywords to your list, adjust your cost-per-click or destination URL for individual keywords, create more ad groups and campaigns, and adjust your campaign settings to fit your style.

In Chapter 29 we'll look at the bells and whistles Google gives you for managing and tweaking your campaigns, and we'll give you some cool tips for getting more clicks and sales from your ads through smarter traffic management.

When you follow these steps, a campaign will grow that is unique to you and your customers. The success is yours, and so is the profit. It's your business, unlike any other, with your fingerprints and personality all over it. Yours alone. Nobody can replicate that.

The Magic Is in the Process

The most important thing you should know about a Google campaign is that it's not a single technique or something that you set up once and forget about.

We have clients whose Google campaigns seem to hum as if on autopilot, but the real power in Google AdWords comes from logging in every few days or once a week and making constant refinements that 2X, 5X, or 10X your traffic. The number of visitors grows even while your cost-per-click declines over time.

This doesn't take a lot of time—sometimes only a few short minutes each week. But you earn compound interest on those efforts because your profit margins get fatter as the traffic grows.

How to Set Yourself Up for Success

Now you know how to build a small, basic ad campaign. The foundation for future success is laid by organizing larger groups and campaigns properly. In the next chapter you'll learn how to do that.

Meet Uncle Claude

If You've Ever Sold Anything on the Internet, This Man Is Your Uncle

Every field of knowledge exists because a handful of luminaries made ground-breaking discoveries and showed others the way. And there's almost always one who stands head and shoulders above the others.

In management it's Peter Drucker. In engineering it's Thomas Edison. In physics, Albert Einstein. In Rock & Roll, it's the Beatles. For saxophone players it's John Coltrane.

In results-driven advertising, it's Claude Hopkins (1866–1932). Whether you know it or not, if your website is generating a profit, it's because you've discovered something that Hopkins figured out, probably before the turn of the century.

Uncle Claude invented the coupon (Did you know he created it so that advertisers could track their results?) and pioneered concepts like split testing, premiums, free samples, and mail-order marketing. In fact his book *Scientific Advertising* is so important we've included it in the online supplement to this book at www.perrymarshall.com/supplement.

In the rest of this book, we take Hopkins' ideas, which in the late 1800s took months to implement and test, and show you how to do the same thing, literally *10,000 times faster*. We've included choice nuggets of wisdom from him in many of the upcoming chapters.

Thanks to Uncle Claude, it's never been easier—or more *scientific*—to make a fortune in marketing.

Chapter 4

Organizing Your Campaign: How to Pay Less and Get More Clicks

We do a *lot* of Google AdWords consultations, both through our coaching programs and with people who come to our site looking for help. We get on the phone with our customer, log into the Google account, and see what can be improved. It's not unusual for us to be able to improve performance by 50 percent or 100 percent in as little as 30 minutes.

■ ■ ■

Want to know what the number-one mistake people make is?

Hastily organized campaigns.

Badly organized ads and keywords will cripple your Google campaigns and cost you a *ton* of money.

WHAT GOOGLE DOESN'T TELL YOU: THE WRONG WAY TO ORGANIZE AN ADWORDS CAMPAIGN

Starting out, it's a temptation to set up a campaign that includes everything but the kitchen sink, one that looks something like this:

<u>Smith Telecommunications</u>
Robust Solutions for
All Your Voice Mail Needs
www.smithtelecom.com

auto attendant
business telephone systems
call management systems
voice mail
voice mail equipment
voice mail service
voice mail systems

The plan would be to send all visitors to the home page, which has a bunch of different options: links to services, equipment, Q&A, About Us, Contact Us, etc.

So if we made a map of that AdWords campaign, it would look like this:

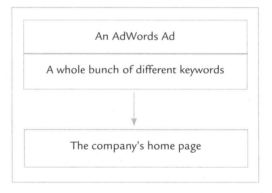

What's wrong with this picture?
Here's why this ad is destined to fail:

- There are too many different kinds of keywords in the same group. Every one of these keywords needs to be in its own group, *along with a list of very similar words and phrases.*
- The ad doesn't match the keywords, and it can't because there are too many different kinds of keywords in the group.

- "Smith Telecommunications"—or the name of almost any business—is a *lousy* headline. The click-through rate (CTR) is going to be very low, and the bid prices will therefore be higher. The ad is about Smith Telecommunications, not what the customer really wants.
- Your ads need to be about your customer—focused on what they're searching for!

THE RIGHT WAY TO ORGANIZE AN ADWORDS CAMPAIGN

Well-organized campaigns get results from the beginning and are easy to adjust and optimize. Over time this makes a huge difference. Here are a few simple steps you can take to organize your campaign.

1. *Define your campaign.* In a single Google account, you can have practically as many campaigns as you want. Some of these campaigns may be on a completely different topic, selling completely different services and sending traffic to a completely different website. In fact, if you have more than one website, it's logical to have a different campaign for each site. A campaign is just a handy way to organize a number of ad groups, usually according to broad topic—for example, a specific type of service or product. So the first step is determining the focus of your campaign.

2. *Define your ad group.* Ad groups are the individual units within a campaign that contain clusters of keywords and ads together, grouped around a single theme. You can have multiple ad groups in a single campaign. How you separate out your campaigns is up to you. How you separate *ad groups*, however, is one of those things where there's a right way and a wrong way.

   In a *perfect* world, you'd have an ad group with an ad written specifically for every single keyword. Since each keyword is different, each ad would be different, too. If you had 50 keywords, you'd have to write 50 ads and track them through 50 ad groups.

   In the real world, that's kind of impractical. So you'll want to cluster similar keywords together with a single ad.

3. *In each ad group, focus on one type of product or service.* If you want to advertise more than one product or service on AdWords, it's important to identify each item that you're marketing and whether they're related. Then differentiate each type of product under a different ad group.

   - A person who searches for "voice mail *service*" needs to be taken to a page about voice mail service.
   - In contrast, a person who searches for *equipment* needs to be taken to a *different* web page—one about voice mail equipment.

These are two entirely different topics. If people have to figure out where to go after they land on your web page, you're making them work too hard. You need to show them exactly what they were searching for.

Now if you structure your campaigns right from the beginning, it's a *lot* easier to make this work. Here's an example of how you can organize your ads and keywords:

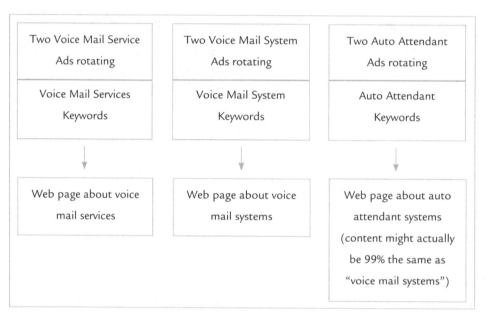

4. *Organize related key words together within an ad group.* To do this, take all of your different keywords and use Wordtracker (http://freekeywords.wordtracker.com; www.wordtracker.com) to organize them into narrow "silos" of very tightly related terms. These silos will look like this:

Voice Mail Services	**Voice Mail System**	**Auto Attendant**
voice mail provider	voice mail systems	answering attendant auto system
voice mail service	voice mail systems for realtors	auto attendant voice mail services
voice mail service provider	telemarketing and voice mail systems	auto attendant
voice mail services	phone systems voice mail	auto attendant phone system
	home office voice mail systems	auto attendant software
	home office telephone voice mail systems	auto attendant system
		auto attendant voice mail
		phone auto attendant

5. *Eliminate negative keywords.* There's another step we need to take before pasting this into a campaign: Consider negative keywords. These are related terms that will cost you clicks without bringing you business. Here's a list of keywords that come from a search on "Voice Mail Software":

> voice mail software
> voice mail business software
> voice mail software for panasonic
> voice mail broadcasting software
> voice mail business software
> multiple voice mail software
> mac voice mail software
> multi line voice mail system software vru
> norstar voice mail software
> software to record voice mail
> free voice mail software

You might not want visitors who want something for *free*. Your company also has nothing to do with voice *broadcasting*, and you don't have anything for *Macintosh* computers. So turn those into negative keywords by putting a minus sign in front of them. The above list now looks like this:

> voice mail software
> voice mail business software
> voice mail software for panasonic
> voice mail business software
> multiple voice mail software
> multi line voice mail system software vru
> norstar voice mail software
> software to record voice mail
> -free
> -mac
> -macintosh
> -broadcast
> -broadcasting

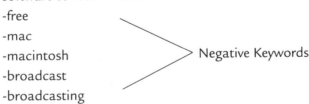 Negative Keywords

When you set up your ad campaigns, each one of these keyword lists is going to go into a different group with its own set of ads.

6. *Cut out irrelevant keywords to improve your CTR even more.* Sometimes in your keyword collecting you'll inadvertently be bidding on terms in your keyword list that

don't belong at all. This example is from a campaign that targets people who are searching on the subject of religion:

☐	●	religion and science	$0.05 ⬚	0	0	0.00%	$0
☐	●	comparative religion	$0.05 ⬚	0	35	0.00%	$0
☐	●	japanese religions	$0.05 ⬚	0	1	0.00%	$0
☐	●	losing my religion lyrics	$0.05 ⬚	0	0	0.00%	$0
☐	●	babylonian religion	$0.05 ⬚	0	0	0.00%	$0
☐	●	spanish religion	$0.05 ⬚	0	0	0.00%	$0

Most of the keywords here are irrelevant to what we were going after. They got zero clicks and nearly zero impressions. Of course, "losing my religion lyrics" takes the cake. We'll delete that keyword and then stick in the term "lyrics" as a negative keyword. We'll now get a higher CTR because now that big fat "0" is no longer bringing down the average.

SPLIT TEST YOUR ADS!

IMPORTANT TIP: The key to long-term success on AdWords—and to keeping your bid prices down—is always testing two ads at the same time (referred to as split testing), deleting the inferior one, and then trying to beat the best one. Always have two ads running at the same time.

The Ads: We'll write two ads. Google will rotate them simultaneously. One will have a better CTR than the other; we'll later delete the inferior one, write a new one, and again split test those. Little by little your CTR will go up, up, up.

Voice Mail Software Make Your Communication Easier With Custom, Expandable Systems www.SmithTelecom.com/VMsoftware	← Headline contains your keywords ← 2nd line contains a BENEFIT ← 3rd line contains a FEATURE or OFFER ← 4th line: Display URL has a keyword in the subdirectory/VMsoftware that will help the CTR

Voice Mail Software
For Any Business & Any Phone System
Same Day Installation & Easy Terms
www.SmithTelecom.com/VMsoftware

Same formula for Ad #2, but we're testing a different message. Notice that we capitalize the important words.

So here's what we've done:

· We've generated a list of various keywords: voice mail system, voice mail software, voice mail service, auto attendant, etc.
· We've used keyword research tools to drill down and generate many variations on these keywords.
· Each family of keywords goes into its own group.
· We rotate two ads at the same time, all the time, and constantly try to beat our best.
· When visitors click on the ad, they are taken to the exact page on your site that has a specific solution to their exact problem—not the home page. No guessing or clicking all over the place to find what they want.

Here's another example of how to cluster keywords into groups and campaigns, for a variety of martial arts-related terms:

	Campaign #1 Self Defense	Campaign #2 Martial Arts	Campaign #3 Fighting	Campaign #4 Security & Safety	Campaign #5 Protection
How to Organize Your Campaigns and Ad Groups					
Ad Group #1	Women's Self Defense	Karate	Wrestling	Personal Safety	Self Protection
Ad Group #2	Defense Class	Tae Kwon Do	Grappling	Women's Safety	Women's Protection
Ad Group #3	Defense Video	Aikido	Hand-to-Hand Combat	Personal Security	Child Protection
Ad Group #4	Defense Tactic	Hapkido	Weapons Combat	Children's Security	Assault Protection

Do you want to make it easy to manage campaigns and match your keywords well to ads within each ad group? Organize your campaigns this way, and it will be. More importantly, you'll get more clicks.

Note: This can also be a sound way to organize campaigns for Google's Display Network (GDN). Just note that search campaigns must be separated from GDN campaigns in order to be effective. (More on GDN campaigns in a later chapter.)

	Campaign #1a Self Defense (search)	Campaign #1b Self Defense (GDN)	Campaign #2a Martial Arts (search)	Campaign #2b Martial Arts (GDN)	Campaign #3a Fighting (search)	Campaign #3b Fighting (GDN)
Ad Group #1	Women's Self Defense	Women's Self Defense	Karate	Karate	Wrestling	Wrestling
Ad Group #2	Defense Class	Defense Class	Tae Kwon Do	Tae Kwon Do	Grappling	Grappling
Ad Group #3	Defense Video	Defense Video	Aikido	Aikido	Hand-to-Hand Combat	Hand-to-Hand Combat
Ad Group #4	Defense Tactic	Defense Tactic	Hapkido	Hapkido	Weapons Combat	Weapons Combat

NEVER, EVER, EVER LET GOOGLE DO THIS

Occasionally, high-spending customers (and sometimes small ones too) get a phone call or an email from a Google rep, offering to "optimize your ad campaigns."

Many customers who had previously built their campaigns according to our precise instructions have taken up Google on its offer. There are very few clients who didn't report to me that it was an unmitigated disaster. It cost a client in the UK about $50,000. Google may have built the greatest piano in the history of the world but that sure doesn't mean it knows how to play it.

The only way to truly understand the Google machine is by spending your own money. It has a funny way of forcing you to learn from your mistakes. Google employees haven't learned anything they know on their own dime, so they generally have no clue how to optimize a real-world campaign.

If you ever take up Google on any such offer, *do not under any circumstances let it touch the campaigns you built*. Ask it to set up separate campaigns that run in parallel. Then compare the performance throttling the daily budget of each campaign. Restore the old ones immediately if the new ones are inferior.

Important tip: Do not pause display network campaigns; it resets the data. Use the daily budget tool to lower the traffic instead. Then you can easily restore the budget and original performance.

THE "PEEL & STICK" STRATEGY: GET A HIGHER CTR
JUST BY MOVING YOUR KEYWORDS INTO NEW AD GROUPS

This is an old example from Google's previous interface, but it still illustrates the point well. Look at this ad group and the fact that most of its keywords are getting CTRs of above 2.0 percent. Notice how some of these keywords could be headlines of their own:

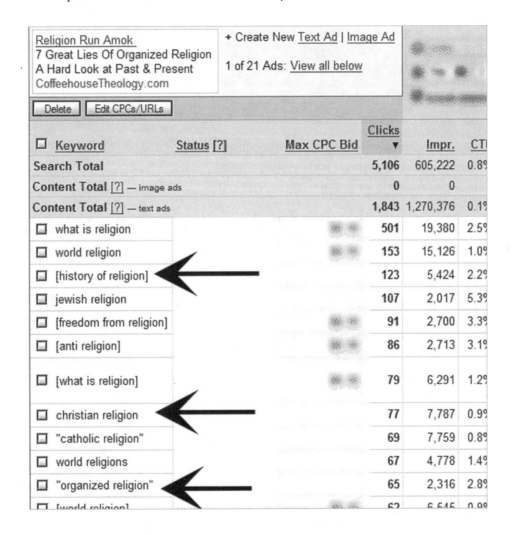

We noticed that. So we did something about it. Pulled those keywords out of that list and came up with several brand-new ad groups. Here's one:

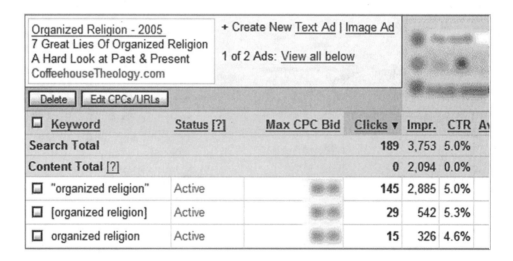

The CTR on [history of religion] jumped from 2.2 percent up to 3.0 percent. That's an improvement of 36 percent, with so little work!

But it gets better:

That improved the click-through rate by 79 percent! Impressive. Plus, you'll notice that the keyword shows up not once but twice in the ad copy. That didn't hurt one bit.

Want a better CTR? Want higher positions on the page without paying any more per click? Want more profit in your pocket at the end of the month? This trick will work for you again and again. It's called Peel & Stick.

You take a high-traffic keyword, peel it out of a group and stick it in a new one, with its own ad. It only takes a few minutes.

Why "Peel & Stick" Is So Simple, So Powerful

Sometimes after you turn on your traffic you'll discover there are keywords in your ad groups that get a lot more hits than you were expecting. And their CTRs, you're convinced, could be a lot higher.

Delete any keyword you find like that and stick it into a new ad group with a clever ad that matches it perfectly.

That's "Peel & Stick." As simple as that. This technique can do wonders for your CTRs.

Why does it work so well? Very simply, it's because people are more likely to click on your ad if they see your keyword in the headline.

Want to improve your CTR by as much as 80 percent? Organize your keywords differently.

More Easy-to-Follow Examples

Here are some ads that some of our associates ran for their businesses, with a sample of a few of the actual keywords they used. Best part is, they're far from perfect. They can be improved even more:

How to Sell Anything
Skills Your Competitors Don't Have
Powerful Secrets You Won't Believe
www.XYZ.com

    how to sell
    [how to sell]
    "how to sell"
    –marijuana
    –devil
    –soul

These negative keywords are kind of funny. You definitely don't want those searches!

Dentures to Be Proud Of
Free In-Office Consultation & More
For a Smile that Wins New Friends
www.XYZ.com

    dentures
    affordable dentures
    denture repair
    same-day dentures
    permanent dentures
    partial denture

How many clicks is "denture repair" or "partial denture" getting? If there are a lot, each of them needs peel & stick.

Power Supplies to Order
Custom Design Requests Welcomed
Any OEM Application, ISO 9002
www.XYZ.com

    power supply
    power supplies
    12 volt power supply
    5v power supply
    class 2 power supply
    ac power supply

Try a separate ad group just for "AC power supply."

A/C Transformers Qty 250+
For OEM Applications, ISO 9002
Custom 1-Day Quote, Fast Delivery
www.XYZ.com

    transformers
    power transformer
    transformer accessories
    power supply transformers
    power transformer tube
    –robots in disguise

Admittedly, the length of some of these search terms might make peel & stick a bit challenging, especially if you're trying to fit the keyword in the headline and be descriptive at the same time.

Toothache Relief, Finally!
Your Local Pain-Free Dentist
Improves Your Health & Much More
www.XYZ.com

    toothache
    toothaches
    toothache remedies
    toothache cure
    toothache relief
    toothache pain

If "toothache remedies" gets enough searches to make a difference, do peel & stick with it.

Day Trading Course
Develop Your Personal Schedule
Maximize Your Trading Potential
www.XYZ.com

    trading course
    [trading course]
    trading training
    [trading training]
    "trading books"
    commodities course
    futures course

If "trading training" is getting enough clicks already, pull it out and put it with a new ad. "Commodities course" and "futures course" belong in their own separate ad groups, no question.

If you organize your Google ad groups so that your keywords call out to searchers from your headline and ad text, you can get more visitors to your site, earn better positions on the page, and pay less money for your clicks.

Do you want to improve your click-through rate by 10 percent, 30 percent, 80 percent, or better and not have to pay a penny more per click? It's all in how you organize things.

As simple as this is—so simple that most people miss it the first time—it's the single most effective secret that has helped our customers get more clicks without paying a penny more.

For a look at a classic old-style ideal ad group that still serves as a good starter model for matching keywords and ads on Google search, visit www.perrymarshall.com/adwords/idealadgroup.htm.

Uncle Claude Sez

You are presenting an ad to millions. Among them is a percentage, small or large, whom you hope to interest. Go after that percentage and try to strike the chord that responds. . . . They will decide by a glance—by your headline. . . . Address the people you seek and them only.

Chapter 5

Develop High-Quality Keyword Lists to Craft Killer Headlines

At my house we've got a wonderful children's book called *No, David!* David is a little boy whose mom is constantly telling him, "No, David!"

David is about to knock over a potted plant.

"No, David!"

David is chewing with his mouth open.

"No, David!"

David is playing baseball in the living room.

"No, David!"

David is about to push the aquarium off the table and spill the goldfish out on the floor.

"No, David!"

From the first moment, my son Cuyler was *glued* to this book. For months it was his favorite book in the whole world.

Why?

You already know why.

It's because Cuyler's Mamma (and Daddy) were always shouting *"No, Cuyler!"* (Maybe it was because he was knocking over potted plants, chewing with his mouth open, playing baseball in the living room, and spilling the goldfish all over the floor.)

The only way to make it better would be to have a book called *No, Cuyler!* Who knows? Maybe somebody will start selling personalized versions of the book.

Cuyler had a favorite part of the story. Know what it was?

It was at the very end, when David's mom says, "Come here, David."

Mamma gives David a hug and says, "I love you, David."

Cuyler *loved* that page. Especially the hug he got every time we closed the book.

Cuyler loved *No, David!* because this book described a day—every day—in the life of Cuyler. *No, David!* is a page from his own diary.

Nothing endears you to your customer like reading him his own diary, showing that you know what it feels like to be *him*.

And *that's* what it means to enter the conversation inside your customer's head. When you step right into his thoughts and talk to him the way he talks to other people and himself, about things that are important to him, he'll listen to you. Just like Cuyler did.

> You'll capture the attention of your customer when you enter the conversation already taking place inside his head. With Google, you do this—and get more clicks as a result—by using your keywords skillfully in your ad. Bid on more keywords, and you can capture the attention of more people.

The keyword they type in *is* the conversation inside their head, at that very moment.

Your ad will capture people's interest when it repeats to them what they're thinking. So putting your keywords in your headline *and* in the body of your ad *and* in your URL is all part of a sound advertising strategy.

The more places in your ad that you have keywords showing up, the better your chances of getting the clicks. That means the headline. That means the body of the ad. It even means the display URL. If someone types in "German" or "Learn German," notice how many times he or she'll see their keyword in this ad:

<u>Want to Learn German?</u>
5 Crucial Principles You Must Know
To Master German, and Fast
www.mastergermanfaster.com

If effective marketing means speaking directly to what people are searching on, and repeating it back at them, how do you go about finding out what people are searching on in the first place? Where do you go to get the good keywords, especially the keywords that are worth the most money?

MORE TOOLS FOR YOUR TOOLBOX: GOOGLE'S FREE KEYWORD TOOL

The quickest place to start looking for good keywords is with Google's free keyword tool, available via the green "Reporting and Tools" tab at the top of your account page. It gives you an immediate sense of how valuable each of your keywords will be relative to the others.

Let's say you provide instruction in German. So you head over to the keyword tool and type in "German":

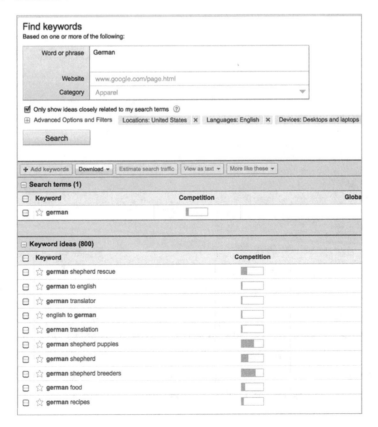

One look at this and it's obvious that there are keywords here that won't serve you a bit.

Negative Keywords: Get Rid of Visitors You Don't Want

You haven't spent a penny yet, and you can already guess what your major *negative keywords* are going to be, if you plan to bid on a broad term like "German." These are words on your list that you specifically do not want your ad to show when people type them in. You can manually enter terms into your keyword list with negatives in front of them:

-shepherd

-rescue

-puppies

-breeders

-food

-dictionary

-translator

-flag

-girls

(etc.)

Or from within the keyword tool you can click on the dropdown menu that appears when you mouse over the space next to the keyword. Click to add negatives in individually:

Now your ads won't show when people include these words in their search. *Tip:* You're going to want to drill down more narrowly. Instead of a broad term like "German" (which, we promise you, even with scores of negative keywords in place will *still* be hard to make convert), start with a keyword phrase of at least two words, such as "learn German" or "speak fluent German." Also, take advantage of the little checkbox that says "Only show ideas closely related to my search terms." That will filter out a good deal of bunk.

The Math of Negative Keywords: Only Good News for Your CTR

Remember that if you include negative keywords in your lists, you'll pull down the number of impressions that your ads get because they'll show for fewer searches. That means that your CTR will automatically go up. But notice the math of this: If you could pull down your number of impressions by 20 percent, your CTR would improve not by 20 percent, but by 25 percent. Likewise,

- When you cut unwanted impressions by 30 percent, your CTR will increase by 42 percent
- When you cut unwanted impressions by 40 percent, your CTR will improve by 67 percent
- When you cut unwanted impressions by 50 percent, your CTR will double.

Negative keywords won't affect the CTR of exact-matched keywords, but they will help your CTR on phrase- and broad-matched terms. If you manage them the right way, there's no way they *can't* help.

Imagine getting the same number of clicks as before, but because your CTR is double what it previously was, Google gives you your clicks at half price!

YOUR ULTIMATE KEYWORD LIST

It used to be that the more keywords you could find, the better. Not so anymore. The most recession-proof AdWords advertisers carefully choose the one hill in their market worth dying on and build their business around it.

But when you want to expand on what you have or enter entirely new markets, the following will point you in the right direction.

Match Your Keywords to Your Website

With Google's keyword tool you have several choices: If you've already got a full website up and you don't want to start completely from scratch guessing all the keywords that are represented there, use the "Website" field in Google's tool and simply enter the web address for one or several pages on your site. Google will search the site and come up with your keyword list for you.

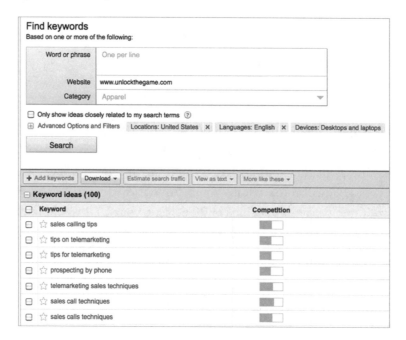

Research Keywords by Topic

Another choice is to find keywords by topic. Click the dropdown button in the "Category" field, and choose a topic or subtopic. Hit "Search," and you'll get a broad swath of results.

This feature ensures that you've left no possible stone unturned. Note also that as with the "German" example, many if not most of these terms you'll want to add in as negatives.

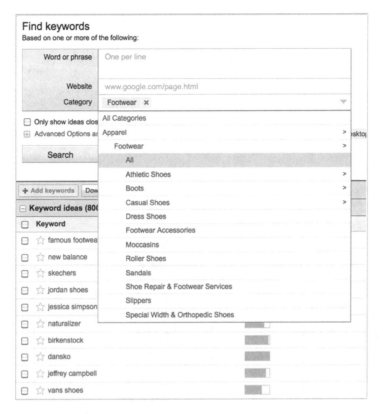

Wordtracker: Another Old Favorite

Wordtracker has been around a great many years and is a good "sanity check" alternative to Google. A free one-search version is available at freekeywords.wordtracker.info:

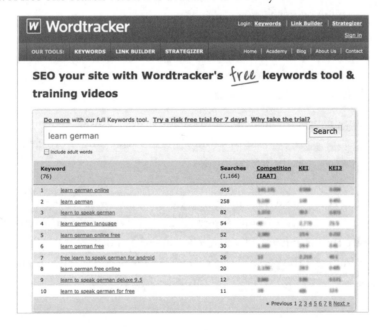

The full version alerts you to all of the possible directions you can take with your keywords. It does this by

1. showing you all the variations people have typed in over the last 60 days, and
2. telling you the number of searches each one has had through Dogpile and Meta-Crawler.

The more keywords you have access to, the merrier.

Now if in fact every keyword is a market of its own, that means that a number of things are true:

· Each keyword gets its own unique number of searches.
· Each keyword converts differently to sales.
· Each keyword has its own level of competition.
· Each keyword represents something slightly different that folks are thinking when they type it in.

SECOND-GUESSING YOUR CUSTOMERS

Bryan here: I'd like to share some insight I've gained from marketing to people who want to learn Mandarin Chinese.

I sell books to expats in Taiwan and Mainland China that teach them how to learn to speak Mandarin by immersion in their environment. Here are some of the search terms people use to find it:

learn chinese
speak chinese
mandarin
learn mandarin
mandarin chinese
learn mandarin chinese

Just the thought process alone behind each of these search terms is different. The person who types in "learn Mandarin Chinese" is already being more clear and specific than the person who types in "learn Chinese."

How so?

The former is someone who knows that he does *not* want to learn Cantonese, the dialect spoken down south in Guangdong Province and Hong Kong. You've already got a more self-aware thinker on your hands, someone with a different set of questions and challenges in mind than the person who's thinking more generically about "picking up a little Chinese."

Never mind the different mind-set for the person who types in "study Chinese" instead of "learn Chinese." Think about it.

Your market is the same way. Every keyword represents a different mind-set, a different set of needs, a different personality. So how do you know who is who?

You can poll the folks searching on the different keywords. At SurveyMonkey.com you can set up surveys and questionnaires in which you ask people specific questions about what they want or need, and then trace their varying answers back through the different keywords they found you on. More on this in a second.

MORE ON THE PSYCHOLOGY OF KEYWORDS

The following strategy is taught by our associate Glenn Livingston, who has a comprehensive method for researching a market before you actually dive into it (www. Glenn-Livingston.com). Glenn points out a key fact about different keywords and how they represent different kinds of thinking: Nobody types in one keyword.

Nobody Types in Just One Keyword

People don't usually just type in one keyword, find what they're looking for immediately, and quit. They type in a series of keywords. So, for example, a person might type in "learn Chinese" at first, and then go back and type in "learn Mandarin" to get more information and see more options. Or it might be the other way around.

So if you can capture the full attention of a person typing in the *first* in a series of searches, you've intercepted him and saved yourself from being pitted against other competitors on his next search.

Find Your Customer's Underlying Motivation

Glenn explains this well. He became known in a number of internet circles as "the Guinea Pig Guru" for his website www.GuineaPigSecrets.com. After doing careful surveys and ask-campaigns, he discovered that the number-one question bugging the folks who typed in that particular keyword was, "How do I keep my guinea pig and his cage from smelling?"

Knowing that, Glenn incorporated a lead-in to that very issue in the headline of his landing page—just for people who came to his website via that keyword—and increased his sales significantly.

You'll win with Google's editors when you hit on that *explicit conversation.* You'll win with your customers—as Glenn did—when you hit on that *implicit conversation.*

This fact is true of online marketing because it was already true of *offline* marketing. It's a principle of human nature that runs back to the days of bows and arrows, flint and fire. Whether you're selling goods and services by using a web page or by direct mail, or if you're simply trying to persuade another person to see your point of view, you speak directly to what he or she is thinking, both explicitly and implicitly.

The Conversation (in Your Customer's Head)

When a guy tells you he wants to lose 50 pounds, he's probably not lying to you. But there's something even he doesn't realize: He really wants to lose 50 pounds *and* still be able to stop at Krispy Kreme every morning, eat Burger King every day for lunch, and sit on the couch watching TV every night with a beer and a bag of Ruffles.

It's the advertisers that speak to *both* wishes who sell the diet pills and weight loss shakes and appetite suppressants, over and over again, year in and year out. Sounds cynical, but it's reality.

So you're aiming to hit people on *two levels*.

There's the "explicit conversation" in their minds, which is the exact keyword they typed in. It's what you want in your ad and, if at all possible, on your landing page. Google will even reward you for doing this with your ad by offering you a lower minimum bid and giving you better positioning on the page by convincing Google's computers that your ad copy is more relevant.

Then there's the second level—the "implicit conversation" in their minds, which is unique to each keyword, the secrets of which you may not discover until you've talked to your customers and done the research.

Glenn did that with his guinea pig site, and he's now impervious to competition.

It's when you hit that second level that your clicks turn into more sales. It's at that second level that you become impervious to cocky competitors who don't understand your customer the way you do.

MORE MARKETS, MORE CASH: HOW TO GET BEYOND THE "OBVIOUS" KEYWORDS

You know about Wordtracker. There are others that give you a different emphasis and have features of their own that make them unique and very much worth having.

Just as your toolbox in the garage has a Phillips *and* a flathead screwdriver, not just one or the other, so, too, do you need more than one of these major keyword tools. Each has its use, and owning more is like having a bigger toolbox.

And there's more to learn still.

The first list of keywords you come up with, even if it's a long one, will be incomplete. AltaVista once reported that 20 percent of all its searches were totally unique in the history of AltaVista. You never know what people are going to hunt for.

So here are some fresh ideas:

1. *Use synonyms.* You'll want lots of synonyms and related subjects in your stockpile of keyword candidates so that you can be sure you're reaching people who are looking for what you've got.
2. *Try bidding on brand names.* You can't use a brand name other than your own in the copy of your ad, but you can bid on it as a keyword. Names of companies, magazines, associations, famous people, and famous places may all relate to your product. For example, for "billiards" you might bid on the name of famous pool player Jeremy Jones. For drums you might bid on "Buddy Rich."
3. *Explore a thesaurus like LexFN.com.* LexFN.com is a website that's been around for awhile, and is one I still find extremely useful and interesting. It's a clever thesaurus that finds scores of synonyms and related concepts for you.

For example, here are LexFN's results when searching on the term "golf." You'll note the long list it gives you. A fun site to play with!

```
golf triggers golfing
golf triggers garment
golf triggers fairways
golf triggers cart
golf triggers arthritis
golf triggers yard
golf triggers woods
golf triggers vuitton
golf triggers vineyard
golf triggers vacation
golf triggers twelfth
golf triggers trunk
golf triggers spikes
golf is a kind of outdoor game
golf is a kind of play
golf is more general than clock golf
golf is more general than match play
golf is more general than medal play
golf is more general than miniature golf
golf is more general than professional golf
golf is more general than round
golf is more general than round of golf
golf is more general than stroke play
golf rhymes with ahlf
golf rhymes with ralf
golf sounds like golla
golf sounds like goller
golf sounds like golay
```

Try These Keyword Variations

Variations on Nouns:	Variations in Hyphenation:	Adjectives:
Shoe	Email	Mini
Shoes	e-mail	Large
	e mail	Red
Variations on Verbs:	firetruck	Blue
Drive	fire truck	Green
Drove	fire-truck	Cheap
Driven		Premium
Driven		Budget
Driving	**Variations on Names:**	2006
Steer	Tolkien	Used
Steering	Tolkein	New
Steered	J.R.R. Tolkien	
	JRR Tolkien	
Wrong Apostrophes:	John Ronald Reuel Tolkien	
Driver's	John Ronald Tolkien	
Tire's	John Reuel Tolkien	
	John Tolkien	

4. *Visual Thesaurus.* Here's a tool that's useful, and entertaining as well. Its power lies in the way it gives you synonyms and related ideas and also shows you other ways your word or phrase can be interpreted.

   For example, "game" can refer to a board game like Monopoly, but it can also refer to a sporting event happening later that day or wild animals for hunting or eating. You can use it to mean you're ready for an adventure. As an AdWords advertiser, you need to be clear about this. Visual Thesaurus ensures that none of these word meanings escapes your attention.

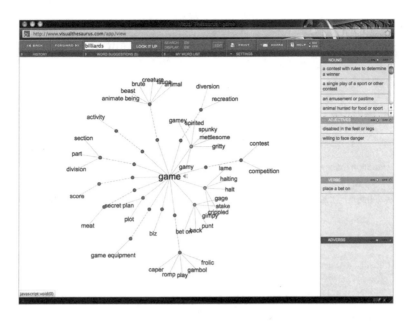

5. *Glossaries and indexes.* We recently built an AdWords campaign for a client in which we went out and got a book on his subject. We went through the glossary and the index and used a large number of the terms in the glossary as keywords. Many of these cost only $0.05 a click, and they get a serious amount of traffic.

6. *The "See search terms" feature.* The best intelligence by far now comes from your own account. Google constantly serves up your ads for searches that don't precisely match the keywords you've chosen. You can see which of these terms got you clicks by using this feature in your Keywords tab. It works for any match type except exact. (More on that in a moment.)

    This allows you to find the precise people who were looking for you and found you. It also gives you terms to add to your negative keyword lists.

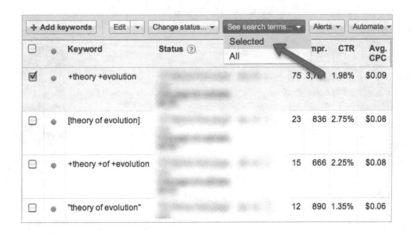

7. 7.*Google's own search box.* Just typing in your keyword into Google will activate Google's auto-suggest feature, which shows you how your term is being used

	Search term	Match type	Clicks ⑦	Impr.	CTR ⑦	Avg CPC ⑦
	Total		**75**	**3,781**	**1.98%**	**$0.0**
☐	evolution theory	Broad match	8	338	2.37%	$0.1
☐	evolutionary theory	Broad match	10	233	4.29%	$0.0
☐	the theory of evolution	Broad match	1	39	2.56%	$0.4
☑	darwin's evolution theory with emotions	Broad match	1	2	50.00%	$0.2
☐	what is the definition of evolutionary theory	Broad match	2	9	22.22%	$0.1
☐	what evolution is from theory to fact science masters	Broad match	1	2	50.00%	$0.2
☑	big bang theory evolution t shirt women's clothing	Phrase match	1	2	50.00%	$0.1

in searches right now, today, in your immediate geographic location. It changes from day to day and week to week, and place to place. It shows you items that are suddenly popping up in the news and in popular culture, and anything related to the current holiday or sports season. Again, it gives you more fodder for keywords you haven't thought to bid on as well as keywords to use as negatives.

EXPANDING YOUR CONTROL OVER YOUR KEYWORDS: UNCOVER KEYWORD NICHES, SAVE MONEY . . . AND KEEP YOUR SANITY

These days, plain old broad-match keywords without quotes or brackets can get your ads shown for a wild variety of sometimes scarcely related searches, unless you tell Google otherwise. If I bid on "German shepherd," Google will show me for singulars and plurals alike, and any and every misspelling. That's usually a good thing.

But sometimes I want more control than that.

That's where phrase, exact, and modified broad-match options come in. These matching options hide more surprises than you might realize.

Here's a rundown of all the matching options.

Broad-Match Keywords

When you insert keywords at the time you're setting up your campaigns, these are the keywords that don't have any delimiters around them. For example:

> used cars
> japanese used cars
> used cars for sale

You need to be cautious. If you don't provide negative keywords, that keyword phrase "used cars" will show your ad for all of the following searches:

> used car
> german used cars
> used car dealer
> used police cars
> cars used in filming dukes of hazzard

And it may show your ad for searches such as "pre-owned cars" or "used trucks" or "repo vehicles" and any of a dozen other less-related searches. You may not want that.

Phrase Matches

These keywords are placed with quotes (" ") around them. For example:

> "used cars"
> "chicago used cars"
> "used cars for sale"

These will make your ad show in searches that include these terms in this order, without extra words inserted. Such as the following:

> used cars
> old chicago used cars
> used cars for sale chicago

Your ad won't show for these searches, however:

> used police cars
> used car dealer

Exact Matches

These keywords are placed with square brackets ([ ]) around them:

> [used cars]
> [chicago used cars]
> [used cars for sale]

With these keywords, only people who typed in these exact phrases, in this order, will see your ad. None of the following keyword searches will show your ad:

> used car
> used cars chicago
> german used cars
> old chicago used cars
> used cars for sale chicago
> used police cars

Modified Broad Match

We recommend that most new advertisers use this option. It keeps Google honest! These keywords are entered with a plus sign (+) in front of one or more of the words in the phrase:

> +used +cars
> +japanese +used +cars

> used +cars for sale +chicago

That plus sign "anchors" the word it's attached to, and essentially says to Google, "If this word isn't used in a person's search, then you cannot show my ad." The phrase still behaves like broad match, but it's limited. So if I use this keyphrase:

> +used +cars

. . . then Google will show me when people type in the following:

> used cars
> german used cars
> used cars in santa cruz
> used kia car dealer

. . . but not when people type in these phrases:

> used trucks
> pre-owned cars
> honda pre-owned vehicles

As an advertiser you're free to use that plus sign in front of any or all of the terms in your keyword phrase.

THE KILLER KEYWORD SECRETS

You've been given some valuable angles:

- There are always keywords that are overloaded with competition, where bid prices are jacked up far beyond their real market value.
- At the same time there are always other keywords that are overlooked but which represent better, more responsive markets—which you can find if you use the right tools.
- Literally every keyword in your list is a market of its own.
- Every keyword represents a mind-set that people have when they type it.
- Behind everything explicit that your customers type in when they're searching, there's some want, need, question, or assumption that they have (but may be completely unaware of).
- Some keyword markets are bigger than others.
- Some keyword markets are more competitive than others.
- Some keyword markets produce more dividends for the winners than others.
- You sell when you match that "implicit conversation" that your customers have with themselves.

A roundup of keyword research tools, with reviews of their pros and cons, is available at www.perrymarshall.com/supplement.

HEADLINES AND KILLER COPY FROM *COSMOPOLITAN* MAGAZINE

We can't say we actually *like* Cosmopolitan magazine; after all, under the guise of supposedly liberating the modern woman, they've degraded her, turning her into a manipulative, greed-driven, appearance-obsessed, fashion-diet sex slave.

But every now and then when we're at the grocery store we might pick up a copy. Why on earth? Because throughout every issue—especially on the cover—are the most visceral lizard-brain headlines found in the publishing business. The fastest route to writing a power headline might be to simply steal one from *Cosmo*.

Recently we met with a client and spent most of the day developing a direct-mail piece. The client sells boring industrial hardware. It would put most folks to sleep, literally. But we brought copies of *Cosmo* and *Redbook* to assist. And it was an amazing process. The guys in the room thought we were crazy . . . until we started to actually apply the formulas. They were amazed at how well it works.

Here's what *Cosmo* did for us:

Cosmo Headline	*Our Headline*
The New Panties He'll Flip For	**The New Fuel Additive That Top Mechanics Flip For**
Selena Gomez She's So Different Than You Think	**Linux** It's So Different than MCSE's Think
Be a Sex Kitten This Summer Hair, Makeup & Body Tricks to Make You Look Hot as Hell	**Be a Speed Demon This Summer** Project, Budget & Staffing Tricks to Make Your Operations Scream
"A Little to the Left" How to Say What You Want in Bed Without Bruising His Ego	**"Budget Cuts Again?"** How to Challenge the CEO Without Losing Your Job
Did the Man of Her Dreams Murder Her? Cosmo Investigates	**Did Bad Polymers Cause the Firestone Fiasco?** ACME Company Investigates

All of these speak directly to issues that engineers—or *Cosmo* readers—think about on a daily basis, sometimes an hourly basis. We just echoed those issues right back at them.

It's a method that works for you time and time again.

Oh—and if you'd like to use this approach without forking over five bucks for a *Cosmo* every month, just visit www.Magazines.com, and click on the magazine covers to get a full-size view.

Uncle Claude Sez

The purpose of a headline is to pick out people you can interest. You wish to talk to someone in a crowd. So the first thing you say is, "Hey there, Bill Jones" to get the right person's attention.

So it is in an advertisement. What you have will interest certain people only, and for certain reasons. You care only for those people. Then create a headline which will hail those people only.

We pick out what we wish to read by headlines, and we don't want those headlines misleading. The writing of headlines is one of the greatest journalistic arts. They either conceal or reveal an interest.

How to Write Google Ads That Attract Eyeballs, Get Clicks, and Earn You Money

Your Google ads are an army of 100,000 tiny salesmen traversing the entire planet for you. And you only have to pay their salaries when the customers crack their doors open to listen to them.

■ ■ ■

Advertising is *selling in print.* That means the words you should use in your Google ads are the same words you use when you're on the phone or sitting across the table from a prospect, convincing him to buy something.

Before you try to write advertising copy, you should try to explain what you're selling to someone who might buy. And then . . . when they raise their eyebrows and lean forward, pay attention to what you just said.

My friend and mentor John Carlton, one of the highest-paid advertising copywriters in the world, spends weeks, sometimes months, researching his clients' products or services, going from person to person or business to business, gauging their reactions and questions. John learns what buyers really want and the certain turns of phrase that make or break the sale.

My own website sports a perfect example of this. I offer a CD called "Guerrilla Marketing for Hi-Tech Sales People" (www.perrymarshall.com/gm). The title of this CD came about exactly as follows. I was walking a trade show floor wearing a "speaker" badge a couple of years ago, and people would ask me what I was speaking on.

I tried a few different titles: "21 Secrets of High-Impact Low-Cost Marketing". . . "The Cold Call Curse". . . "Advertising Strategies for Technical Sales". . . but the one that provoked positive reactions was "Guerrilla Marketing for Hi-Tech Sales People." And that's what it's been ever since.

Those tiny Google ads will succeed for exactly the same reasons. The only challenge is your limited space. The headline is 25 characters or less, and each line of the body is 35 characters. The website URL displayed in the ad can also be up to 35 characters long.

So those are your limits. And that's OK, because your goal is not complex: just be *clear, simple,* and *relevant.* Claude Hopkins understood this well:

> *Literary qualifications have no more to do with it than oratory has with salesmanship. One must be able to express himself briefly, clearly and convincingly, just as a salesman must. But fine writing is a distinct disadvantage. So is unique literary style. They take attention from the subject. . . . Fine talkers are rarely good salesmen. . . . Successful salesmen are rarely good speechmakers. . . . They are plain and sincere men who know their customers. . . . So it is in ad writing.*

English majors and Ph.D.s (and even MBAs) generally suffer from severe marketing debilitations. In advertising, an academic education is more of a liability than an asset! You don't need to be a literary genius.

Google Ads are the language of the street, not the ivory tower. Speak to your customers in the language they respond to in everyday conversation, and they'll click.

GREAT HEADLINES: RIVETING TO YOUR CUSTOMER, DEAD BORING TO ANYONE ELSE

Just as in print advertising and on web pages, your headline swings the biggest difference in response. It's in that split second of reading your headline copy that your customer first makes up his mind whether or not you're really relevant.

Start with that keyword your customer just typed in and fit it into your headline. That will be the first signal to him that you're truly relevant. This means that you'll want to create enough different ad groups that each of your major keywords can have an ad of its own.

Let's say that you sell custom power supplies. There's certainly more than one way potential customers might come looking for what you sell. They might search for "adaptors." They might search for "power supplies." They might search for "transformers."

So you'll go to your major keyword tool, such as Wordtracker or Google's keyword tool, and you'll come up with all the possible major variations and related terms for your market niche. Then you'll separate them out into smaller groups that you can match to specific ads. For example:

Custom Power Adaptors

www.xyzadaptors.com
Record-Speed Custom Production Time
Get a Full Quote in 1 Business Day

    adaptor
    adaptors
    ac adaptor
    power adaptor
    custom adaptors

Custom Transformers, Fast

www.xyzadaptors.com
Inventory Cost, Lead Time Advantage
Get a Quote in One Day or Less

    power transformers
    electrical transformers
    voltage transformers

Note: This ad group will need a strong set of negative keywords to block out traffic looking for Transformers® movie or toy information.

Power Supplies to Order

www.xyzadaptors.com
Inventory Cost, Lead Time Advantage
Get a Quote in One Day or Less

    power supply
    power supplies
    switching power supply
    dc power supplies
    ac power supply

These ads aren't very flashy, are they? They're not loaded with over-the-top language. In fact, to folks like you and me they're, frankly, boring. But that's okay. They aren't meant for the average guy on the street.

This particular company caters to engineers. It speaks the language that engineers would understand, relate to, and appreciate. It matches its audience just fine. And it gets a good click-through rate. (Too good, in fact.)

Use your major keywords in your headline, and create as many different ad groups as you need to do this with all of your biggest keywords. That's what makes the formula work.

YOUR AD TEXT: WHERE YOUR INNER SALESMAN COMES ALIVE

After your headline, you've still got a second chance to convince your customer even further that you've got what he wants and get more clicks. This is where your inner salesman comes alive.

There's a second secret that makes this work. Check out the difference between these two ads:

Popular Ethernet Terms 3 Page Guide—Free PDF Download Complex Words—Simple Definitions www.xyz.com **0.1% CTR**	Popular Ethernet Terms Complex Words—Simple Definitions 3 Page Guide—Free PDF Download www.xyz.com **3.6% CTR**

The second ad got *36 times* the CTR as the first! What happened? What was the secret?

Look closely at the two ads. They both have the exact same wording. There's only one difference between them. What is it? The first ad listed features and offers first, benefits second. The second ad listed benefits first.

This secret is just as true in long-copy print advertising as in those little thumbnail Google ads.

Features and offers are what your product has or what you're going to do. They describe it, what it includes, and how big or small or robust or thorough it is. Benefits, on the other hand, are the emotional payoffs your customer gets from using your product.

Define the Features

So the list of *features* for a book-and-video course you sell may include these items:

- 12 timeless principles
- 17 brief, easy-to-understand video tutorials
- 24 chapters, 222 pages of rock-solid content
- 64 full-color photos
- Helpful, easy-to-read charts and graphs
- Step-by-step tips and instructions
- Fascinating stories, anecdotes, and personal experiences
- Introduction by Malcolm Gladwell

Show Them the Benefits and the Payoff

But your list of *benefits* will tell your customer how she'll actually be helped by what you've written. Sometimes there's a little bit of crossover between these and the features:

- Achieve a 46 percent improvement in less than 30 minutes.
- Reach your goals in one-fourth the time using the 80/20 principle described in Chapter 5.
- Apply any one these 12 techniques immediately, and see instant results.
- Catapult energy levels, convert fat into muscle, develop strength, endurance, and flexibility all at the same time.
- Discover how making *more* mistakes along the way becomes a strategy in itself that will grow your skill level even faster.
- Get compliments from your friends as they ask you again and again (jealously), "What has *happened* to you?"

There's no way to pack all of this kind of content into a Google ad, granted. But the principle of dividing benefits from features is universal. Your Google ad is about benefits (emotional payoffs) more than anything else. And when you describe benefits *and* features both, it almost always serves you to put benefits *first*.

The second ad did exactly that. Switching the order gave us a 3,600 percent improvement! We know this because we tested it. Will it work this way in your market? That's for you to find out.

You don't have to be a poet or a master copywriter to convince your customer that he or she will get something of value. State your case simply and clearly, and test to see if putting the benefits up front and the features second will boost your response.

Test Your URL and Grow Your Ad's Effectiveness

The display URL is the second most visible element in your ad. If you're lucky enough to have a domain name that uses the exact keyword phrase people are searching on, you're virtually guaranteed a high CTR. If you can *buy* such a domain, you could potentially double your CTR.

Regardless, with your existing URLs we recommend you test other variations like these in your display URL, including use of keywords as subdomains (which replace the "www") or subdirectories (which are always followed by the "/" slash), and capitalization within those subdirectories:

· www.healyourmarriage.com
· www.healyourmarriage.com/forgiving
· www.healyourmarriage.com/ForgiveHim
· forgiving.healyourmarriage.com

THE "GOLDILOCKS THEORY": WHY THE BEST ADWORDS ADS ARE NEVER OVER-THE-TOP

We thought we'd get ultra-creative one day, and we wrote up an in-your-face ad that would shock Google users into clicking. We were just sure it would work. After all, the number-one worst thing you can do is bore the hell out of people, right?

Here's what happened. It's the second ad below:

<u>D.I.Y. Sales Leads</u>
www.perrymarshall.com
Don't hire telemarketers
Make prospects chase you instead
42 Clicks | 1.0% CTR

<u>Escape Voicemail Jail</u>
www.perrymarshall.com
Get Customers to Chase You Instead
with Savvy Guerrilla Marketing
20 Clicks | 0.3% CTR
Deleted

We thought it was great. Our customers didn't. This happened again and again, and we learned a valuable lesson: Google searchers do not generally respond to hype. Nor do they respond to messages that are too plain. What works is something in the middle—intriguing, yet not pushy. Swipe ads from *Cosmo,* but do it with caution.

Andrew Goodman, the author of *Winning Results with Google AdWords*, calls it the "Goldilocks" principle. Not too hot; not too cold—you want the temperature to be *just right.*

Avoiding the Google "Slap"

Here's an ad that was very bold, *and* performed well at first . . .

> ### Prospecting Sucks
> www.perrymarshall.com
> Make B2B clients call you first
> with smart guerrilla marketing
> 1.1% CTR

> ### Disapproved

. . . until Google's editor saw it and *disapproved* it. Google doesn't let you use inflammatory words like "sucks" or "hate." We did get away with the word "stinks," however:

> ### Prospecting Stinks
> www.perrymarshall.com
> Telemarketing Annoys People
> Guerrilla Marketing is King
> 1.3% CTR

All-Time Most Successful Google Ads (These Will Surprise You)

The ads that bring in record-high numbers of clicks are never the most flashy, the most outlandish, the most brilliantly composed copy you'll find. Never. They're simply a function of saying the right thing at the right time to the right people.

Here are some real-life examples of ads that our coaching clients wrote—ads that brought in record-high click throughs. You'll notice how unspectacular their language is, how they're specific rather than general, they never completely follow all of the "rules," and they're sometimes not even the best English!

But these were tested *rigorously*. We worked and worked with our clients to help them create a message that perfectly matched what their customers were looking for, and their high CTRs show it:

Light Folding Tables So Strong and Durable you get an Unconditional Money-Back Guarantee www.mobiliteuk.com 24.5% CTR *—David Morgan* *Oxford, UK*	**Kona Condos for Sale** Big Island MLS and Agents Search Property Listings www.MarylRealty.com 18.2% CTR *—Claudia Hafner* *Waikoloa, HI*

The Lupus Recovery Diet
New Book! Learn how I overcame
Lupus without drugs or supplements.
www.LupusRecoveryDiet.com
9.5% CTR

—Jill Harrington
Mill Valley, CA

Mens Hair Growth Solution
25 Facts You Don't Know About Your
Hair Growth Problem. But Should!
HowToStopHairLoss.com
25.1% CTR

—Ed Keay-Smith
South Perth, WA, Australia

More Rules of the Road

Our friend Richard Stokes and his team over at AdGooroo.com share some examples of affiliate ads that perform stellarly on Google and therefore get solid positions and low bid prices and which get served well above 95 percent of the time on searches. Here are a couple:

Keyword "FTD fruit baskets":

Fruit Gift Baskets, FRESH
capalbosOnline.com/Since-1906
Always Fresh! Register & Save 5% on
Every Order. Nationwide Delivery.

Keyword "fashion sneakers":

Fashion Sneakers & Shoes
www.zappos.com/Fashion-Sneakers/
Upgrade To Free Overnight Shipping
By Ordering One Item of Clothing!

Why do these work?

· Both include the keyword phrase in the ad's headline.
· Both make careful use of exclamation points.
· The second has an implicit call to action ("Upgrade to . . .").
· Each word is capitalized, and the first ad makes use of all caps.
· The second ad makes careful use of the word "free."
· Specific, concrete numbers are put to use wherever possible.

FOCUSING YOUR ADS TO SAVE $$$ ON CLICKS

Your Google ads are an army of hardworking salespeople whose job it is to bring as many of the best prospects possible to your website. But you don't want just anybody.

You don't want tire kickers; you don't want the looky-loos. You want genuinely interested people.

After all, you have to pay every time they click.

What to Do When a High CTR Is *Not* Your Goal

Sometimes you find yourself in a very crowded marketplace attempting to single out only a small percentage of people who you know are a real fit for what you offer.

That was the case with the adaptors example we showed you earlier. The business we were promoting provides custom-built electrical adaptors, converters, and transformers for high-tech original equipment manufacturers, and only deals in large-quantity orders.

You can imagine how many different types of people go looking on the internet for adaptors or converters or transformers in any given day. Even after we've used negative keywords (which we talked about in Chapters 4 and 5) to filter out the searches that we don't want—such as Transformers® toy robots or online dollar-to-yen currency converters—we've still got people searching for the same terms we're bidding on who aren't looking for what we offer.

The guy who's just looking for a replacement power adaptor for his personal IBM laptop, for example. He's not our man.

So it's up to our Google ad to filter out the rest of that traffic, to get as many *good* clicks as possible but as few of every other kind. The more is not the merrier.

Connect with Your Niche Customers

The key is being clear and specific. We're going to write an ad that addresses precisely the type of customer we're after:

AC/DC Converters for OEMs

xyzadaptors.com
Qty 250+, Rapid Custom Production
1-Day Quote & Overnight Delivery

This ad won't win any awards for high CTR or stunning copy, but it knocks out three criteria: 1) it's for people wanting *custom* design, not off-the-shelf, 2) it's for OEMs (original equipment manufacturers) only, and 3) it's for orders of 250 units or more.

A lot of people are going to see this ad and pass it up. And that's okay. All we want are clicks from people who match these criteria. The ad will do its job.

Again, there's no black magic. Just tell your story. Be clear, be straightforward, interesting, customer-centered and, most importantly, relevant. Sell on the computer screen just like you'd sell in person. And people will see that you're for real, and they'll click and buy.

IF THE GUYS AT THE BAR WILL BUY IT, YOU'VE GOT A WINNING AD

John Carlton tells the story of the highly paid, highly sought-after copywriter who writes sales letters aimed at blue-collar men. Before he delivers a project, he takes the draft down to the neighborhood bar, buys a round of drinks for all the guys, and then reads them the letter. Then he gets their comments.

They chime in and tell him to tweak this, fix that, change the wording here or there. But he knows he doesn't have a winner yet until one specific thing happens:

One of the guys in the group asks where they can get what the letter is offering.

That's when he knows he has a sales letter that's working. That's when it's ready for press. He's moved them from being critics to being buyers and they don't even realize it.

Take your copy—your Google ads, your sales page, your direct-mail pieces, your email blasts—and test them in other environments, other venues, with friends or out on the street. When people are salivating over what you offer, then you've got a winner.

Uncle Claude Sez

The uninformed would be staggered to know the amount of work involved in a single ad. Weeks of work sometimes. The ad seems so simple—and it must be simple to appeal to simple people. But back of that ad may lie reams of data, volumes of information, months of research.

So this is no lazy man's field.

Like Uncle Claude says, Google advertising isn't for lazy people. However . . . high performance ads can run with zero maintenance for months, even years. (Yes, even on the internet!) There are few assets more valuable than a system of effective ads that bring customers to your website—and deposit money in your bank account—24/7/365.

Knowing Your Numbers = Money in the Bank: How Google's Conversion Tracking Tells You What's Working

Josh was burning up the pages on Google. He had a fine-tuned herbal supplements AdWords campaign that was breaking new CTR records literally every week. Traffic was screaming. Product was moving. People were buying. Money was changing hands.

■ ■ ■

But then the credit card statements came in.

Josh compared his credit card statement from Google with his sales reports. The ship was leaking! He was losing money, lots of it, fast.

The left hand didn't know what the right hand was doing. He had no tracking system set up. No way to trace sales back to clicks, no way to know where to plug the leaks.

Josh called us in a panic.

So we set up Google's conversion tracking for him. We even went over to www.Hypertracker.net and set him up with an account there. He tracked every sales dollar back to the ad group it came from. He had put in place a system that was lean, mean, ruthless. Every penny going out accounted for. Every dollar coming in measured for profit down to the cent.

With this newfound knowledge Josh beefed up his Google advertising even more, trimmed off the fat, and in a ferociously competitive herbal supplement market (where new competitors show up daily and soon drop like flies), he went on to solid profitability.

Now Josh can take his supplements business wherever he wants. He can reinvest his profit and expand, or he can put it on autopilot and pursue other ventures. Josh has succeeded because he keeps close tabs on every number, all the time.

> You're a smart Google user when you know your numbers: how much each click is worth, what you can afford to spend to get a customer, and the return on investment for each ingredient in your AdWords mix. This is a well-oiled machine that can generate profit for you night and day for years.

BLOATED CORPORATE ADVERTISING BUDGETS VS. YOUR LEAN, MEAN TRAFFIC MACHINE

If you called up your stockbroker and asked him, "How much is IBM selling for today?" what would you think if he mumbled, "Oh, IBM's up a few points," and dodged the rest of your questions?

You'd get a new stockbroker! You want to know exactly how much your stock is worth, in dollars and cents. That's the only way you know if you're making money or not.

The same applies to the operation of any aspect of your business—your website, your mailings, your employees, your phone and utilities, everything.

You may have heard it said, "I know that half of my advertising dollars are wasted; I just don't know which half." If you were Coca-Cola and you did image advertising on a mass-marketed consumer product, that might be the hard reality of things. But you're not Coca-Cola. *You* can do far better.

The mail order business has known this secret for decades: *One really good ad in the right place can make money for you month after month for years, with no changes or alterations.*

That's because if you use rigorous methods to identify advertising formulas that work, then you'll have formulas that you can apply as often as you wish. More, if you're in a recession.

If advertising is the great hidden waste in corporate America, effective, results-accountable advertising is one of the great secrets of small-business success.

Business for us is strong because we put in tracking mechanisms. We can glance at a few key numbers and see where we're at. We teach our clients how to succeed in marketing themselves and their businesses the exact same way we market ourselves and our business.

You can track your own Google clicks and advertising dollars using the same systems, the same mechanisms, the same techniques, and the same criteria that we use.

HOW TO SET UP GOOGLE TO TRACK YOUR CONVERSIONS AND GROW YOUR BUSINESS

Google makes it kindergarten simple for you to track your conversions and sales all the way back to every keyword in your list. You can turn up traffic where it's the most profitable for you, and trim back dollars where they're being wasted.

Tracking clicks to sales is not optional, by the way—it's mandatory if you want to get all the profit that's available to you. In competitive markets it's the only way to survive.

There are a host of conversion programs and subscription services you can buy that do conversion tracking, split testing of landing pages and sales letters, web analytics, and more. However, Google's tracking is effective, it's free, and it's integrated right into the AdWords system itself.

How Google's Conversion Tracker Works

For us—and for you—Google's Conversion Tracker follows three steps:

1. When you search one of our keywords, our ad shows up at the top or on the right on the first page. If you click on the ad, Google will stick a little "cookie" in your internet folder to track you. It's like stamping your hand at the amusement park: It tells Google you've been there.
2. Google then sends you to our opt-in page. You read it, and if you like our offer, you'll enter your name and email address:

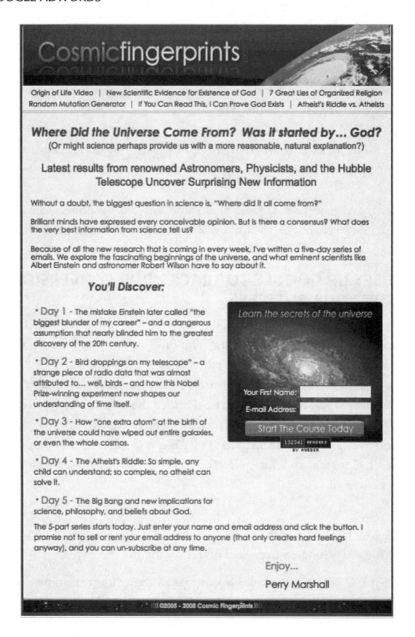

3. Our site will then send you to a thank-you page (usually with a free download or some type of bonus). Encoded in this page is a little piece of JavaScript generated by Google that we have entered into the source code for our thank-you page.

Remember that "cookie" Google stuck in your internet folder? Google tracks that cookie, and matches it to this JavaScript when you land on our thank-you page. Presto! It records your sign-up as a conversion.

Setting Up the Tracking Code

Google's conversion tracking is simple to set up. On the toolbar at the top of your campaign summary page, click on "Reporting and Tools," and select "Conversions" from the tool list you're given. Click to create a new conversion,

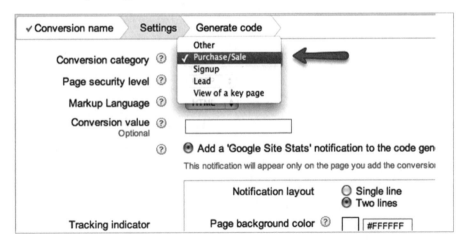

and Google will let you name, and then define, the action you want to track:

From there you can generate a simple piece of JavaScript that you'll stick in the code of your thank-you page. The only people who will be visiting this page are those who have joined your list or made a purchase:

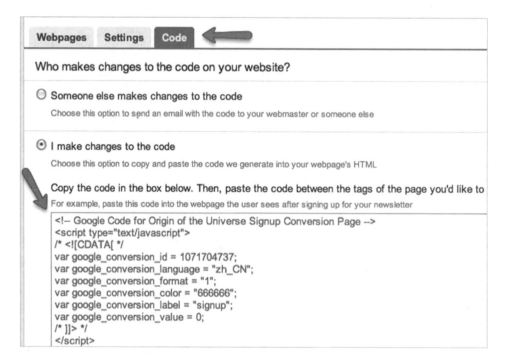

```
<!-- Google Code for Origin of the Universe Signup Conversion Page -->
<script type="text/javascript">
/* <![CDATA[ */
var google_conversion_id = 1071704737;
var google_conversion_language = "zh_CN";
var google_conversion_format = "1";
var google_conversion_color = "666666";
var google_conversion_label = "signup";
var google_conversion_value = 0;
/* ]]> */
</script>
```

The Glorious Benefits of Tracking Conversions

As people opt-in to your site or as they buy, Google will tell you how well you're turning clicks into sales or actions. You'll be able to see which keywords are generating conversions and which are converting better than the others. And you can tell which of the *ads* you're writing are turning into conversions.

Want to make your engine hum? This is where you tweak and test more, and hone your advertising to perfection:

· You can bid more on keywords that are highly profitable, and get even more good traffic from them.
· You can delete irrelevant keywords that are wasting your money.
· You can trim spending on ad groups and campaigns that have thin margins.
· You can identify whether Display Network advertising is making you money or losing it.
· You can spot which sites you're advertising on that are bringing in the most cash.
· You can tell which ads are attracting more paying customers.

This is where the cost-cutting happens in Google AdWords!

A Quick Example of Conversion Tracking

Here's a set of keywords that showed up in the same ad campaign. All were bid at the same price. All triggered the same ads. But I knew I had a limit on bids—I could not go over $1.00 cost per conversion—otherwise the campaign would be losing me money.

So I started by deleting one of the keywords that violated my $1.00 rule:

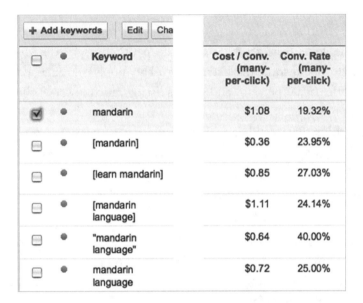

		Keyword	Cost / Conv. (many-per-click)	Conv. Rate (many-per-click)
☑	●	mandarin	$1.08	19.32%
☐	●	[mandarin]	$0.36	23.95%
☐	●	[learn mandarin]	$0.85	27.03%
☐	●	[mandarin language]	$1.11	24.14%
☐	●	"mandarin language"	$0.64	40.00%
☐	●	mandarin language	$0.72	25.00%

. . . followed by others. Once I did this, I made more money the following month. Google gave me the information I needed to streamline my marketing strategy even more.

COUNTERINTUITIVE BIDDING STRATEGIES

If you've got keywords that are doing screamingly well, do you just up the bid price on them and aim for the top positions on the page?

It sounds logical, but experience sometimes tells you otherwise.

It's All About Ranking and Position on the Page

Don't assume that you'll make the most money by being in the top positions. In many cases the opposite is true: You could *lose* the most money by being in the top positions.

It's because of 1) the price you pay to get into those highly competitive positions and 2) the low-quality traffic you might get from them. Lower positions on the page convert to sales better, generally, because they attract fewer click-happy people. So if you're on a limited budget, it's better not to worry about being first. Just go to the right side of the page and convert more often.

One of our clients, John Jaworski of X-Streamers, sold confetti and party supplies for large events and venues. He was doing conversion tracking just as we've described here, and words like "party confetti" and "wedding confetti" were doing just fine. But he was paying $0.65 per click for a high-ranking position on "confetti" and had gotten 1,200 visitors . . . with zero sales.

Some people would consider $0.65 to be cheap. Compared to the $10 and $20 prices you pay for keywords in some markets, that's a bargain. Nevertheless, we advised John to cut his bid price by 90 percent, and get his listing much lower in the search results. He dropped his bid to $0.07.

You might think that would have killed his traffic and sales. Amazingly, the opposite happened: his traffic started *seriously* converting! This is not always the case.

Outsmart the Law of Diminishing Returns: Why the More You Pay, the Worse Your Traffic May Get

Sometimes premium positions work best. But Richard Stokes at AdGooroo confirms that often the number-one premium position converts poorly because it attracts the "happy clickers," and the number-two and number-three premium positions work best. Sometimes positions four to seven work best. Whether top listings or side listings work best seems to depend mostly on whether you're selling to an *impulsive market* ("I just want a plumber and I'll take the first thing that looks good") or a *research everything market* ("I just found out I have stage 1 prostate cancer and I'm going to click on every link for the first three pages of Google results and scour everything I find").

Real savings and money well spent comes in finding that "sweet spot" between paying a *low price* for clicks (which generally improves the conversion rate) and still getting a *good position* (which increases your traffic). You have absolute direct control over this because you set the price. And as you watch your campaigns over time, you can move that CPC up or down to hit the perfect middle ground between price and position.

Of course, this will vary from market to market—some advertisers (like plumbers, for example) make the most money in the topmost positions simply because those are the most visible and they attract people in a hurry to solve an immediate problem.

Nevertheless, you'll know you've hit that "sweet spot" when your net profit is the highest. This is something you can set and tweak individually for literally every single keyword in your entire account.

Realistically you only need to do this for the top 10 to 30 individual keywords, which for most people will represent 95 percent of the traffic.

How a Higher CTR Helps You

Getting a higher CTR than your competitors means you pay less money per click than they do.

Your position on the page is a function of your bid price times your click-through rate. That's a simplified explanation of Google's whole "quality score" formula, but it's fundamentally true. The higher your CTR, the higher up on the page Google will place you, without charging you more for each click.

That can only help your bottom line. As your CTR goes up, either you'll be able to get more traffic without having to pay a higher rate for it, or you can lower your bid prices and keep the same volume and quality of traffic but pay less.

Sound like a good deal?

Using the 80/20 Rule to Tweak Your Numbers and Save More Money

More than 80 percent of your sales will come from fewer than 20 percent of your campaigns.

Some keywords and ads are naturally, almost automatically, going to bring in good, consistent sales, while others simply never will.

When you know which ones are which, you can put smart money and effort into those campaigns that produce sales and take your time and money away from the ones that don't.

It might even be that 90 percent of the traffic comes from 10 percent of the keywords. Most of the time the most productive 10 percent to 20 percent of keywords will be obvious to everyone, and there will be bidding wars.

One way around this—and it is an extreme measure—is to turn the 80/20 principle on its head. If you can get by with less traffic, you can cut your costs dramatically.

Cost-Per-Action Bidding

As your campaigns mature, Google may give you the option of using CPA (Cost-Per-Action) bidding, which means paying for conversions instead of clicks or impressions. This is an advanced topic. You'll find more information on an interview with CPA expert David Rothwell and a guide sheet at www.perrymarshall.com/supplement.

THE SAVVY MARKETER: HOW TO TRACK
YOUR SALES NUMBERS AND GO ON AUTOPILOT

Perry here: I'd like to share a story that proves the value of tracking your numbers. For almost 30 years LT Sound has sold a forerunner of the Karaoke machine—a product called the "Vocal Eliminator." The Vocal Eliminator is a small unit you use with your own CDs. It eliminates the original vocals and inserts your voice as you sing. So it's like Karaoke, but with your regular CDs.

It runs classified ads in *Popular Science*, music and entertainment magazines, and audiophile periodicals year after year. Here are two ads for this product, an early version and one that's run continuously for more than two decades:

The owner of the business, Lacy Thompson, has tested these ads for years. He knows his numbers. He knows which ads pay and which ones don't. He knows which magazines get a response and which ones don't. He knows which sizes, which copy, which descriptions, which *everything* pulls the best response.

The older ad above was published in *High Fidelity* magazine in October 1978. You'll notice how the mailing address is "LT Sound, Dept. HF." The newer ad ran in *Popular Science*. Sure enough, readers of this magazine who want the free demo are told to write to "LT Sound, Dept. PS-1." In other words, these ads are carefully traced back to the magazine they appeared in.

Lacy Thompson keeps the money flowing by knowing his numbers. And now he's got a marketing machine that runs almost on autopilot and puts cash in his bank account month in and month out, winter and summer, year after year.

The product has been redesigned a few times, but the business has not essentially changed in 30 years.

Is this a "dream" business? Maybe not, but it ain't a bad business either. Steady. Predictable. The FTC and FDA won't be going after Lacy for anything. It's a lot better than most people's jobs, and there's no pink kool-aid to make him frustrated with his lot in life.

If he wants to grow this business by introducing other products or exploring new distribution channels, he can certainly do that. And since his advertising is largely offline, he's more immune to competitors who suddenly show up than if he were only online.

Marketers who can do this are the marketers who know their numbers. Are you one of them? Once you learn how to do this, you'll control your game.

Savvy marketers keep an eye on the numbers that matter: How much each customer is worth, what they can afford to spend to get each customer, and the return on investment for each ingredient in their marketing mix. This is true online and offline, for internet startups and brick-and-mortar businesses alike.

Uncle Claude Sez

Never be guided in any way by ads which are untraced. Never do anything because some uninformed advertiser considers that something right. Never be led in new paths by the blind. Apply to your advertising ordinary common sense . . . .

The only purpose of advertising is to make sales. It is profitable or unprofitable according to its actual sales. It is not for general effect. It is not to keep your name before the people . . . . Treat it as a salesman. Force it to justify itself. Compare it with other salesmen. Figure its cost and result. Accept no excuses which good salesmen do not make. Then you will not go far wrong.

Take the opinion of nobody who knows nothing about his returns.

How to Triple Your CTR (and Cut Your Bid Prices by Two-Thirds, if You Want)— No Genius Required

AdWords rocket scientist Howie Jacobson kicked off a new campaign a couple of years ago, driving salespeople to his site where he teaches them how to turn cold calling into a profitable sales process. He started out with a simple Google ad:

> **Stop cold calling forever**
> www.leadsintogold.com
> Small business marketing system.
> Free report and 2 chapter download.
> 33 Clicks | 0.8% CTR

Today he's making traffic scream with killer ad copy that has more than *tripled* his click-through rate:

Cold calling not working?

www.leadsintogold.com

Discover a powerful alternative.

Free report and 2 chapter download.

368 Clicks | 2.7% CTR

What's Howie's secret?

He's just brilliant, right? A copywriting genius, a Merlin, a sorcerer of the printed word, yes?

Howie will tell you no. (We think he's brilliant, as does every one of our customers who consults with him on their Google campaigns. But for this example he would argue otherwise.)

Seriously—what was his secret?

Answer: Howie just tested ad copy. That's all he did. You've seen the first and the last of his ads, but you haven't seen the score of other tests that he ran, that inch by inch grew his CTR by tiny percentage points over a two-year period. Here are just a few samples of the ads he put up for testing:

Stop cold prospecting.

www.leadsintogold.com

Small business marketing system.

Free report and 2 chapter download.

42 Clicks | 1.0% CTR

End cold calling forever

www.leadsintogold.com

Attract customers automatically.

Free report and 2 chapter download.

145 Clicks | 2.0% CTR

End cold calling forever

www.leadsintogold.com

Lead generation system explained.

Free report and 2 chapter download.

338 Clicks | 2.2% CTR

Howie's full collection is available at www.LeadsIntoGold.com/genius. When you look over these ads, you see nothing spectacular. No shocking content, no in-your-face power words that jump off the page, no mind-blowing sales hooks.

Even more importantly, if you looked over all these ads by themselves and tried to *guess* which one would get the most clicks, I'll bet you couldn't. Not among these ads. *Only the market could tell you which one would be the winner!*

Howie knows his customers quite well, but he never had any brilliant flashes of insight, and he never consulted on these ads with any of the geniuses of the copywriting world.

Frankly, they couldn't have helped him anyway.

Instead, he did what all successful Google advertisers do: He ran two ads at a time. He compared their results. He deleted the loser and wrote another ad to try to beat the winner. He followed his nose, people clicked on what resonated with them, and the market told him what worked.

As the saying goes, "It is a fool who looks for logic in the chambers of the human heart."

AdWords is no focus group. The magic of AdWords is that nobody normally sits and ponders an ad before clicking on it. A person sees your message, her brain runs an instant gut-reaction 0.1-second process, and the decision is made. She clicks, or she doesn't.

It won't do you any good to pontificate long hours over ad copy. Calling in focus groups to sit and discuss their feelings and reactions is a waste of your time, and theirs. In the Google world, decisions are instantaneous, and you can never predict with 100 percent accuracy what the market is going to react to. Your good common sense will tell you what "should" work. And then the market will tell you what actually *does* work.

HOW TO SET UP A SPLIT TEST: IT'S A NO-BRAINER

Google lets you set up a split test with ease. When you've got an ad written, you can write a second one as well, just by clicking on the "Create new Text Ad" link next to the ad that you're currently running. Google will rotate this with your other ad, and you can compare the click throughs and eventually delete the loser and try to beat your best again:

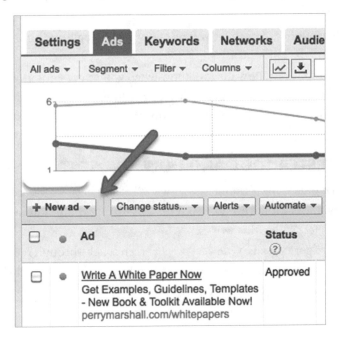

Statistical Significance: Sounds boring, but it's *Really* important
(So important, one coaching student put himself out of business by ignoring this!)

During our Bobsled Run personal AdWords coaching program (www.BobsledRun.com), we got a very frustrated email from a member whose sales had gone south, not north, since the program started.

Not exactly what he was hoping for when he signed up, right?

This gentleman was getting a few sales a day and was rewriting his sales page on a daily basis. He'd get two sales on Tuesday and assume the changes were bad. He'd change something. Then he'd get five sales on Wednesday and assume the changes were good.

But little by little his sales started going down the toilet, heading toward zero.

By the time he sounded an alarm he was in dire financial straits. Furthermore, he hadn't saved the early versions of the sales page when it *was* working so it wasn't even possible to go back to what was working.

About a month later, he let go of his employee and shut the business down.

As they say in Spanish, *¡Qué lástima!*

Again, by the time we found out about this campaign, it was too far gone to save. Here's what he failed to do:

1. He didn't use our SplitTester.com tool to figure out if his winning sales page was really a winner.
2. He didn't keep a detailed record of his modifications and copies of all the versions along the way.

This problem applies to *anything* you test—not just Google ads but also opt-in pages, sales pages, etc.

When you do split test, how do you know when you've got enough results to be sure that your winning ad didn't just "get lucky" or the loser didn't just have a bad day or a bad week? How many trials do you need to run?

THE SPLIT-TESTER TOOL AND HOW TO USE IT

With the help of our friend Brian Teasley (www.Teasley.net), we created a split-testing tool on the web at www.SplitTester.com. With this tool, you can find out how likely it is that it was luck. Here's how this works:

Let's say we've got two ads. One gets a 1.2 percent click-through rate with two clicks total, and the other gets a 2 percent click-through rate with five clicks total. Was the better one really better, or was it luck? Let's see:

Enter Your Numbers Here:

Number of Clicks (First Ad)	1.2	Number of Clicks (Second Ad)	2
CTR (First Ad, in %) *	2.0	CTR (Second Ad, in %) *	5

* Your CTR must be entered as a simple percentage.
For example, enter 3.1% as "3.1", and not "0.031";
Enter 0.7% as "0.7"

Calculate   Reset

When we click "Calculate," it says:

You are **not very confident** that the ads will have different long-term response rates.

But now let's say we've got 20 clicks for one and 35 for the other, not just 2 and 5.

Enter Your Numbers Here:

Number of Clicks (First Ad)	1.2	Number of Clicks (Second Ad)	2
CTR (First Ad, in %) *	2.0	CTR (Second Ad, in %) *	5

* Your CTR must be entered as a simple percentage.
For example, enter 3.1% as "3.1", and not "0.031";
Enter 0.7% as "0.7"

Calculate   Reset

We click "Calculate," and it tells us:

You are **approximately 95 percent confident** that the ads will have different long-term response rates.

Ninety-five percent confidence means that if we ran this test 100 times and got these results, the results would lead us in the right direction 95 times. That's pretty good—I'm willing to bet on those kinds of odds.

Here's a real simple rule of thumb: When your response percentages are fairly close between two competing ads, you need 30 or more responses to each one before you can declare a winner. And maybe even 50. But if one is already doing considerably better than the other, then it doesn't take as long—after 10 to 15 actions have been taken you can be fairly sure. Use www.SplitTester.com to find out.

When you do proper split testing, when you test two things side by side and make sure you're 90 percent, 95 percent, or 99 percent sure of your results before you go on, you're dealing with hard numbers and good, high levels of certainty. Your progress isn't squishy and uncertain. It's measurable and reliable.

Not only does that make for very effective marketing, it makes for a healthy company, good morale among the troops, and a happy bank account.

Uncle Claude Sez

Now we let the thousands decide what the millions will do. We make a small test, and watch cost and result. When we learn what a thousand customers cost, we know almost exactly what a million will cost. When we learn what they buy, we know what a million will buy.

We establish averages on a small scale, and those averages always hold. We know our cost, we know our sale, and we know our profit and loss. We know how soon our cost comes back. Before we spread ourselves thin, we prove our undertaking absolutely safe. So there are today no advertising disasters piloted by men who know.

Chapter 9

The Winning Method the World's Smartest Marketers Stole from the Wright Brothers

The boneyards of modern civilization are littered with "great" marketing ideas that never got off the ground.

Think of the billions and trillions of dollars companies spent developing products, only to find out that their products weren't what people wanted in the first place.

■ ■ ■

Let's not assume you're a corporation with billions of dollars to spend. Instead let's assume you're a regular person who quit a cushy job to pursue an entrepreneurial vision. As you calculate it, you've got to start making a profit in six to nine months or else you'll run out of money.

If that's you, then you can't afford to make a mistake. You can't spend three months developing a product and later find out in month six that the product has to be totally redesigned. That'll kill your business and send you back to the J.O.B. with your tail between your legs.

We're going to make sure this never happens to you.

How can you prevent this? By testing your product idea and even your website itself on the cheap, using Google, before you've spent a lot of money on it. With the internet, you can find out if a product idea will succeed or fail for a few hundred to no more than a few thousand dollars.

If you do this, you will be sure that the product you develop will be well received.

HOW THE WRIGHT BROTHERS' SAVVY TESTING METHOD MADE THEM "FIRST IN FLIGHT"

The year: 1903. The place: a houseboat on the Potomac River, U.S.A.

Just weeks before Wilbur and Orville Wright were to fly the world's first airplane at Kitty Hawk, North Carolina, Samuel Pierpont Langley, a well-funded engineer and inventor, was launching an airplane of his own—with the assistance of an entire staff.

Langley's assumption: Put a big enough engine on the thing, and it will fly. He focused all his effort on that one project: creating an engine powerful enough for the plane to go airborne. On October 7th, 1903, Langley tested his model for the very first time.

The plane crashed immediately after leaving the launch pad, badly damaging the front wing.

Two months later, just eight days before the Wright Brothers' successful flight, Langley made a second attempt.

This time the tail and rear wing collapsed completely during launch.

Langley was ridiculed by the press and criticized by members of the Congress for throwing away taxpayer dollars on his failed projects. (Can you imagine the cynicism? I'm sure many sneering reporters believed that nobody could or would ever fly.) Disillusioned by the public response, Langley abandoned his vision.

Wilbur and Orville Wright, meanwhile, had a completely different approach: build a glider that would glide from a hilltop with no engine at all. They focused their energy on balance and steering. Power was almost an afterthought. Only after the glider worked by itself would they try to put an engine on it.

After three years of tedious experimentation the glider was working well, so they commissioned bicycle shop machinist Charlie Taylor to build them an engine. It was the smallest engine he could design—a 12-horsepower unit that weighed 180 pounds.

And on December 17, 1903, at Kitty Hawk, North Carolina, Wilbur and Orville Wright made history.

The Wright Brothers changed the world and became famous historical figures, while few have ever heard of Mr. Langley. Their approach of making the plane fly before applying high power was the winning idea.

Langley had spent most of four years building an extraordinary engine to lift their heavy flying machine. The Wrights had spent most of four years building a flying machine so artfully designed that it could be propelled into the air by a fairly ordinary internal combustion engine.

—SMITHSONIAN MAGAZINE, APRIL 2003

Skill comes by the constant repetition of familiar feats rather than by a few overbold attempts at feats for which the performer is yet poorly prepared.

—WILBUR WRIGHT

Samuel Pierpont Langley died in 1906, a broken and disappointed man.

PEOPLE WHO TEST, FLY. PEOPLE WHO RELY ON BRUTE FORCE, DIE.

You don't want to die a broke and disappointed person. You want to die rich and famous.

Or at least rich, right?

Then there is a direct comparison between the Wright Brothers and your career as an internet marketer.

The search engine is the motor. Your website is the glider.

A motor without a good set of wings does you no good. When you put an engine on a glider, you have a plane. When you feed traffic to a website that can "fly," you have a business.

And as smart marketers like "Uncle" Claude Hopkins have known for over a century, you get the wings to work through careful, systematic testing.

This is not a new concept. For more than 100 years, smart, savvy marketers have followed these time-tested principles of proven good sense, and made their dollars go many times further.

In 1923, Claude Hopkins said:

Advertising and merchandising become exact sciences. Every course is charted. The compass of accurate knowledge directs the shortest, safest, cheapest course to any destination.

We learn the principles and prove them by repeated tests. . . . We compare one way with many others, backward and forwards, and record the results. . . .

Advertising is traced down to the fraction of a penny. The cost per reply and cost per dollar of sale show up with utter exactness.

One ad compared to another, one method with another. Headlines, settings, sizes, arguments and pictures are compared. To reduce the cost of results even one percent means much.

So no guesswork is permitted. One must know what is best.

Building a business online doesn't have to be guesswork. It's not a crapshoot. It's a science. Wise men and women before us have taken the risks, tested the limits, learned the hard lessons for us, and laid down a clear path that we can follow with confidence.

Whether your business is all online, or only partly so, the foundation remains the same: Start small, test carefully, make modest improvements, get deeper insights into your market, test some more, and you'll know that your business is going to grow.

This well-worn path builds a sales process that works. And when you have a persuasive website, you have a glider. Just like the Wright Brothers, all you need to do is put a lightweight engine on it and you can fly.

Add Google traffic the smart way and you've got a business that soars.

Google AdWords can bring you a lot of traffic, and that traffic is valuable to the extent that your website can convert the traffic to leads and sales.

When you're getting started, Google is like a lightweight engine that you can turn on and off instantly. You can test your glider safely without crashing, killing a potential joint venture partnership, or blowing a wad of money.

MARKETING MISERY IS *NOT* NECESSARY

Thousands of people go to bed every night wondering Why? Why can't I make any sales? Why can't I earn any real money at this?

This is not necessary, but it's a lesson that the scorched Dotcoms in 1997–2000 learned the hard way. They were a lot like Langley. They focused on the engine instead of the wings. When it didn't take off, they just poured more gas into the engine. When that didn't work, they put it on a rocket launcher and forced it up into the air.

You don't have the time or the money to pour into product ideas and sales messages that, in hindsight, were "almost right." Your spouse won't let you blow the grocery money or college savings on a lark.

Reality is a great teacher, if you let it speak its piece. The people who click on your ads will tell you what they want, if you ask them. They'll show you what they want, if you watch them.

Uncle Claude Sez

The time has come when advertising has in some hands reached the status of a science. It is based on fixed principles and is reasonably exact. The causes and effects have been analyzed until they are well understood. The correct method of procedure has been proved and established. We know what is most effective, and we act on its basic law.

Once a gamble, advertising has become, under able direction, one of the safest business ventures to undertake. Certainly no other enterprise with comparable possibilities need involve so little risk.

Chapter 10

Triple Your Traffic with Google's Display Network

At first I was leery of traffic from Google's Display Network. Even now, when I start a new campaign, I almost always turn it off. (You should, too. It throws off your split tests. You get an uneven mix of Google and syndicated traffic in your ads, and you can't compare the CTRs.) Furthermore it frequently brings lower-quality visitors who are less inclined to buy.

■ ■ ■

But not always!

Sometimes the Display Network brings *better* traffic. In fact, as I've developed my AdWords chops, I've come to enjoy buying Display Network traffic much more than search. It brings a more diverse cross section of buyers; it's much harder for your competitors to reverse-engineer what you're doing. It allows you to use images instead of just plain text ads. You have far more creativity in what you say in your ads because quality scores and keyword relevance are much less important to Google on the Display Network. It's a more challenging game for more experienced marketers. It's possible to achieve branding with display ads even in small niche or local markets. For some advertisers, prodigious amounts of traffic are available there.

A couple of years ago I had a project that was running on Google traffic alone. I'd tested and tweaked the ads, and I thought it was doing fine.

Then one day, by accident, I turned the Display Network on.

It produced a sudden *avalanche* of traffic. Good traffic, too. The number of visitors to that website grew by a factor of 5X!

> Odds are, there's even more traffic waiting for you on Google's Display Network and through image ads and on targeted sites. Test it, and find out if you can make it profitable. You could potentially double or triple the number of quality visitors to your site through these new venues of advertising.

Some of our customers have been able to double, triple, even quadruple their traffic just by turning on Display Network sites in addition to the regular Google and search network traffic. But what is the Display Network?

Google shows your ads on Google. They also show your ads other places, unless you tell them not to. One possible place is the *search partners network*—the partner search engines that display Google's results, such as AOL, Ask.com, Earthlink, etc.

But this chapter isn't about that. It's about Google's Display Network (GDN)—any and every website across the entire internet that displays AdSense, those "AdChoices" ads. And that can mean a ton of traffic for you. Here's a shot from a major news website with Google ads served on the left:

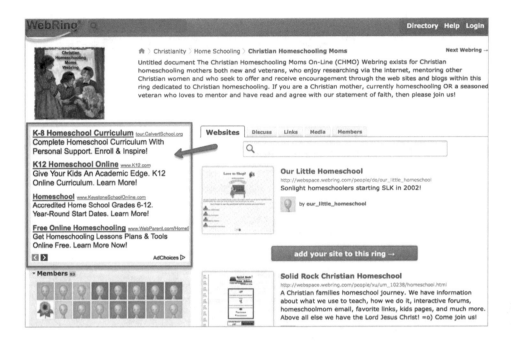

HOW IS THIS DIFFERENT FROM REGULAR GOOGLE SEARCHES?

Google Search is like the Yellow Pages; a person who searches there is looking for a specific solution to his problem and is often in a spending frame of mind.

The Display Network, on the other hand, encompasses all the sites where people go to spend time. It's like a giant coffee shop, a magazine rack, bookstore, or even a TV network. It shows ads where visitors are reading articles, watching videos, commenting on forums and blogs, and not necessarily thinking about a particular solution to a particular problem. A person in this case is less likely to be in an immediate buying frame of mind.

Success on the Display Network is more about distracting people, catching them unexpectedly, and guiding their attention to your product, service, or cause.

A major success strategy for ads on GDN is to tickle the reader's curiosity. Use words and language and imagery that are unusual, interesting, curious, compelling, even mysterious. Display Network ninjas employ this whenever they can.

HOW TO TURN IT ON AND OFF

Google turns on the Display Network in your account by default. To change this, go into the campaign you want to adjust, and click on the "Settings" tab:

Then find "Networks and devices" and click "Edit." An additional box of options will open up, and you'll select "Let me choose":

You can then uncheck the box next to "Display Network." This setting will affect all of the ad groups in the campaign. Google will warn you that your ads won't show on the Display Network, but that's the way you want it.

Google lets you bid different amounts for GDN traffic. This way you don't overspend. (Get it wrong, and you could rack up thousands of dollars in click costs in a matter of days!)

Three Things Could Happen, None of Them Necessarily Bad.

When you turn *on* Display Network traffic, you could find that:

1. You get ten times as many clicks here as on Google search.
2. You get low CTRs of 0.1 percent or 0.01 percent or worse (but these low numbers won't negatively affect your account).
3. One or two keywords or ad groups could convert superbly while the rest fall flat.

ROLLING OUT A SUCCESSFUL DISPLAY NETWORK CAMPAIGN

First off, this tip will save you confusion and heartache:

You should always manage your Display Network in a new and separate campaign from your Google search traffic.

And we *do not* recommend duplicating your Google search ad groups into a new GDN-only campaign and turning on the traffic. There's more nuance than that.

So the following sections tell how you turn this information into a solid Display Network campaign.

GOOGLE WANTS "THEMES"

To find pages to show you on, Google looks at your keyword, plus your ad, plus your landing page, and infers a "theme" that they're about. Then it finds pages across the internet that match it.

We recommend you start by making a short list of the keywords most directly relevant to what you sell: "Learn Spanish online" or "high school science curriculum" or "natural migraine remedies." Not extremely long-tail keywords, just keywords that are specific to you.

Then for each of those keywords, go to Google, and search on it. Scroll down to the end of the results page, and notice the collection of additional search phrases that Google lets you click to view results on:

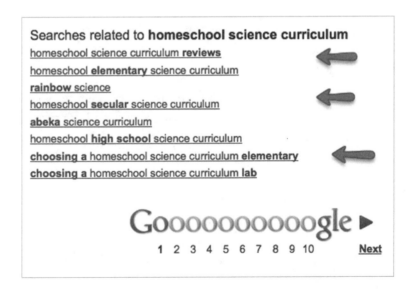

Each of these related searches is a separate "theme" in Google's system. Collect as many of these search phrases as are directly relevant to you, and create individual ad groups for each one: *one keyword phrase per ad group* and two ads to split test.

Why just one keyword? That way it's easier for Google's computers to identify *the theme,* and they have more latitude for finding pages that echo it. Cast your net wide early on, and Google will reward you with more placements.

Your next step is to remove the bad placements. (See later in the chapter for an explanation of how to do that.) When you're done, 2 to 3 percent of the sites Google showed you on will actually be productive. Keep those, and you're good to go.

Don't try to tweak this merely by adjusting your bids. That will shorten your reach. Keep your bids where they are, and eliminate sites where you don't convert. You'll end up with 6 to 12 ad groups that are performing genuinely well.

It's a long-term strategy that works.

THERE'S MORE THAN ONE WAY TO TARGET TRAFFIC ON THE DISPLAY NETWORK

Everything we've described up till now encompasses just one way to target people on GDN. You choose a keyword or two for each ad group, and then Google selects the sites and pages where you show. Those pages are what we call "automatic placements." Google chooses them, but you have veto power.

There are *three* ways to find your audience on GDN, not just one:

1. by targeting keywords (as already described),
2. by targeting "managed placements," and
3. by targeting topics.

Managed placements are the second way to find your audience. You give Google specific websites—even specific directories or specific URLs on those sites—and Google then displays your ads there.

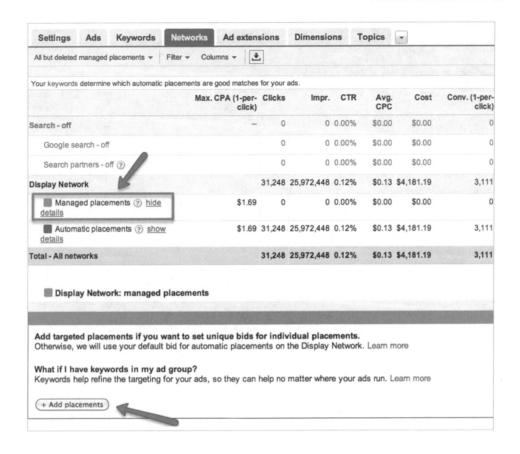

The third way is called "topic targeting," formerly known as "contextual targeting." You choose one or several of Google's broad classifications of website themes, and it finds the pages for you. More on this in a bit.

Every other possible way of setting up ad groups and campaigns on GDN is just a combination of these three types.

HOW DO I FIND OUT WHERE GOOGLE IS SHOWING MY ADS?

Just click the "show details" link next to "Automatic placements" and what unfolds is a list of sites where your ads have shown:

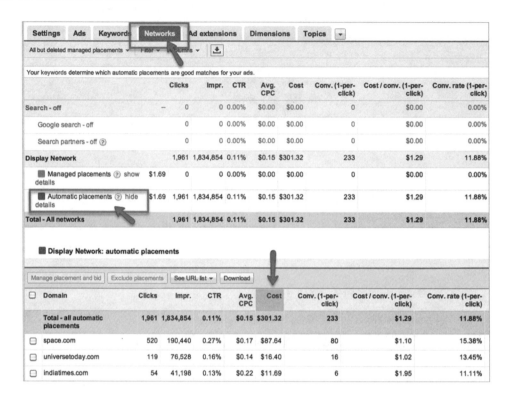

Don't want to show up in all those places? Just select the sites or domains you don't want, and click "Exclude placements":

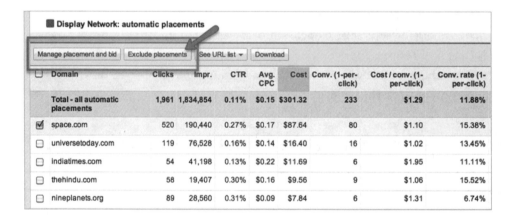

HOW DOES GOOGLE DECIDE WHERE TO SHOW MY ADS?

We talked about this earlier in the chapter: For any single ad group Google's system identifies a "theme" based on the keyword(s) you've chosen and your ad copy (and website) and then picks sites that fit.

But there's a growing, expanding process to this. Google is constantly looking for new and more relevant sites to show your ads on. That way you get more clicks, Google AdSense publishers get more commissions, and Google gets more revenue.

Google has a method for this. If you bid on "red wagons," then, of course, it shows you on red wagon sites. But it's going to expand on this, in two directions:

1. It digs down and starts testing your "red wagons" ads on more specific pages about specific niches: Radio Flyer red wagons, red wagon toys, red wagon wheels, plastic red wagons, etc. If ads placed on these pages get clicks, Google keeps trying.
2. It goes wide. Instead of just "red wagons" Google aims for pages and sites about wagons of all kinds:

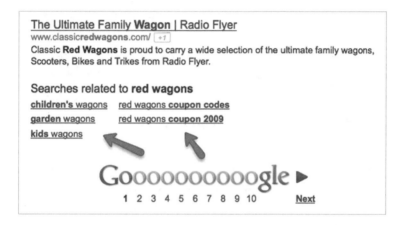

If in new keyword markets you get good CTRs, Google keeps expanding until the good CTRs stop . . . or until you hit the Jet Stream.

THE WILD PHENOMENON WE CALL THE "JET STREAM"

Only a tiny percentage of AdWords ads ever reach the Jet Stream. It's the point at which an ad gets served nearly everywhere across the entire Display Network because it gets clicks no matter where Google shows it.

Let's say you sell goldfish. You're clever with copy, and you come up with an ad that gets a high CTR on every goldfish site and page where Google shows it. Google will now do several things:

1. It'll run your ad on pages and sites about other kinds of fish. If that works . . .
2. It'll run your ad on pages and sites about other kinds of pets. If that works . . .
3. It'll run your ad on any pages or site about animals. If that works . . .

4. It'll run your ad on pages or sites about any and every other topic.

If that works, congratulations! You've hit the Jet Stream. You could get hundreds, thousands, even tens of thousands of clicks a day from around the internet.

But remember that you've got veto power over any site or category of site that you're showing up on. Use the "Exclude placements" feature as often as you need to in order to stay off sites that waste your money.

Ads that hit the Jet Stream typically have universal appeal, or stroke some sort of universal desire or curiosity. Obviously some markets are more Jet-friendly than others; dating or weight loss or nutrition or social causes are more likely to get clicks everywhere than very narrow-interest niche markets like model airplanes. Ads for metal-bending equipment don't have a chance of hitting the Jet Stream, nor would you want them to. But regardless, curiosity is power, and the ability to stimulate it means more clicks from more places.

We provide to new members of our Renaissance Club a full report on Google's Jet Stream, available at www.PerryMarshall.com/club.

WHAT ARE MANAGED PLACEMENTS?

By using managed placements (formerly called "site targeting" or "placement targeting"), you choose the sites, instead of Google. And you can do it with or without keywords. (You can also choose to bid on impressions rather than clicks.)

Any site on the internet that's set up to run Google ads is available for you to advertise on. Plus you can run display or banner ads as well as text ads.

To set up managed placements, choose the campaign you want to start with. It will need to have the Display Network enabled (and Search turned off). From there, you set up placements by ad group.

You've got a choice: You can either create a new ad group (which we strongly recommend) or add managed placements into an existing one.

To create a new ad group with managed placements, click to create a new ad group. Once you've entered the copy for at least one ad, *skip* the keywords section, and click "Select managed placements" instead:

You can now enter the sites you want to show ads on.

To add managed placements to an existing keyword-based ad group, click on the "Networks" tab in the middle of the page. Next to "Managed placements," click "Show details." It will now give you the option to add your own managed placements to the ad group:

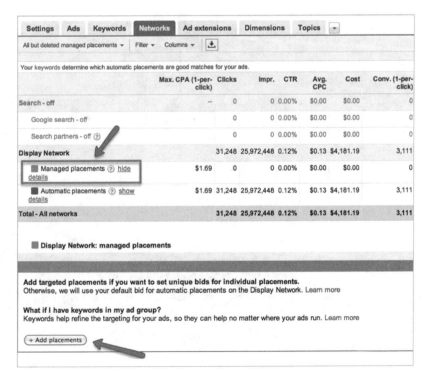

From here on, this "Networks" tab is where you'll go to see impressions, clicks, and other performance statistics for your existing managed placements.

KEYS TO MAKING MANAGED PLACEMENTS WORK

Just as with Google ads, the key to success is persistent split testing. Peel & stick works here, too, but we're now peeling and sticking *domains and URLs.* Not keywords.

Targeting individual pages can allow you to write laser-honed ads that are tailor-made just for visitors to that page. And again, using language and imagery that's unusual, interesting, and compelling, which plays on the reader's curiosity, is one of the first things you'll want to test.

THE THIRD WAY TO FIND YOUR AUDIENCE: TOPIC TARGETING

Google categorizes all its sites and pages by topic. You can go after a topic Google has specified and show your ads on appropriate pages.

You may not even have the "Topics" tab enabled yet. To add topics, navigate to an ad group you've created, and first click the dropdown button to add tabs:

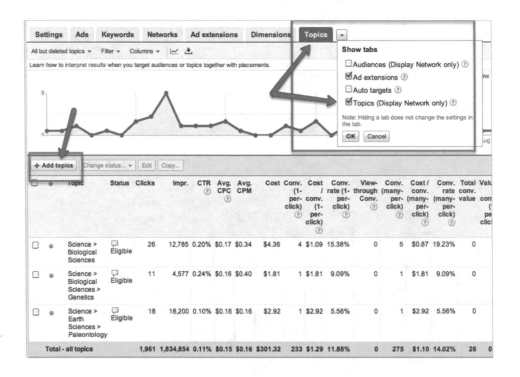

Then click on "Add topics." A dialog box opens up that lets you choose from a wide array of categories and subcategories:

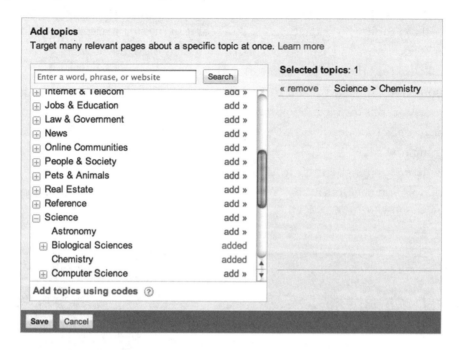

And now within this ad group these topics will look and behave just like keywords, with impressions, CTRs, conversions, and more.

(Hint: You can add a couple of keywords to a topic-targeted ad group as well, and further narrow Google's selection of pages in a way that's useful to you.)

By the way, you'll find one of the most valuable metrics in your interface to be your *cost-per-conversion.* How much does it cost you to get a real customer, from each of the different sites or pages or topics you're aiming at? That determines what you keep, and what you throw out.

HOW GOOGLE'S BOTS FIND YOU NEW CUSTOMERS

Google starts by showing your ads in "obvious" places. Google is looking at not only your keywords but also your ad copy and your landing pages to decide what it thinks your site is about. Google immediately starts seeing if your ads get clicks because its job is to maximize clicks for its advertisers and maximize its own revenue.

You sell goldfish; so Google puts your ads on various goldfish sites and sees if people click.

If your ads make the cut, Google starts testing your ads in wider circles. If your ads are really good, your ads eventually might even show up on dog sites and parakeet sites. Maybe. It's a matter of how broad your appeal is. If you sell the kind of product that can appeal to people who weren't even looking for it in the first place, your ads could go quite far. This is why the Display Network can fetch far more traffic than search.

You'll also find that Display Network traffic takes time to grow. It's like a garden; there's something "organic" about it. The process I described can take weeks or months to mature. As it rolls forward, Google accumulates more and more data. Meanwhile you can split test ads (not nearly as fast as you do on search because Google takes its time distributing new ads).

Google even pays attention to which ads work on which websites in the Display Network, so if you have lots of ads, Google can distribute diverse messages across diverse ranges of syndicating websites.

Uncle Claude Sez

Human nature is perpetual. In most respects it is the same today as in the time of Caesar. So the principles of psychology are fixed and enduring. You will never need to unlearn what you learn about them.

We learn, for instance, that curiosity is one of the strongest of human incentives. We employ it whenever we can.

Chapter 11

Google Image Ads: Banner Advertising Is Here to Stay

Back in the internet Bubble Days of 1999, banner ads were one of few routes a small startup could take in order to get paid traffic online. Everyone and his chalupa-eating chihuahua were buying and selling banner space online, and if you wanted visitors to your site, banner ads were the only medium that promised any significant volume.

■ ■ ■

Then up jumped Google, and soon after, AdWords.

The internet has since come full circle. Banner and display ads are far from being the only way to buy traffic now. But with Google they're one of the best bargains you can find. We've seen Google's image ads bring in hundreds of clicks per day for, in some cases, as little as $0.03 a click.

WHY BANNER ADS GIVE YOU THE EDGE

At our AdWords Elite Master's Summit in Maui, Hawaii, Richard Stokes of AdGooroo.com shared some fascinating numbers. Google doesn't release this kind of information to the public, but according to AdGooroo's database, in Spring 2011 Google AdWords had:

- 1,265,047 advertisers on the Search Network
- 273,879 advertisers on the Display Network
- 26,080 Display advertisers who use banner ads

AdGooroo also counted the number of ads in rotation:

- Text ads on Search: 30,411,236
- Text ads on Display Network: 1,993,765
- Image ads on Display Network: 145,964

You can instantly see why the Display Network is less competitive than search and why banner ads have such an edge over text ads. Advertisers who use banner ads are the sharper pencils in the box, but there're so many fewer of them competing with you.

Rare, yes, but not at all unheard of. All provided courtesy of Google's Display Network, which by design finds and grows traffic, impressions, and clicks for you automatically until you tell it to stop.

Oh, and one more thing: If you study those numbers, the average search advertiser is running 25 different ads. The average Display Network advertiser only has seven. If you test dozens of image ads over a period of months, odds are you're going to hit pay dirt with a killer ad. *One killer ad can bring you tens of thousands, hundreds of thousands, even millions of dollars. It's a huge asset.*

ARE DISPLAY ADS ON GOOGLE A HUGE DEAL? YUP.

We estimate that 20 to 30 percent of Google's AdSense advertisers are willing to allow image ads—so there are *tons* of places where your ads can show. Text ads don't catch the eye like image ads do. Text ads limit you to 130 characters; image ads don't. The only limitations in display ads are the size you happen to be working on at the moment and what sorts of things users will and will not click on.

Display ads give you an infinite range of variables to test. And they bring you CTRs better than regular content-targeted text ads by 3:1. This is because 1) visuals are more compelling than mere words and 2) you could be the only Google ad that shows on a page.

It's quite simple. The same principles of good ad copy apply to image ads as well. Take a text ad, tweak a couple of phrases to make them complete sentences, decide what graphics will go in it, and you're done.

The point still is to enter the conversation inside your customer's head.

Be relevant, compelling, and credible. Use language that attracts. See if including numbers and statistics works. Put in a brief testimonial. Add a visual that supports your copy. Test and see what pulls best. Some elements you can try:

· Color vs. black-and-white images
· Images from nature
· Pictures of people (including famous people)
· All of the copy variations you'd test in text ads
· Photos of your product
· Graphs
· Computer screenshots

We've tested numbers of ads for both for-profit and nonprofit markets. Here's how different image ads performed in one of those markets:

Ad	Clicks	Impressions	CTR	Cost	Rate
SCIENCE ASTRONOMY & GOD	3,538	848,398	0.42%	$114.90	17.35%
MARS, THE STARS, & PLANETS	879	317,343	0.28%	$22.07	11.04%
THE HUBBLE TELESCOPE	1,283	144,719	0.89%	$49.49	14.65%

Note the different conversion rates. And note that the average cost-per-click in all cases came to less than $0.04. Not bad.

HOW TO SET IT UP

Choose the sizes that matter. The 80/20 rule applies here: Start with the 250 x 300 rectangle. That's where you'll get shown the most, followed by the 728 x 90 leaderboard. YouTube can be a huge source of impressions for the 250 x 300 ads:

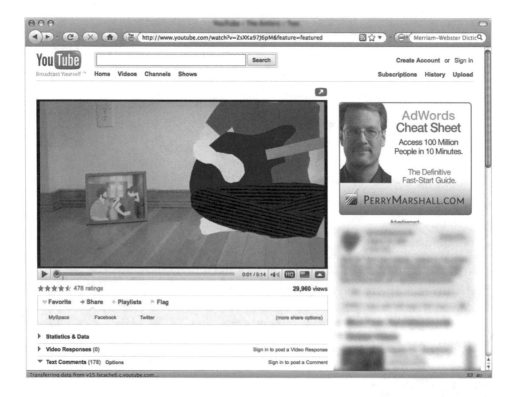

Remember that YouTube is the number-two search engine in the world. Some people can generate huge amounts of traffic just by carefully crafted campaigns that target YouTube users exclusively.

Create ads that catch the eye. There are nine sizes available. You can create ads in as many of them as you like. However, when you're split testing, only compare CTRs among ads of the same size; otherwise you might delete an ad that "lost" only because it's a different shape.

Add them in to your ad group. From the "Ads" tab in your AdWords interface, click on the "New ad" button and select "Image ad."

Upload your ad and wait. An editor will have to approve it.

You can, of course, set custom prices and choose where to show your display ads. Google's interface gives you special leverage with managed placements when image ads are involved:

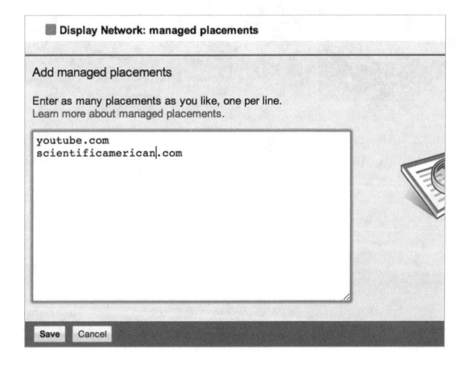

GETTING ADS MADE

You may not be a graphic designer and need help creating ads. We've appreciated our friend Laura Jennison at www.BannerAdQueen.com and the vibrant, click-worthy ads she creates.

If you can't afford to hire a designer, Google's Display Ad Builder is an alternative solution. From the "Ads" tab, click on "New ad," and select "Display ad builder":

From there you can choose a topic or theme and be provided with existing ad templates that you can rework—or simply add your own copy to—and submit for approval.

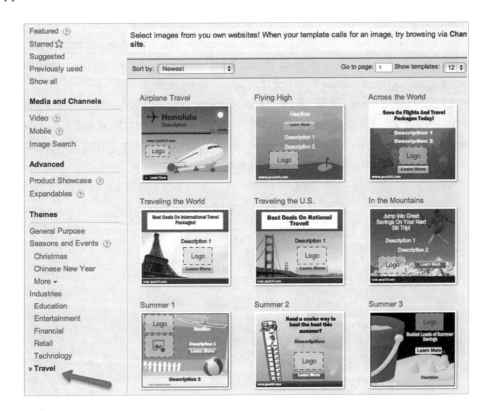

The advantage of Display Ad Builder is that you're using Google's existing images, which means that you only need editorial approval on the copy you add. In most cases this makes the approval process much faster than if you submit your own image ads.

RARE FIND: A NEWBIE ADWORDS ADVERTISER READY TO DO IMAGE ADS

As I write this, I just finished an AdWords consultation earlier today with Paul, a sharp young advertiser who was eager to start from scratch with new campaigns promoting his self-help products on Google.

Every month that goes by we do scores of one-on-one phone consultations with AdWords users in every market imaginable. And one odd thing they all seem to share in common is that they *rarely* ask us about display advertising on Google, despite the fact that this has been readily available to AdWords users for more than five years.

Paul was different. He hadn't turned on any traffic yet, but had three text ads already up and ready to go on Google, along with two handsome banner ads that promoted his landing page offer. He hadn't purchased a single Google click yet but knew he wanted to do Display Network advertising primarily and get as much traffic as possible from banner ads. He figured he could get banner ad clicks for less than he'd pay on text ads.

Good for him. He's right.

What I told Paul, I'm telling you now: In so many established, competitive markets these days you're likely to find it *easier,* not harder, to cut out a patch of ground for yourself on the content network rather than on Google search.

And Paul is also more likely to get clicks on his image ads for a third of the price of clicks on his regular text ads—and arguably a tenth of the price he'd pay for clicks on those ads on Google search. I told him that I look forward to seeing how this works for him because I'm convinced he's going to be more than pleasantly surprised.

Uncle Claude Sez

Pictures in advertising are very expensive. . . . Anything expensive must be effective. . . .

Pictures should not be used merely because they are inter-esting, or to attract attention, or to decorate an ad. Ads are not written to interest, please or amuse. You are writing on a serious subject–the subject of money spending. . . .

Use pictures only to attract those who may profit you. Use them only when they form a better selling argument than the same amount of space set in type.

Chapter 12

Local Advertising on Google: Mostly Virgin Territory

How Retailers, Restaurants, and Service Businesses Can Beat the Yellow Pages

According to the Kelsey group, 60 percent of all internet searches are local. Other estimates run as high as 75 percent. But even if it were only 20 percent, that's still a *lot* of searches. Tens of millions a day, at least.

■ ■ ■

Whatever the number is, local search is undoubtedly the most untapped opportunity in pay-per-click marketing. You want to sell weight loss plans, MP3 downloads, high-definition TVs, or mortgages nationwide on Google? You can do it, but you'd better strap on your gladiator helmet and prepare for a fight.

But if you're an accountant, plumber, painter, repair shop owner, or podiatrist, it's a much easier victory. In most local markets, your internet competitors have no idea what they're doing. Rarely will they read a book like this.

For example, my friend Bill is a minister who does weddings, and he gets more business than he can handle, bidding 50 cents to a dollar on simple terms like "wedding officiant." His wedding officiant brethren aren't exactly the green berets of the marketing world.

This is also a great place to consult, setting up campaigns for neighboring businesses, because it's so underserved. Think about it:

- Hundreds of local businesses in your city spend upwards of $1,000 a month just on Yellow Pages ads—so these people are already spending money!
- The Yellow Pages reps are also selling internet Yellow Page listings, creating more awareness of online marketing. Some of them are selling warmed-over pay-per-click porridge in the form of badly managed, overpriced Google campaigns.
- For companies like Google that are so busy dealing with existing opportunities, putting reps on the street to sell PPC to local businesses is a *long* way off at best. (There are rumors of partnerships with Yellow Pages companies though.)
- Large pay-per-click aggregators focus on specific niches (dentistry, home repair, restaurants) and sell one-size-fits-all solutions.
- Web-savvy local advertisers are rare, but this situation is changing. Running a retail store and running an online store are two entirely different things. If you're selling locally, now is the time to learn and act.

If you can accept the fact that many keywords will only produce a few local clicks a month, the ROI on what you do get can be extraordinary. And if you use all the options available to you to get premium listings (site extensions, click-to-call, high Quality Scores), the amount of traffic available can sometimes be surprising.

> A giant fraction of Google searches are local. Advertise your business locally, and you'll get traffic and customers for a fraction of the cost of other media. This may sometimes reach more people than Yellow Pages ads. It's more traceable than billboards, and it costs you less than mailings and fliers.

Google uses IP addresses and other clever technologies to figure out where people are when they search, and it serves up local ads. Local Google is perfect if you're in any of these markets:

Real estate
Hotels
Private investigators
Wedding planners
Storage
Home furnishing
Dentists
Churches
Hospitals

Beauty salons
Telephone service
Attorneys
Bid auctions
Cars and trucks
Printing
Construction
Movers
Pets

Funeral planning
Heating/Plumbing/Electricity
Landscaping
Doctors
Counselors
Assisted living
Restaurants
Clothing
Photographers

YOU'RE REACHING TWO KINDS OF PEOPLE, NOT JUST ONE

It seems like we give the following advice to real estate people the most, but it applies in a lot of places. There are *two* kinds of people looking for your business:

1. A person who lives in your area—your city, your state—who types in "real estate" or "dentist" or "churches" or "restaurant" and expects that the results he sees will be area-only. You'll be there when he comes looking for you.

2. A person may not be in your area at all (or else Google's system can't tell where he is) but is still asking for your area's services. He goes to Google and types in "movers in Palo Alto" or "Palo Alto real estate" or "hotels Palo Alto," hoping to get Palo-Alto-only results. He may be traveling on holiday; he may be planning a move; he may be an investor.

He may in fact be from Palo Alto. But he could be down in San Diego. Or way out in Orlando. Or in Montreal. Or Sydney. But he's still searching on Google for you, and he identifies Palo Alto by name.

Either way, you want to be there, ready to open the door when he comes knocking.

HOW TO REACH THE FIRST PERSON

Because you're aiming at these two kinds of people, you can set up *two* Google campaigns for them, not just one.

Here's how. When you're first setting up your campaign, tell Google the location(s) you want to target:

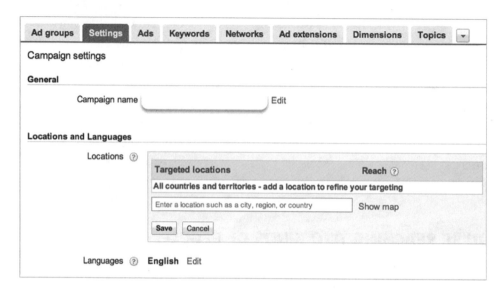

From this point forward, everything else you do in this campaign is the same as described in the rest of the book, but your ads will only be seen in the local area you choose.

HOW TO REACH THE SECOND PERSON

If you were advertising for real estate in California, you'd set up a *nationwide* campaign—possibly even an international campaign—but with local terms like "Visalia real estate" and "Yorba Linda real estate." After all, there are likely people from all over the country—and maybe even outside the country—who are doing searches on these terms.

So you'd grab a map or a listing of cities from a website and create a keyword set like this:

California real estate
LA real estate
Healdsburg real estate
Villa Real real estate
Santa Monica real estate
Buy homes California
Buy homes San Francisco
Buy homes Bakersfield
Buy homes Sausalito

To do this the best way, you would combine a large list of general keywords (the same ones you used on the regionally targeted campaign) with a large list of cities and towns, and then use a spreadsheet to mix and match them together.

Either way, you'll end up with a huge keyword list; 95 percent of them will never get searches, and the other 5 percent may only get a few. However, it doesn't cost anything to bid on these keywords if nobody clicks, and when people do click, they'll only be 10 or 20 cents. Not much traffic, but what you do get will be bargain priced.

You should still buy generic keywords in your local campaign, but these local keywords in a nationwide campaign will bring very cheap clicks, mostly.

Your real estate Google account would be arranged like this:

Campaign #1: California Targeting Only
Group 1: Real estate
Group 2: Buy homes

Campaign #2: National Targeting—entire USA
Group 1: California real estate
Group 2: Buy homes California

Now you have both bases covered, and you'll be getting as much traffic as possible for your local market. The key is that you're not leaving out people in other geographic locations who are seriously looking for what you offer.

Under the geo-targeting tool's "Custom" tab, you can also use your business's address or latitude and longitude, and target all searches within a radius that you select. Google even gives you the advanced option of choosing your own customized set of coordinates to target.

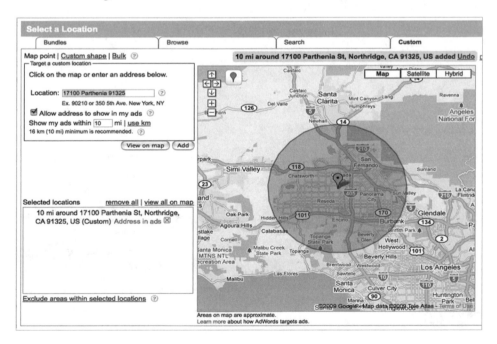

HONE YOUR CHOPS ON A LOCAL TEST CAMPAIGN BEFORE YOU GO NATIONAL

Time-honored advertising practice is to test ideas in a smaller market before you spend big bucks to try them out in a larger one. Nowadays the risks of going national instantly if you have a good product may seem small. After all, you're paying for one click at a time, and you can set a daily budget and turn your traffic on and off at will. But that doesn't undo the value of trying your product in one small geographic area first.

For example, if you sell advice to investors, you might start just with investors in New York State. The advantage? You don't need to worry nearly as much about your daily budget.

If your cash reserves are limited, you can choose this smaller market to start off in. If in the first few weeks or months it's not profitable, you're not forced to shut the entire thing down for fear of quickly going bankrupt. Make the sales process profitable in a smaller market, and then go national.

At that point you're able to take on the big boys in the worldwide market because you know that the mechanism works like clockwork in the small market, and every dollar you send out comes back with more dollars attached.

(Oh—this is also an excellent way to keep competitors from knowing what you're up to—if they don't live in the cities you're targeting.)

SOMETHING CALLED "GOOGLE PLACES"

If you're selling locally, head over to www.google.com/places, and sign up for an account if you haven't already.

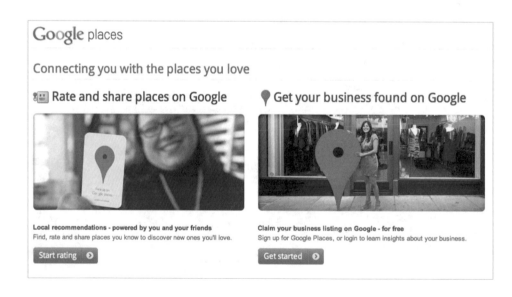

Google Places lets you create a page for your business that makes your information easy to find by people searching for you. You get tremendous SEO benefits from this, for one thing. The advantage to your AdWords campaigns is that Places lets you add extensions to your paid ads with key information about how to find you. Here's a San Fernando Valley search for Starbucks:

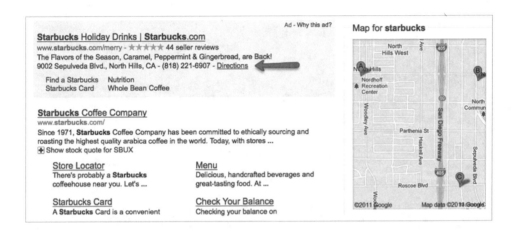

How do you incorporate these data points into your ads once you're set up with Google Places? The key is the "Ad extensions" tab, and selecting "Location extensions" from it:

From here you can link up a Google Places account:

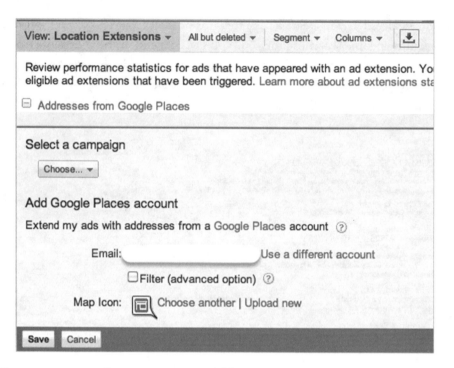

Or you can manually enter your own address.

The point here is not to send paid ad clicks to your Places page; the point is to have a Places page to link to which will allow your regular AdWords ads to display additional information about you, and tip the scales in your favor.

HOW TO BE SURE PEOPLE FIND YOU ON THEIR MOBILE DEVICES

One other element of ad extensions is the ability to target mobile devices intelligently. This is a game-changer for local businesses. If your customer is out and about, finds you on his smartphone, and ends up walking through your door and buying from you, that's a huge win.

You can do this via "Call extensions":

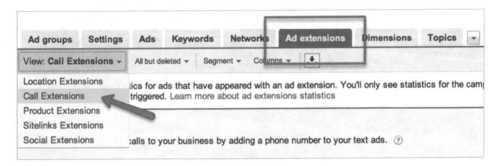

There is an ever-expanding menu of options for you here, but we'll single out just one: click-to-call-only ads for mobile devices. This is where your ad shows up (alone!) at the top of a search results screen, and clicking the ad calls your phone number directly. No clicks through to your webpage, in other words. That's a relief if you don't already have a mobile-friendly site. And it gets people talking to you.

Set this up by selecting "Allow only clicks-to-call" from among the high-end mobile phone options:

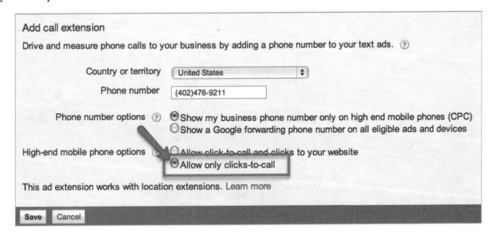

Every action local folks take, you can measure, all the way down to the phone calls you generate. And what works in one local area, you may be able to expand into other areas. Perhaps even take your business nationwide.

Uncle Claude Sez

We usually start with local advertising, even if magazine advertising is best adapted to the article. We get our distribution town by town, then change to national advertising.

Whether you advertise few or many dealers, the others will stock in very short order if the advertising is successful.

Slashing Your Bid Prices: Quality Score and How Google Rewards You for Relevance

"Which One Do You Think Will Get Us to the Martinis Faster?"

My friend and mentor Dan Kennedy was in a conversation over cocktails with an ad agency exec. The discussion was about two different ads that were each scheduled to run in a national magazine.

■ ■ ■

One was a down and dirty, old-school ad with an in-your-face headline and dense, carefully worded body text followed by a call to action and a clip-out coupon to be mailed in.

The other was the ultra-modern, ultra-sleek gigantic full-page ad with the irrelevant photograph and blurb at the bottom in tiny, whittled-down, vague text about how hip XYZ Company was. The usual ad agency fluff.

Dan pointed to the old-school ad and explained to the ad exec that it had been run before and was carefully tested and tweaked for maximum response, and it was virtually guaranteed to make the client's phone ring. "How would you like to run this one against your corporate-style ad and see which one got more sales?" he asked. "What would your client think?"

The ad guy chuckled. "To be perfectly honest with you, Dan, I could run either one. Makes no difference to me. But if I have the choice of showing one or the other to the CEO, which one do you think is going to get us to the martinis faster?"

Glitz and puffery is the secret sauce in most ad agencies. The goal is not ROI or to make the client's phone ring. The goal most certainly is not to be relevant.

The object in an old-school ad agency is to goose the CEO's ego, get invited out for drinks, and get the guy to invite you back and write you another round of checks next month.

IT AIN'T HIS NECK UNDER THE GUILLOTINE BLADE

When you're the person laying out the cash yourself and it's *your own* business and *your own* risk and *your own* credit card that Google is dinging every month, you don't have time for your own ego stroking. Your customers don't have the patience for it either.

Nowhere is this more clear than in Google AdWords. Putting your own money on the line has a funny way of wising us up to what gets clicks and what doesn't.

> People are drawn to you when you're relevant. The formula for success on Google is relevance. When you're relevant, people will click on your ads, Google will explicitly reward you for it, your costs will drop, and your profits will grow.

HERE'S HOW GOOGLE REWARDS YOU FOR RELEVANCE

Traditionally, you get higher positions on the search page by bidding more. But when your click-through rate goes up, Google actually gives you better positioning without charging you more per click. It rewards you for being relevant.

Roughly speaking, the first position has always been given to the highest bidder. But Google has long maintained an ingenious little twist. Here's a simplified version of its formula:

Your Relative Position = (Your Bid Price) x (Your Click-Through Rate)

Google now has a fuller version of that formula that it calls Ad Rank—your bid price multiplied by your Quality Score. More on the Quality Score later. Either way, in this case your CTR swings the biggest difference, apart from the price you bid.

Google's chief economist Hal Varian has a useful series of short videos to help you understand Ad Rank. To see them, just go to www.perrymarshall.com/adrank.

If you have a high click-through rate then you don't have to bid as much for the position. A simplified example: I bid $1.00, and my ad gets a CTR of 1 percent. Your ad gets a CTR of 2 percent. In theory you can get the same average position as me by bidding $0.50. If you bid $0.51 then you'll get the position above me.

If you're already in top position, Google will automatically charge you a lower bid price as your CTR improves. Not bad.

This really works. Our customers who buy our online e-book (www.PerryMarshall.com/adwords) tell us this all the time:

> *Before I purchased your program, I was averaging about 50 clicks a day, paying at least 25 cents each for them. But after implementing your strategies: 402 Clicks, average cost per click of 14 cents, average position of 3.3 with my ads. My traffic is much more targeted, so my conversion rate almost doubled. I don't think my first impression of Santa Claus was this good!*
>
> —Michael Mettie, Simple Streams, The Colony, TX

> *I've been doing internet marketing for a little over four months now and I just have to say that your Guide has been the best course I've bought because it has allowed me to spend a fraction of what I used to pay and get more than 5x the visitors for less money.*
>
> —Andres Cordova, Salinas, CA

This isn't magic, even though it looks like magic. Our customers are just writing straightforward, relevant ads, and their cost-per-click is going down.

That's what will happen to you. It means you're coughing up less money to Google every month, and you're putting more in your own pocket every day.

THE QUALITY SCORE STORY

AdWords ads are little salesmen. You know as well as I do that you rarely get straight, unfiltered info from a salesman. It's even worse when the website it takes you to doesn't give you what it promised.

Google knows this, too. It knows its users are cynical about its sponsored ads. But it also know that if it can slowly alter this trend by ensuring better landing pages after you click, more people will trust its paid ads and click them.

Google won the first round of the search engine wars by making its organic searches more relevant than anyone else's. Its owners became billionaires in the second round because its CTR-based ranking system made its pay-per-click ads more relevant than anyone else's. (Plus it had a far better user interface.)

And it continued to kick the other engines' butts in the third round by having its paid ads send users to more relevant, higher-quality *websites* than anyone else's.

In 2005, Google introduced the idea of *Quality Score,* where it gave each of your keywords a secret, Google-only-knows ranking based on how well your ad copy matched your keywords. If your Quality Score was low, you were forced to pay a high minimum bid of $1.00 and sometimes more, otherwise your ads wouldn't show.

Then in July 2006 Google issued its first major "slap": your keywords' Quality Score was now based on keyword-to-ad-text relevance *and* landing-page relevance both. If your ad and website were not up to snuff, Google would deactivate your keywords and require a minimum bid of $5.00, $10.00, or more in order to get your ads to show again.

Since then Google has updated and revised the Quality Score algorithm numerous times. Nowadays it won't make your keywords "inactive" per se; instead it names a minimum bid that you have to pay in order (it claims) to show on the first page of search results.

THERE'S LOW QUALITY SCORE, AND THEN THERE'S BEING "SUSPENDED"

This chapter is about helping you earn a higher Quality Score and have your ads show in better positions for less money. But the biggest penalty from Google comes when you don't have a good website to send people to in the first place.

Google frequently has human reviewers look over sites and suspend the ones that violate its terms of service or which appear to be borderline risky or shady, such as sites that offer ways to get rich, make questionable medical claims, etc. Suspensions can be temporary or permanent, depending on how severe the infractions are and how often an advertiser keeps committing them.

It used to be that Google would suspend all traffic going to the site and label associated keywords with a Quality Score of 1/10. Now it simply marks a keyword as "site suspended." Suspension is no longer directly tied to Quality Score.

Nevertheless, many of the steps that Google encourages you to take to get your site unsuspended will also earn you better rankings.

The Grandma Factor

As we mentioned, human editors look over sites and flag for suspension anything they find questionable. The single biggest factor in the decision? Every editor asks, "Would I be comfortable sending Grandma to this site?"

If your site is making outrageous claims, if it's promising health benefits that the products sold there cannot deliver, if it handles mature content in an offensive manner, then the human editor certainly wouldn't want to send his poor grandmother there. He'll flag it.

At this point an email or a call to Google's customer service may not yield answers any more specific than what's already in the online documentation. That's why high-volume Google advertisers are frequently assigned personal account representatives, who often have access to the real reasons for low Quality Scores and can sometimes get them reversed.

QUALITY SCORE: WHAT IT IS, HOW IT'S MEASURED, WHEN IT MATTERS, AND WHEN IT DOESN'T

Google takes a look at your keyword, then at the ads directly associated with it, then at your landing page, and then at the rest of your website. From there it does two things:

1. It gives you a number ranking from 0 to 10.
2. It determines what percentage of the time it's going to show your ads when people search on that keyword, and at what position on the page and what click price.

Hint: Often (1) above has little bearing at all on (2). More on this later.
Quality Score (QS) is reflected in:

· How much you pay. Higher score = lower actual cost per click
· Where on the page you show. Higher score = higher positions on the search results page
· How much exposure you get. Higher score = higher impression share, i.e., your ads show a higher percentage of the times people search on your keywords.

When you first introduce new ads and new keywords, Google's system will take a quick look and guess how it thinks you'll perform. If your ads match your keywords and your website has minimally relevant content on it, Google will start you off with a 7/10 or 10/10 QS. When clicks start rolling in, you may see your QS drop suddenly if your CTR is significantly below that of your competitors.

QUALITY SCORE IS A TRAILING INDICATOR, NOT A LEADING INDICATOR

Interestingly, we've seen campaigns with QS of 3/10 or 4/10 that are nonetheless strong and perform well. In other words, Google may tell you that you have a QS of 3 or 4, but still show you a high percentage of the time. So before panicking over a low QS, check first to see if your CTRs or impression shares are low and if you're showing in poor positions on the page.

How Do I Find My Quality Score?

There are two ways to see your QS:

1. Mouse over the little speech bubble under the Status column next to your keyword. A small popup tells you the QS number and briefly summarizes what is or isn't working.

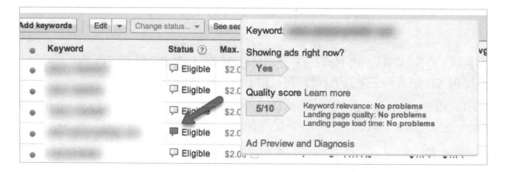

2. Or, in the ad group view, click the "Columns" button below the tabs and above the graph,

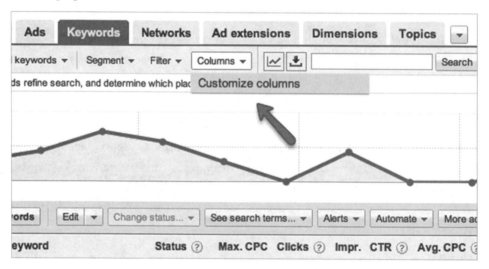

and you'll be given the option to add a column showing Quality Score:

```
Select columns
☐ Attributes          ☐ Performance  ☐ Conversions
☐ Dest. URL           ☑ Clicks       ☑ Conv. (1-per-click)
☑ Qual. score         ☑ Impr.        ☑ Cost / conv. (1-per-click)
☐ Est. first page bid ☑ CTR          ☑ Conv. rate (1-per-click)
☐ Est. top page bid   ☑ Avg. CPC     ☑ View-through Conv.
☐ Match type          ☐ Avg. CPM     ☐ Conv. (many-per-click)
                      ☑ Cost         ☐ Cost / conv. (many-per-click)
                      ☑ Avg. Pos.    ☐ Conv. rate (many-per-click)
                                     ☐ Total conv. value
                                     ☐ Value / conv. (1-per-click)
                                     ☐ Value / conv. (many-per-click)
```

How Exactly Does Google Determine My Quality Score?

Here's how we understand QS to be calculated:

- 50–60 percent of QS is the CTR of the individual keyword plus the ads in your ad group, over the entire time you've had that keyword in your account
- 5–10+ percent is the quality of your landing page (and as of this writing that percentage is increasing)
- 5 percent is your account history, measured by the CTR of all the ads and keywords in your account
- 5 percent is how well you matched the keyword to the ads in its ad group
- Other factors account for up to 25 percent of your QS, many of which, to be perfectly honest, are still opaque!

So the CTR of your keyword-plus-ad is the single biggest factor. Never overlook negative keywords, as these help cut out unwanted impressions.

Note also that history is a big deal. Advertisers with older accounts perform better than newer advertisers. A high CTR right off the bat can be golden, as it can take one week to four-plus months to shake off a "bad history." (This is often called "account level quality score.")

Two quick diagnostic questions you can start with may help boost a low Quality Score.

1. Does the slapped keyword match your ad perfectly? Does it show up in the headline of the ad?
2. Is your landing page clearly about that keyword, and is the keyword used repeatedly on the landing page?

Of course, you want Google to conclude that the entire *site* is about your keyword's topic as well and that yours is the best site people could go to in order to learn about the topic.

Great, interesting content is the best way to keep people arriving and staying put. Blogs, online calculators, audios, videos, and other "involvement devices" keep people around longer. Do whatever you need to in order to keep people there in larger numbers and for longer times.

ACTING ALL UPPITY WON'T EARN YOU A PENNY MORE

Do you like to see impressive, amazing things? Do you like to see jaw-dropping, astonishing situations and events?

Of course you do. Everybody does. And it only costs ten bucks. That's right, for ten bucks you can go to a movie theater and watch Matt Damon, Vin Diesel, or Angelina Jolie deliver two solid hours of stunning imagery, special effects, action, and thrills, splashed across the big screen in blazing color and Dolby Surround. And these days, with a few thousand dollars of audio/video equipment, you can see the same thing, maybe better, at home.

Yes, people like to be wowed and impressed, and Hollywood thinks nothing of spending $100 million on a picture so it can give the people exactly that. And it does a great job.

But one of the worst things you can do is deliberately try to impress your customers. Why? Because when you try to impress instead of building trust, educating, and persuading, your would-be customer shuts you off. Her guard goes up and she stops listening to you.

Help her solve problems and capitalize on new opportunities, however, and she's yours for life.

Most businesses these days are trying hard to impress. But impressing people never makes a positive contribution to customers' needs. Nobody cares how many billions of dollars of assets some company has.

Your customers would much rather know that you'll go to the mat for them when there's a problem. They'd much rather know that you're there to help them.

Your customers want to be spoken and written to in a conversational, layman's tone of voice that strives to build trust, educate, and persuade them, rather than dazzle and impress them.

So the best of the best Google ads are never the ones that jump off the page and knock you over. The ones that get the most clicks are simple, engaging, straightforward, and honest, and they speak in a voice that their unique market recognizes and understands.

If you want CEOs to buy you martinis, New York ad agencies might be just your thing. If you want to stand tough against your competitors and sell to customers who trust you, just be relevant.

Uncle Claude Sez

Ads are not written to entertain. When they do, those entertainment seekers are little likely to be the people whom you want.

That is one of the greatest advertising faults. Ad writers . . . forget they are salesmen and try to be performers. Instead of sales, they seek applause.

When you plan or prepare an advertisement, keep before you a typical buyer. Your subject, your headline has gained his or her attention. Then in everything be guided by what you would do if you met the buyer face-to-face.

Don't try to be amusing. . . . Don't boast, for all people resent it. Don't try to show off. Do just what you think a good salesman should do.

Chapter 14

The Dark Side
of Google

Google is a magnificent invention. You might well argue it's the single most powerful technological tool of our generation. Its capacity to connect people with information and resources, to facilitate commerce and research—not just the advertising but the organic listings as well—positively impacts trillions of dollars of business and most of the world's population.

■ ■ ■

But there is a dark side.

The dark side is, if you're a small advertiser building your business on Google traffic, you can get body slammed. And Google won't care.

In this chapter I'm going to tell you what can go wrong.

As long as you know your place in the food chain . . . as long as you're cautious and savvy and don't view Google as some kind of "savior" . . . you're going to be OK.

But this chapter is a stern warning: If you look at Google through rose-colored glasses, you're gonna regret it. Here's an example—an Amazon review from the previous edition of this book:

> 6 of 12 people found the following review helpful:
>
> ★☆☆☆☆ **Nothing about how easy it is to be suspended!**, December 30, 2010
>
> By <u>Gina Kamentsky</u> - <u>See all my reviews</u>
> REAL NAME
>
> This review is from: **Ultimate Guide to Google Ad Words, 2nd Edition: How To Access 100 Million People in 10 Minutes (Paperback)**
>
> One fatal flaw in this book, there's nothing covering how easy it is to have your account suspended by Google. I followed the guidelines in this book AND was very careful to adhere to Googles rules and woke up Christmas morning to find 6 months of hard work down the drain and I'm now banned for life from marketing using adwords. In addition I know a few other people who were suspended on the same day. There is no recourse when this happens, Google knows the computer you used, your identity and credit card info so I will have to buy a new computer and open up an account through an associate if I wish to continue with this. In conclusion, I would not put much energy into an adwords program and concentrate on organic search instead. Google has become too big, lost their connection with the "little guy" and evil. There whould be some big warnings and cautions in this book!

My apologies to Gina for not saying much about this in the 2nd edition of this book. I certainly talk about it a lot on my blog and in my emails!

(This might be the best reason of all to subscribe to our email updates at www.perrymarshall.com/supplement/. You can't get everything you could possibly need to know in one book.)

In our "Bobsled Run," a 12-week intense training that starts with Google clicks and refines your entire sales funnel, I begin by telling people:

> *If 12 months from today you're still getting all your traffic from Google, then I have failed. Because the whole point of this course is to perfect your sales funnel so you can affordably buy traffic from all kinds of places, not just Google.*

That's the Unlimited Traffic Technique in action. When you build a great sales funnel, you naturally make it easy to diversify. My own business was heavily dependent on Google in the beginning, but it's not anymore. We have SEO, referrals, affiliates, Facebook ads, publicity, articles across the web, and the book you're reading now, each sending us new customers every day.

Now when we get hassled by Google, the effect on our traffic is less than 10 percent. You should aim to do the same.

THE MOST DANGEROUS NUMBER IN ANY BUSINESS IS: "ONE"

Dan Kennedy famously said the most fatal number in business is one. One traffic source, one advertising medium, one web page, one product, one star salesman, one means of communicating with customers, one critical business partner, one bank account, one merchant account.

When all you have is one of any of these things, somebody can kill you dead. Your sales tank overnight. You don't own your business. THEY do. Big mistake.

In the next few pages I'll tell you

- why Google behaves the way it does,
- who's got a bull's-eye painted on their forehead and who doesn't,
- how to deal with Google slaps and Google bans, and
- how to sanely diversify when you're getting started.

A Brief History of Google Advertising

A little history is in order. I wrote the first edition of *The Definitive Guide to Google AdWords* in the summer of 2003. At this point, AdWords hadn't quite caught on. Then a young surfer dude named Chris Carpenter wrote a book called *Google Cash*.

Google Cash explained how you could sign up for an affiliate program, sign up for Google AdWords, give Google five bucks, and start sending traffic through your affiliate link. You could be an invisible traffic broker, pocketing the difference between your click cost and your affiliate commission.

All you had to do was find a combination of keywords and affiliate programs that was profitable, and you had an instantly profitable business. You were now an invisible traffic broker.

Google Cash caught on like wildfire. Within six months, hundreds of thousands of people all over the world were bidding on every conceivable word and phrase in the English language—and quite a few other languages—and driving traffic to eBay, Amazon, ClickBank, and thousands of other sites.

It was a massive, underground gold rush. The thing about it was, it *worked*. Honestly, I thought it was stupid at first. (I also thought pay-per-click was perverse, too. I was wrong.) To me it was just too simple.

Well it *was* too simple, as I shall explain later. But actually it was too simple *not* to work. Some percentage of the time, it was bound to succeed. A lot of people were making a lot of money with this, and there were a lot of keywords available for 5 or 10 cents.

Affiliates created the magic that made Google go supernova. Because after awhile, no matter what you typed into Google, you saw ads. Every company president, every marketing and sales manager, every webmaster saw somebody showing up on Google, and it wasn't them.

This sucked 'em into Google AdWords against their will.

Ya think clicks should be free? Too bad. Cuz your competitors are buying space where you ought to be showing up.

Google hit the tipping point and exploded. I had customers making $100,000 a month, just brokering clicks.

The genius of *Google Cash* was:

You have zero commitments. It's way easier to go find another product to promote than it is to own a product or change your own product. Or even change your website, for that matter. The name of the game is speed and testing.

Google cashers embraced speed and testing overnight. So a new, billion-dollar industry—pay-per-click affiliate marketing—sprang up out of nowhere. At light speed.

This Is Where the History Lesson Starts to Kick In

The history lesson has everything to do with pretty much anything else you do in marketing or advertising. This speed/testing combo was like crack cocaine. It was addictive, and it was shallow. It created lots of problems, including the following:

- An invisible affiliate business is extremely fragile. It's very easy to knock off. (Within a year or two, people started selling software that helped you detect and copy successful affiliate campaigns.)
- You own zero assets in a business like that. A $1 million-per-year direct linking affiliate business is equivalent to building a mansion on the side of a hill in Sao Paulo, on rented land. The next rainstorm could wash that mansion away in a mudslide. You have nothing to show for it.
- Invisible affiliates often have no ethics. Some of them promote horrible products.
- Thousands of affiliates all do exactly the same thing at the same time. They have no advantage over each other; they just drive bid prices up.
- Affiliates cluttered the internet with all kinds of lousy offers. Sometimes you'd search for something, and ten people were all promoting the same thing at the same time. It took awhile for Google to eliminate duplicate offers from its search results, but it did.
- Content is king, and most affiliates create no content.
- Click for click, the most profitable offers are generally overpriced, overpromised products. In the short term, "edgy" offers with unrealistic claims, obnoxious websites with pop-ups and no back button, and abusive return policies make twice as much money as sane, honest offers.

- Websites like *The New York Times* don't like "edgy" advertisers. Neither does Google or Facebook. In the early days, edgy advertisers were all they had. They accepted the money for awhile, but as soon as sites like Facebook or Google have enough legitimate advertisers, they kick out the edgy ones.
- From the perspective of Google—or Facebook—affiliates are disposable. "Thank you, Mr. Affiliate, for your giving us so much money for these last few years. Now that you've helped us attract 'real' businesses, we're done with you. Happy trails, you poor pathetic scumbag."
- Google and Facebook don't like affiliates all that much. After a couple of years, Google started tightening the screws on affiliates. Facebook will too.

Please understand that some affiliates are really cool and very likeable. At the same time, average, unsophisticated, garden-variety affiliates are the trailer trash of the internet. Just tellin' it like it is.

Much of what I said about affiliates applies broadly to all advertisers in "troublesome industries." The following markets consistently have problems with Google slaps and bans:

- Weight Loss
- Alternative Health
- Illness "cures" of any kind
- How to Make Money in {Anything}
- Marketing, Direct Marketing & Sales of {Anything}
- Multilevel Marketing
- Affiliates
- Turn Key Businesses
- Free Software Downloads
- Anything related to gambling, adult sites, or weapons
- Employment and Jobs
- Self-Help

These are mostly unregulated, low-barrier-to-entry, low-startup-cost industries that attract some percentage of psychopaths. Heck, we get hassled by Google about once every six months—and they know who we are. It still happens. It's because we're in the direct marketing category, and we make bold claims and guarantees on our website.

It just goes with the territory. In some of these categories, Google just more or less refuses to take people's money for very long. I have a theory that Google is paranoid about getting nailed by the federal government for being complicit with some advertiser's fraudulent scheme because it sold that advertiser the ads.

"Google Bans" Mostly Have to Do with Your INDUSTRY, Not YOU

The number-one factor in whether you get hassled by Google isn't your website or your opt-in page. It's what you sell and who else sells it too. If you sell riveting machines or ping-pong tables, odds are you'll never have a single problem with Google, ever.

If you're in one of the suspect categories and get a nasty email from Google, don't take it personally. And don't get mad at the person at Google either. Most of those emails come from low-wage overseas employees who would rather eliminate you with one click of their mouse than hear your bitter tirade.

In my opinion Google is making a big mistake by putting hundreds of $50,000-per-year accounts under the control of a $5,000-per-year, uneducated employee, but that's what it does. Hey, you can't blame 'em for following the 80/20 rule. So deal with it.

During one round of "Google's not happy with Perry's site," the rep sent me an email. At the end of the email it said, "And please stop scams."

Like I said, don't get mad at 'em. They're just clueless.

The way to get nonclueless account reps is to get yourself a "Google rep." This normally involves spending hundreds of thousands of dollars per year. Google's top 1,000 advertisers generate the vast majority of the revenue and the other million advertisers are the "long tail." Google knows who butters its bread.

Some advertisers have escaped these problems by aligning themselves with an agency, to whom they pay money for a share in its "My Client Center" and access to its Google rep. Agencies may be reluctant to work with you if you're a problematic account or if you're in a problematic industry—as discussed above. If you're in compliance with all of Google's policies, however, this might work very well for you.

TEN TIPS FOR BUILDING A ROBUST, STABLE, LONG-TERM INTERNET BUSINESS

1. Build a presence over time that's difficult or impossible to knock off. Any business that can be replicated with "cut and paste" is the online equivalent of a shantytown. A trailer park in Tornado Alley. You want original content, extensive sales funnels, and a unique selling proposition that's hard for others to attain.

TEN TIPS FOR BUILDING A ROBUST, STABLE, LONG-TERM INTERNET BUSINESS, CONTINUED

2. Build assets: email lists, snail-mail lists, unique products, unique processes, unique experiences. You want your business to run on systems that you own, not rent. You want to build a brand. Better if there's more to those systems than meets the eye. By the way, you can do all of those things as an affiliate.

   You can build a website, and content, and systems. All those things are hard, tangible assets. Intellectual property. Technology. Patents. Things that aren't easy to replicate. Amazon is nothing more than a sophisticated affiliate for a third of the things they sell. All those product reviews on Amazon are a huge asset.

3. Consider the value of your product. Google's staff that manually reviews websites uses this criteria: "Would I send my grandma to this site?" Your criteria should be: "Would I sell this to my grandma? Or my sister-in-law?"

4. Use a different style than everyone else. You are always developing and sharpening your USP.

5. Sell different things than everyone else.

6. Create great content.

7. Remember that solid, dependable, and honest beats edgy every time—in the long run.

8. Make your product something other sites, including Facebook, would feel proud to advertise. Every shopping mall in the country would be delighted to have Nordstrom as its anchor store. Become Nordstrom for internet sites.

9. Do not look like, taste like, or smell like an affiliate—even if you are an affiliate. You should add value to the equation.

10. Understand how media companies tighten the screws on affiliates and "thin" advertisers.

"MY SITE IS SUSPENDED. WHAT DO I DO?"

Your goal is to get as many people as possible to stay on your site as long as possible. Here are some essentials to ensure that your website passes muster with Google:

- On pages where you ask for opt-ins you must have additional navigation links so that people can see the rest of the site and find out more about you. See the homepage at www.CosmicFingerprints.com for a simple example.
- Provide a link on the landing page to full contact information that includes your company name, a physical address, and a working phone number.
- Make it crystal clear who you are, where your business is located, what you sell, and how your money is made.
- Provide clear links on your landing page to your privacy policies and legal disclaimers.
- Turn teaser bullets into paragraphs with helpful, meaty information.
- Offering an email series: Put it on your site and make every installment accessible by (non-obvious) links for folks who don't want to opt-in.
- Put up a site map that links to every relevant public page on your site so that Google can easily find your public content.
- Post articles. Put the kids to bed, promise your wife you'll make up the quality time, go lock yourself in your study, and start writing articles and content like a banshee.
- Add a blog.
- Get comfortable with the essentials of SEO, that is, search engine optimization. We highly recommend getting on the list of our friends at Planet Ocean (http://www.SearchEngineHelp.com).

Other Reasons for Suspensions

There are other scenarios as well that can trigger a suspension. Here are some questions you can ask:

1. *Is a large number of affiliates bidding on keywords and sending Google clicks to your site?* Google doesn't want 10,000 affiliates all buying clicks, placing ads, and sending traffic to one single website. It doesn't even want ten affiliates doing that. It would turn Google into a warring ground over which site owner can amass the most paying fans. Not what it wants. Ideal Google world: one site per advertiser, no more.
2. *Is your site heavily templated or pre-fab content?* Google wants every new ad to point to fresh, new content. If your site was provided to you by an organization or service

that provides near-identical sites with near-identical content to other site owners, Google can easily tell. And you'll get slapped.

If every word, phrase, and sentence on your site is entirely your own original content, you have nothing to be afraid of.

3. *Is your site a review site that compares multiple products, and you're an affiliate for any or all of them?* This is another model Google dislikes. A major telltale sign for Google is when your landing page is heavy with affiliate links to other vendors and sites. It wants visitors to hit your landing page, find good quality, and stay on your site—not just get herded off to some big vendor.

(Google dislikes this for good reason, by the way. The majority of such sites hawk high-commission, low-quality products. "Fake review sites" are spam. Google wants people to own their products and their customer experience, take a stand, and not be anonymous.)

4. *Are there overbold or outrageous claims on your site?* If your target market is health and nutrition, moneymaking and business opportunities, sexual issues or adult content, or anything remotely dicey or high-visibility, then Google is exercising double, triple scrutiny over your content. Anything overstated, exaggerated, or outrageous will get a human editor behind the scenes at Google to tag or rate your site negatively.

IS GOOGLE "EVIL"?

Google's motto is "Don't be evil." Is it really evil? I'll leave it to you to decide. But the fact is, it's *tempted* to be evil a thousand different ways every day.

Google knows who butters its bread: its top 1,000 advertisers. It bends over backwards to give them great service. If you're one of its bottom 100,000 advertisers, don't expect good customer service.

Expect Google to do what's good for Google.

Don't waste a lot of time trying to decide whether Google is evil or not. Understand that everybody—including Google employees, including you—everybody does what makes sense to them.

If Google seems indifferent to your tiny little corner of the world, it's all just part of serving up a million search results each minute for a billion people. Remember that thousands of webmasters are trying to unfairly game Google's system every day. Even if you think Google is trying to screw people, don't forget that millions of people are trying to screw Google. Google's job is not an easy one.

Remember that few people actually get banned for life. It's not uncommon for someone at Google to change his mind six months later. There's nothing to keep you from sending Google an email every month or so and politely ask to be reconsidered.

And don't build a business that is exclusively dependent on Google.

HOW TO DIVERSIFY IN A WORLD WHERE GOOGLE IS KING

Having said all this, I *still* maintain that Google AdWords is the best first step for 75 percent of all online businesses. Why? Because it's the most instantaneous, most sophisticated advertising system in the history of man.

And remember, most businesses—pet shops, metal foundries, coffee shops, massage therapists—will seldom if ever have any of these problems.

Here's how you build a stable business that's immune to the daily whims of Google:

1. Build an email list, so you can directly market to your own prospects and customers. Collect snail-mail addresses, too.
2. As soon as you're getting specific keywords to convert to sales with reliable data, start doing Search Engine Optimization for those keywords.
3. Copy your campaigns to Yahoo/Bing. It'll probably increase your traffic by 10–15 percent.
4. Explore Facebook ads. See Chapters 16 and 17 on Social Media and Facebook.
5. If what you sell has mass appeal, test other advertising networks, such as Advertising.com. If you have a large budget, buy your Google display ads through DoubleClick, which is owned by Google. You'll probably get better customer service there.
6. Rent space in e-zines. Recruit affiliates. Rent mailing lists. Explore offline marketing opportunities like direct mail and radio.
7. Publish articles. Get publicity. Make a product that's so great people tell their friends about it.

And above all else . . .

BUILD A SITE THAT CONVERTS *ALL* FORMS OF QUALIFIED TRAFFIC

The ultimate key to being immune to Google slaps and bans is a site that converts well. If people make more money sending you traffic than sending it to someone else, then in the long run, you'll always wind up on top.

Chapter 15

Google, Vegas, and Those Who Live by Gaming the System

If there is any such thing as a historian of Direct Marketing/Information Marketing, it's Phil Alexander from Toronto. Phil and I have been friends since 1998, and he's one of the most insightful guys in the business. It's kind of nice having a guy like him in my pantheon of secret weapons.

Phil wrote a brilliant piece on the subject of Google bans, which puts Google's behavior in its proper place in history. For those who study history knowing that those who don't will repeat it, I offer this to you:

EVERYONE'S BEEN TALKING ABOUT THE GOOGLE BANS—AS IF IT'S SOMETHING NEW

It's not. It's been done before, almost exactly.

You know what this is EXACTLY like?

Blackjack, circa 1962. Just after *Beat the Dealer* (the first real book on card counting) was published.

Back then, blackjack was a small game. The men, mostly ex-veterans, played craps. And the slots were growing, but not like the late '80s.

Beat the Dealer came out and showed people how to win . . . and like all "easy winning" systems, it wasn't all "easy." The dealers didn't throw money at you any more than $20 bills come out of your disk drive when you buy an e-book!

Many people bought the book. Few people read it. Fewer people practiced it, and fewer people mastered it. (Sound familiar?)

And of course blackjack profits went up. Way up. Poorly trained players do *not* do well at the tables!

Slowly, though, players improved.

The casinos panicked. They tightened the rules so no one could win and, more importantly, made the game look impossible. More decks. More shuffling. Tougher rules. Take note: It wasn't just tougher; it *looked* tougher.

Now if you're a student of marketing—as you should be—can you guess what happened?

Can you guess what the customers demanded, and what the gurus developed?

Enhanced strategies? *Check.*

Systems to overcome casino rule changes? *Check.*

Newsletters? *Check.*

Coaching? Boot camps? Even *franchises* for blackjack schools? *Check, check, and check.*

To some casinos, the rule changes weren't enough. Every winner was a dreaded "counter." And when you won too much, even if you were just lucky, a casino could walk over and bar you from the premises. No rhyme. No reason. Why not? The casinos were riding high, and it looked like the ride would never end.

Sound familiar?

Yes. Just like Google. AdWords isn't quite like blackjack—blackjack is seven people against the dealer, while AdWords is hundreds, even thousands of bidders against each other—but the analogy is still spot-on.

Casinos, in a nutshell, were happy to ban you if you so much as *looked* like you were a card counter. Did this hurt the casinos? Not a bit. The Vegas casino business was and is a license to print money. There are always more suckers to fill the tables, so who cares if you occasionally ban a legitimate player?

Yes, Google = Vegas.

And Card Counters = Good Google Advertisers.

But note: A good AdWords advertiser is far more dangerous to Google than a good player is to a casino.

How so?

A good advertiser who has "nailed" the market with exactly the right ad and keywords can reduce the number of clicks the other advertisers get . . . making competitors' investment of time and money no longer worth it.

Their campaign goes on permanent "hold" and the Google universe is one advertiser poorer.

Every Google advertiser has one or more campaigns on hold until he "figures it out."

Look at history: What has the blackjack community with its Gurus and Customers and Casinos done over the last 40-plus years?

1. *The illusion of a beatable game* is more important to attracting players than anything else. Any Vegas casino could cook up an unbeatable game if they wanted to. But whenever a casino attempts this, their competitor across the street loosens the rules. The "tight" casino starves . . . until it follows suit.

   Casinos can cook up what *appears* to be a beatable game, but isn't. Bob Stupak was a master at this, at the old Vegas World Hotel.

   Intelligent advertisers diversify their traffic streams.

2. There will always be a parade of so-called experts with their scam of the month. They come, they hawk their wares, and they leave.

   Good riddance.

3. There are always a few truth tellers in every market. Those who spend their own dime mastering AdWords for themselves before taking a single dollar from anyone.

   (In blackjack, Arnold Snyder is a self-taught expert whose honesty and gift of analysis is well regarded.)

4. As the market has matured many blackjack gurus have of necessity moved to other pastures.

5. Constant ebbs and flows: As soon as a new rule is made, another guru comes out with a new report that teaches how to exploit it. The rule then gets repealed or tightened. Rinse and repeat.

So let's summarize the last 40 years. The gurus who stick around have:

· *Longevity.* Most true experts spent years in the trenches, incognito. In mature markets, up to *four decades.* There is no substitute for this kind of experience.
· *True breakthroughs of their own.* We all borrow ideas, but in the end, you have to add something original to the equation if you want to be more than a mere copycat.

Your customers want to know that you've walked your own path and taken your own medicine.

· *A charming ambivalence.* Bertrand Russell said it best: "The trouble with the world is that the stupid are cocksure and the intelligent are full of doubt."

· *Willingness to warn newcomers of pitfalls.* Rainbow chasers won't want to hear about risks. But good business people will listen and pay attention.

· *Good guys they cluster together with.* The bad guys hang together; the good guys do, too.

· *Flexibility.* They have their ear to the ground, they get good info from sound sources, they take rational risks when genuine opportunities arise, and they're ready at any moment to cut bait and move—into entirely new games or niches if need be.

The latest bans have a justifiable percentage of people annoyed at Google. And you and I will never know what Google's master strategy is. But we do know this: Many of those cut loose are not just good people; they're good marketers.

And good marketers will seek out new sources of traffic. They'll build solid businesses with a wealthy back end that gives them resilience against sudden shifts in traffic.

And maybe, just maybe Yahoo!-Bing will become better sources of traffic too.

Maybe.

Amen, Phil.

DEAR READER, I HOPE YOU READ THAT TWICE

One more thing: There will always be players gaming the system. There will always be casinos rigging the game in their favor. There will always be "B" players who try *too hard* to game the system, and get chewed up and spit out.

And there will always be deep players, "A" players, feral men who cannot get tossed off the bronco no matter how hard the bronco bucks.

FERAL

A feral animal is one that has escaped from domestication and returned, partly or wholly, to a wild state.

Be a feral man. A feral woman.

Oh, and one last thing: Take full advantage of all the intelligence Google gives you. Build your campaigns, optimize them. But most of all, *learn from them.* And apply your knowledge to getting other forms of traffic.

A WARNING AGAINST "GAME THE SYSTEM" MENTALITY

There's a percentage of people out there who seem to view the entire world as something to be hacked, a system to be gained, a trick to be learned.

Some such people make a *lot* of money.

For awhile.

Inevitably, though, the house of cards comes down.

The best question you can ask before you start anything is, "How long will this last?"

If it's only going to last three weeks or three months, you might want to reconsider.

Listen, I've made a lot of money teaching people to game the system. None of it was black hat, but certainly many things I've taught over time had a limited shelf life.

It's OK to execute limited shelf-life projects if you know that's what you're doing. All of us have to sometimes. But that's not anywhere near as valuable as building and marketing a business with a great USP that serves people for the long haul.

Please understand that this chapter isn't really about Google at all. It's about the upside and downside of the "game the system" mindset.

My friend Joe Sugarman, who built the famous innovative mail order company JS&A in the 1970s, was the first to take credit cards over the phone, the first to put 800 numbers in ads, and went on to build BluBlockers.

Joe says, "In business, the most valuable thing you can do is build a brand. A brand is a huge asset, it can make you millions of dollars, and it can outlast you."

You don't build great brands by gaming the system. You build brands by building legions of happy customers and a consistent, recognizable message.

Chapter 16

The Butt-Ugly Truth About Social Media, and the Beautiful Untold Story

How to Convert the World's Number-One Time-Suck into a Treasure Trove of Customer Insights

In 2010 I wrote a blog post: "Social Media: Anyone actually making money with it?" I asked for hard, measurable numbers.

I sent it to more than 20,000 people. I got 65 replies.

Half dodged the question, saying things like, "I've seen this stuff work occasionally as a reinforcement to sales activity."

Only 14 contained any kind of "yes" and only four gave a definite answer that inspired confidence.

■ ■ ■

The rest said no.

- "I love the 'measurably' stuff as much as you do, Perry. But some things are valuable and difficult to measure . . . love peace joy." (As though love, peace, and joy could make your car payment.)
- "Our company has been using social media to supplement our sales efforts and as 'reputation building.'"
- "I've gotten a few people to some of my blog posts using Twitter where they have actually bought software that I recommended through my affiliate links."
- "This is a great question, but one that is tough to answer fully."
- "I've heard of a local restaurant using Twitter to build a local following and then tweeting specials. . . . I think this is brilliant."
- "No. But I think the value of social media is in the contacts that you make."
- "Reading this article will help your readers know what they can achieve through social media. . . . Honestly so far we have not made any money directly from social media."
- "I have used Twitter in the past but only for communicating with current clients, I wasn't getting new clients that way. I've since stopped and am focusing more on Facebook—I can see my friends and family there AS WELL AS clients . . . "
- "Me—yes. . . . **But not buckets of money. Just gained a couple of paid accounts and a lot of great contacts."

Suppose I'd said, "Is anybody out there making money with Google AdWords?" It would've been a stupid question. I have *tens of thousands* of customers who are advertising on Google profitably. Even though lots of people lose money with Google, a lot of my customers would think it was a trick question.

You can use social media to overthrow despot regimes in the Middle East; there's a lot of money to be made *talking about* social media. As an author, I've had publishers offer generous advances to write books on LinkedIn and Twitter.

But few businesses are actually making money using social media to sell products and services for real-world businesses.

Still, a small number of people *are* making money with social media. Tons of it in a few cases. I know this because Tom Meloche and I wrote the *Ultimate Guide to Facebook Advertising*. It's the sister to this book. We did three years of intensive research before the book went to press. My students and I have successfully used Facebook advertising to profitably acquire many customers and generate sales leads.

In this chapter I'm going to explain who's making money with social media, who's not, and what they're actually selling. I'll show you what kinds of businesses are never going to make money with social media.

Most importantly, I tell you how to use social media *indirectly* to make all your other marketing more profitable, especially Google AdWords. Social media can make your AdWords campaigns 10 to 15 percent more profitable, even if you're not a "social media friendly" business. Stay tuned and I'll show you.

The number-one reason social media is a lousy place to sell stuff is that people don't go to Facebook to make decisions. They go to Facebook to *avoid* making decisions!

This might be the most important thing you can know about Facebook. The only things that are *easy* to sell on Facebook are forms of escape.

What kinds of businesses help people escape "normal life"?

· Bands and music
· Movies and TV shows
· Fiction books
· Audio/video equipment
· Travel
· Restaurants
· Spirituality
· Hobbies and special interest communities

We created a free tool at www.IsFBforMe.com. It asks you ten questions you can easily answer in 60 seconds and gives you a score of 1 to 10.

Businesses that sell entertainment and experiences sometimes get *more* traction from Facebook than from Google. If you have a band, I can assure you it's easier to get strangers to buy your CD from a Facebook ad than a Google ad.

On the other hand, if you sell asbestos brake pads to car manufacturers, selling them on Facebook is gonna be a tough slog.

Please go to IsFBforMe.com on your computer or smartphone right now and take the quiz. It will return your score instantly. Enter your email address, and we'll also send you a detailed customized report that explains your score.

But here is a general explanation:

1: *Danger.* If you bought my Facebook book, see if you can get your money back.

2–3: *Caution.* If your final score is 2 or 3, then finding new leads and customers through paid advertising on Facebook is likely to be difficult, time-consuming, and expensive. If you are a small company or a startup, it may be a losing proposition. You should focus your advertising dollars elsewhere to find new leads and customers.

However, you should probably use some Facebook paid advertising to feature events, market to existing customers, and collect customer and lead demographics. Facebook is an amazing tool simply for what it can teach you about your own customers, such as their age, gender, location, affiliations, favorite books, favorite music, favorite movies, political affiliations, and other likes and interests. This is useful for AdWords, as I'll explain below. Buying some Facebook advertising may be useful just to help you collect this data.

4–5: *Helpful.* If your final score is 4 or 5, then paid advertising on Facebook has the potential to bring you more customers, but it will take a bit of work. It probably should not be your primary source of traffic. The biggest benefit of being on Facebook is to provide you another channel to connect to existing customers and to collect detailed customer demographics you can use on Google AdWords.

6–7: *Significant.* If your final score is 6 or 7, then you are definitely in the Facebook sweet spot. Facebook paid advertising may be a new way for you to attract significantly more traffic to your website. In addition, at least for the next few years, you may be able to get this traffic very affordably.

8–10: *Jackpot.* If your final score is 8 to 10, then you have hit the Facebook jackpot. It is possible that Facebook paid advertising may even become your number-one traffic source.

EXAMPLE SCORES

Dentist: **8**

Vinyl Records-Only Store: **8.4**

Musical Venue that Hosts Events: **9.2**

Summer Day Camp with Religious Affiliations: **9.6**

Industrial Network Software: **3.6**

Automated Tutors to Home-Schooling Families: **8**

Hipster T-Shirts: **6**

Businesses that are making a lot of money with Facebook advertising are ones with scores of 8 or above. If your business has a score of 5, then Facebook is very unlikely to be a key part of your *direct* sales strategy. But it will still be valuable *indirectly* – and not the way most people think.

Because people on Facebook are not in a decision-making mode, it is *essential* that you market to them outside of Facebook. Every single successful Facebook marketing campaign that we've studied uses an autoresponder sequence (see Chapter 20) because people are in decision-making mode at other times when they're not on Facebook. Like when they're checking their email.

Facebook is not the only form of social media, of course. There's also Twitter, LinkedIn, the various bookmarking sites like Reddit and StumbleUpon. There are blogs and YouTube. YouTube is half social site, half search engine. It can be very powerful. LinkedIn can be great for business-to-business. Many businesses that score low on IsFBforMe.com are great for LinkedIn.

If you want detailed instructions for advertising on Facebook, buy our *Ultimate Guide to Facebook Advertising*. Meanwhile, the next chapter is about harnessing social media *data* so you can sell to your existing customers much more effectively.

HOW TO USE SOCIAL MEDIA TO DO MARKET RESEARCH AND GET GREAT COPY BULLETS

You can also use social media to tap into conversations. One of my favorite services is http://tweetgrid.com/search. It uses Twitter to generate snapshots of current conversations. You get them in 140 easy-to-browse characters at a time.

I typed "Sinus Infection" into Tweetgrid:

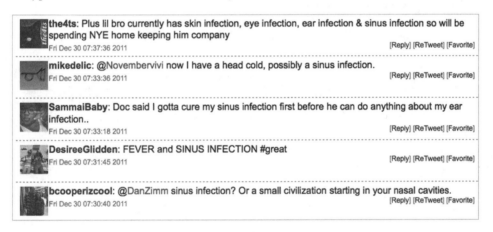

You find humorous quips, with insight into the situations people are in. Like "Small civilization starting in your nasal cavities." And "I'm spending New Year's Eve taking care of my lil bro who has a sinus infection."

I searched "Migraine" and one gal said, "Im sick to my stomach, all stuffed up, i have a bad migraine, Im stressed & I work 11–8. If I don't get through today, I'm gonna die tryin." Prime example of "Entering the conversation inside your customer's head."

Reddit goes a step deeper and gives you easy access to actual conversations. When you search "migraine headache" on Reddit.com, you get this:

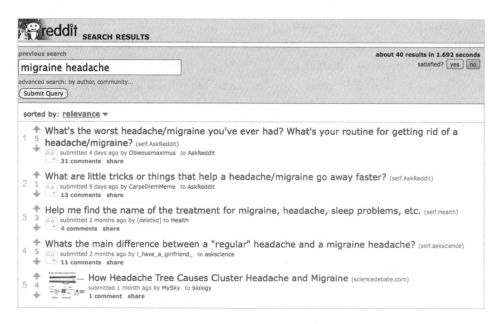

When you click on a link, you get this:

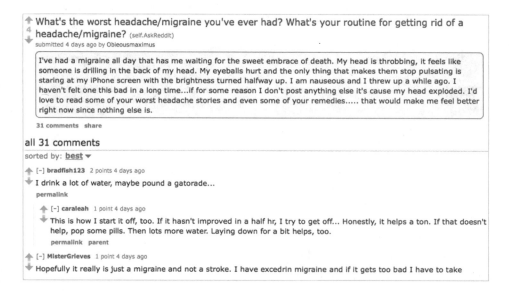

Find the Problems That Remain

Solutions that are easy to find everywhere else, maybe even for free on Reddit or Google—nobody's parting with their dinero for those. Too ordinary.

When you're doing market research through social media, you're looking for problems that remain unsolved after everyone has offered their advice. "I looked everywhere but it was impossible to find ____." If you can provide a solution to that problem, if you can deliver *that*, people will give you money. Obviously those are the hardest problems to solve, but the bleeding neck is always where the money is.

In the next chapter I'm going to show you how to reach d-e-e-p inside your customer's head—not just the itch they're trying to scratch right now, but how they scratch itches in general and the stories they live in every day.

It's Not About Having Fun

Despite what all the social media hypesters tell you, your number-one job as a marketer is to buy advertising for $1.00 and get $2.00 back. Your job is NOT to Like, Tweet, Facebook, banter, interact, bookmark, answer questions, and schmooze all day. That is a freakin' waste of time for 80 to 90 percent of businesses.

When you add the rich intelligence and enormous eavesdropping power of social media to your direct marketing campaigns, you'll write better ads. You'll find targets you would have never thought of, and you'll spike your leads and sales by double-digit percentages.

Chapter 17

How to Harness the Psychic Power of Social Media in Your Google Campaigns

Before the web took off, people mainly dated and married people who lived in the same town. Only a few pioneers embraced the idea of dating and marrying strangers. Not many hardy souls were relationship pioneers, but my friend Bob was one who was. Bob ran a mail-order bride service for Christian, single men. He helped connect Christian, American men with Christian, Filipino women.

■ ■ ■

Bob ran advertisements, did lead generation, and sent letters to guys talking about how it was hard to find a woman who shared their values. "Wouldn't it be nice to find a woman with character who wasn't just a gold digger and wouldn't dump you when the going got tough? Are you sick and tired of our lying, decadent society where people are so disloyal and divorce is so common?" This message resonated powerfully with his audience.

Bob advertised in all of the easy-to-spot locations. Specifically, in magazines read by Christian men. Also newspapers like *USA Today*. The business was a success. Connections were made. Marriages resulted. Bob wanted to figure out how to grow the business even more.

RIGHT-ANGLE TARGETING

We were in a group with Dan Kennedy. Dan asked Bob a "right-angle" question:

"Are there any idiosyncrasies that your customers have in common? Where they hang out? Hobbies? The type of work they do? Anything other than just being Christian single men?"

Bob said, "Well, I don't know."

Dan said, "Why don't you find out?"

So he did.

When they got together again, Bob had discovered something significant. Over half of his customers had the same job: They were *truck drivers*!

Bob had never noticed this before. In hindsight it made perfect sense. Driving over the road is a hard and lonely job. Lots of time away from home, which is hard on existing relationships and makes it even harder to start new ones. Truck drivers, as an occupation, needed relationship help. The need was so acute that these men were willing to try brides from overseas.

Advertising to truckers was a right-angle approach to reach potential customers. A right angle totally changes your approach to a market.

Bob could now post ads in trucking magazines and stock literature racks at truck stops. (Right between the cigarette machine and the condom machine next to the men's restroom.)

Bob wrote new ads in the language of trucking, making his prospects feel immediately at home. His business skyrocketed, and his advertising cost dropped.

This is a prime example of "right-angle targeting."

Right-angle targeting, up 'til now, has been a rather advanced marketing concept. Only very sophisticated marketers habitually think this way. However, Facebook makes it easy to find idiosyncrasies that would otherwise require a lot of thought and expensive research.

Most customer bases have something in common that is not initially obvious, just like Bob's. Once you learn this new connection, a whole set of new opportunities emerges. Not only can you place new ads in new locations, but you can also write ad copy to appeal to the specific psychographic. You, just like Bob, can leverage right-angle knowledge everywhere in your business.

HOW WE USED FACEBOOK RIGHT-ANGLE TARGETING TO IMPROVE GOOGLE CAMPAIGNS BY 11 PERCENT OVERNIGHT

Bryan Todd was driving traffic to the website www.CosmicFingerPrints.com. This site discusses the intersection between science, astronomy, and religion. Bryan was running ads on Facebook driving traffic to the page and seeking an opt-in to "Learn the Secrets of the Universe."

After a while, Bryan ran a Facebook responder profile report and noticed that his responders had an interest in science fiction, history, and really liked the books *Brave New World* and *1984*. So, he split-test two landing pages, which were identical except that one page inserted the following two lines:

This ultimate question touches the distant past, and—with the forewarnings in Orwell's 1984 and Huxley's Brave New World—it touches the distant future as well.

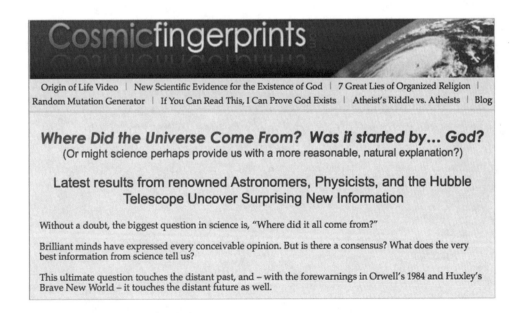

Bryan recognized that people who like science fiction think about the distant future and the distant past, and he already knew specifically that his prospects liked these two books.

In hindsight, like most right-angle marketing connections, they all go together. If you're inclined to click on an ad that says "Where did the Universe Come From? Did it come from God?" you probably do all of these things. Bryan added this one sentence to the page.

The conversion rate for the page increased by 11 percent. That 11 percent improvement worked across the board, not just Facebook traffic but Google AdWords traffic as well!

To prove the right-angle concept, at no time during this experiment did Bryan ever specifically target fans of *Brave New World* or *1984*. He didn't change his targeting at all. He only proved that people we targeted for completely different reasons also responded to these book titles.

(Of course we do use right angles to laser-in on new target audiences, too! But that wasn't the point of this experiment.)

THE REVOLUTIONARY "ONE SENTENCE" PRINCIPLE

Most people would never expect one sentence to improve conversions by 11 percent, the way this did. Especially one that's just innocently added to the third paragraph, with no change to the headline, pictures, or offer! This worked because it pressed invisible buttons in the reader's mind and heart. This technique works in almost any market.

There is a sentence that will increase your conversions 10 to 15 percent. All you have to do is find out what it is and add it to your landing page. But you'll probably never discover it without the assistance of social media.

This is the most powerful thing about Facebook marketing. It's not the ability to post free status messages. It's not the ability to have 10,000 fans for free. This is so non-obvious, it doesn't surprise me that hardly anyone else is talking about it. But it's astonishingly powerful. Because Facebook tracks thousands of bits of information, like peoples' favorite:

· Books
· Music
· TV shows
· Artists
· Movies
· Personalities
· Politicians

It gives you a profound sense of "what kind of story these people live in."

WHY FACEBOOK DATA AND GOOGLE ADWORDS ARE A SUPER-POWERFUL COMBO

Google AdWords targets people based on *what they're looking for right now*. Facebook targets people based on *their identity, their beliefs, and the tribes they belong to*. AdWords and Facebook slice the world two entirely different ways.

When people search Google for information on astronomy, they want to know about astronomy *right now*. They're scratching an itch. Even if they're reading an online newspaper and your ad manages to catch their eye, it's still usually about *right now*.

When they type into Facebook that they're female, that they're a Democrat, a Methodist, a Grateful Dead Fan, those things have much more to do with who they are and what they believe in. These things are much more permanent than the fact that they happen to have a sinus infection at the moment.

When you combine **the itch they're trying to scratch right now** with **who they are and what kinds of things they're into** you earn compound interest on everything you do in your advertising. You strengthen the emotional bond.

Fans of the Cosmic Fingerprints site also liked battle movies and science fiction flicks like *Star Wars, Lord of the Rings,* and *Fight Club*. They were mostly male. Fans of Coffee.org, a coffee distributor's website, on the other hand, were mostly female and preferred movies like *Steel Magnolias* and *Bridget Jones's Diary*.

You talk to guys who like *Lord of the Rings* and science fiction much, much differently than you talk to ladies who like chick flicks. They're living in completely different stories! Until you understand these kinds of things, you really don't know your audience.

HOW TO GLEAN RIGHT-ANGLE INSIGHTS FROM FACEBOOK

We got our book and movie information from Facebook's "Responder Profile Report," which tracks the profile information of people who click on your ads. Facebook has since taken that report away. Now you have to get this information using other, cleverer ways.

The most "obvious" way is to page through the profile information of your Facebook fans. This requires that you have a fan page and fans. You can look at the pictures of your fans, click on them one at a time. If that person has made his or her profile information public (two-thirds of people do), then you can go through the menus and find an entire list of likes and interests.

When you check this profile information, you find a "like and interest" list that looks like this:

> A2 Breaking News, Realize Your Business - Finding Your True Fans, ~The Knights of Ni~ Fraternity, Fidelity, Shrubbery, Robert Pasick's LeadersConnect, Better Homeschools, Ann Arbor SPARK, Workantile Exchange, Homeschool Advantage, New Missions (official page), Pure Visibility, 1960s Pop and Rock Music Trivia™, Homeschool, OnStartups, Get Your Church Fan Page, Double Your Likes, Kirtan Central, DoubleYourLikes.com, ASAP Checks, Joplin, MO Tornado Recovery, Zingermans, In Loving Memory of Sharon Tate, IFrame Apps, Welcome Applet, North Social, Pepsi, Victoria's Secret, RedBalloon, BRUT, GNOME ENTERPRISES, Zingerman's Delicatessen, Zingerman's Roadhouse, Support Japan, Sizzle Bop, Adrenalin Experiences Melbourne, Steve Spangler, Red Bull, Adrenalin Experiences Sydney, Like Button, Click "like" if you love reading to your kids, I love someone in the military, Geekbox Computers, Personalized Children's Books, ABtests.com, Over The Top Marketing, Sunny Hills "The Affirmations Genius", Tom's Golden Cafe, Social Graph, Where 2.0 Conference, Working Michigan, The Ark - Ann Arbor, The Cupcake Station, You: "I'd like a Coke." Waiter:"Is Pepsi ok?" You: "Is Monopoly money ok?", AnnArbor.com Photo, Charcot-Marie-Tooth Association: The Time is Now, Schoolhouse Expo, MountainOcarinas, Puppies, U.S. Naval Forces Central Command / U.S. 5th Fleet, FamilyMint, MamasHealth.com: easy, simple to understand information about health, SOAR Study Skills, Allstate Insurance,

If you go through enough of these pages, you begin to see patterns. There are three problems with this:

1. Facebook does not allow you to scrape this data or download it. It also took away the report that analyzed it for you. Scraping it with an automated bot is against its Terms of Service. Not only is it extremely hard to get around this technically, it can also get you banned from Facebook real fast.
2. Doing this by hand is very tedious, and it's almost impossible to see all the important patterns if you do it manually.
3. The most important data is always masked by the most "common" data. Millions of people like Barack Obama or NPR or the Bible. But knowing someone likes one of those three things doesn't tell you nearly as much as knowing that they like Karl Marx or Al Franken or the Left Behind book series. That's because many fewer people like Karl Marx, Al Franken, and Left Behind. The second list is more extreme than the first list, so it tells you more.

THE "HANDSHAKE" TOOL

We wanted to find a way to access right-angle Facebook data legitimately and analyze it easily. So we created a web application called Fanalytix™, which gathers this data for you and presents it to you. It's a Facebook application that's easy to use and conforms to Facebook's Terms of Service.

Fanalytix™ gives you a button called a "Handshake™," which is the Facebook equivalent of an Opt-In.

You put the "Handshake" button on a page next to an offer (for a free item, video, a white paper, etc.) instead of an opt-in box. When people click on it, they confirm that it's OK to share their email and publicly available info with you. When they click the second link, it automatically adds them to your autoresponder program (Infusion, 1ShoppingCart, Aweber, others) and puts their data in the Fanalytix™ database.

Fanalytix™ is available to buyers of this book at www.perrymarshall.com/ supplement/. It analyzes that data and shows you the eccentricities of your audience. The data shown below is for a very specific campaign I used to analyze part of my own customer list:

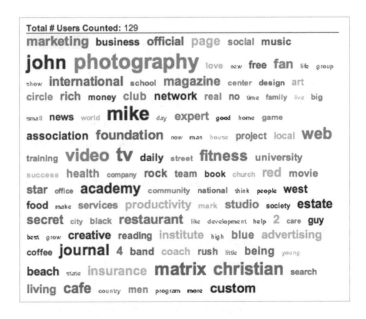

Even though this is a pretty small segment, it gives me a clear idea what kind of magazines they like to read:

Like Name	# Users
Entrepreneur Magazine	6
Website Magazine	3
SUCCESS Magazine	3
Surfer Magazine	2
Inc Magazine	2

It also shows you, when the word "Business" appears, what kinds of pages they're liking:

Count: 49	FB Freq: 0.208%	Impact: 4.7

Like Name	# Users
Business	8
Crowd Conversion Transforming Your Business Through Social Currency	7
Small Business Saturday	5
Harvard Business Review	4
Guerrilla Marketing Coaching Low Cost Strategies To Grow Your Business	3
Social Media for Business – Powered by Dell	3

Fanalytix™ gives an excellent idea of what your fans like to talk about, and also where to get more of them. Yes, you can more or less target fans of *Success* magazine on Facebook. But you may also be able to target Google ads to *Success* magazine's web page if *Success* magazine participates in the Display Network. Or you might go directly to the magazine website and talk to its advertising department. You have an excellent chance of finding more customers similar to the ones you already had, but from a new source.

Let's say you sell asbestos brake pads to large companies. You have a IsFBforMe score of 2.4. Facebook is a lousy place for you to look for new customers. Is Facebook useless then?

No. You could offer your existing email list something free in exchange for clicking a Handshake™ button and collect this kind of data. You will inevitably find out something about your customers that you did not know before.

I have a campaign called "Marketing Secrets of Rush." I use it to advertise to fans of the band Rush, fans who are also interested in marketing. I discovered some really interesting quirks about these fans:

· They overwhelmingly like gangster movies like *The Godfather*.
· Their favorite TV shows are *South Park* and *The Simpsons*.
· 24 percent of them like Dos Equis beer.

Who knew?

This is hugely valuable information for direct marketers and for brand marketers as well. It means that if I add stories about *The Godfather* or *The Simpsons* to my autoresponder sequence, a disproportionate number of people will engage with me and respond emotionally. Brand marketers can use this to select stories, colors, fonts, images, customer icons, retail channels, and advertising media.

How to Get Fanalytix™ Free

All buyers of this book get access to a basic version of Fanalytix™ at no charge. You can access it through www.perrymarshall.com/supplement/. If you like it and want to use the full suite of capabilities, you can easily upgrade to the paid version.

WHEN YOU ADD SOCIAL MEDIA INSIGHTS TO YOUR DIRECT MARKETING AND ADWORDS PROJECTS, ASK YOURSELF THESE QUESTIONS

- What story are these people living in?

- What tribes do they belong to?

- What is their identity? When they say "I am a _____," what kinds of things do they put in that blank?

- Who do they admire? Who are they fans of?

- How can I connect the dots between the itch they're trying to scratch right now with their identity and the story that they're living in?

- How do they want their story to change?

Uncle Claude Sez

Every campaign that I devise or write is aimed at some individual member of the vast majority. I do not consult managers and boards of directors. Their viewpoint is nearly always distorted. I submit them to the simple folks around me who typify America. They are our customers. Their reactions are the only ones that count.

Chapter 18

How to Get Customers to Eat Out of Your Hand

Get the Biggest Money from Your Market When You Give Your Customers Exactly What They Want to Buy

Next time you roll out a new product, you can have a 75 percent or better chance of success by using Google to measure your traffic. You can know exactly how much demand there is for your idea. You can test your headlines and copy, and have your potential customers tell you exactly what kind of product they're looking for.

Google makes this far less expensive and far less risky than ever before.

■ ■ ■

HOW WE USED GOOGLE ADWORDS TO PICK A TITLE FOR A SEMINAR

Do you know what's wrong with most "market research"? It's not market research; it's opinion research. Opinions are what people *say*. Markets are about what people *do*.

In his landmark book *Blink*, author Malcolm Gladwell talks about this very issue: People's buying decisions are usually an impulse act, and the reasons they *tell* you after the fact for buying a certain item or liking a particular product may have nothing whatsoever to do with their real impulse in the moment.

Most focus groups won't tell you the real reason. Most in-depth surveys won't get to the bottom of it. Often the only way to know what attracts customers is to give options and let them act in real-time. Then go with what works, even when you don't know their inner reasons why.

Here's one such example of powerful, real-time market research on the internet.

PERRY MARSHALL

How Google Quickly Assessed the Viability of an Event Name . . . for Two Dollars and Seventy-Eight Cents

I'm the marketing and publicity director of TruthQuest, which is a local nonprofit group that hosts speakers and discussions on a variety of hot topics in religion and theology.

After the smash success of *Lord of the Rings*, its sequel, *The Two Towers,* followed suit the next winter. We found ourselves a speaker, Professor Jerry Root of Wheaton College, who could talk about this movie and the philosophical point of view of its author, J.R.R. Tolkien.

No matter how great the speaker may be, it doesn't matter if nobody shows up. So the title of the event was crucial.

Somebody suggested a preliminary title: "Is *Lord of the Rings* Christian?" But I didn't like it. Not intriguing. Too easy to say "No" or "Yes" and forget about it.

The more marketing I do, the less I trust myself even to pick a good title. So our group brainstormed four titles and let the world vote on them. I used Google AdWords and had an answer in just 18 hours.

What Happened When We Ran the Overnight Test

I took our proposed titles and made four ads, all rotating simultaneously. I purchased the keyword "Tolkien," as well as "Tolkein"—a common misspelling that people often mistakenly search on.

I started running the ad on Google at about 3 P.M. on a weekday and stopped it at 8 A.M. the next morning. Here's what the ads looked like, along with their results:

The Two Towers
Tolkien, The Two Towers, and
Spiritual Symbolism
tolkiensociety.org
11 Clicks | 1.0% CTR | $0.06 CPC

Lord Of The Rings
and The Spiritual Powers
of Hobbits
tolkiensociety.org
8 Clicks | 0.7% CTR | $0.06 CPC

Spirituality of Tolkien
Hidden Messages in
The Two Towers
tolkiensociety.org
20 Clicks | 1.9% CTR | $0.05 CPC

Tolkien Spirituality
Is There Hidden Christianity
In The Two Towers?
tolkiensociety.org
16 Clicks | 1.5% CTR | $0.06 CPC

Keyword	Clicks	Impressions	CTR	Cost
tolkien	48	3,878	1.2%	$2.43
tolkein	7	252	2.7%	$0.35
Overall	55	4,130	1.3%	$2.78

What We Found Out

1. Click-through rates were dramatically different for different titles. The winner was "Spirituality of Tolkien: Hidden Messages in *The Two Towers*."

2. This was *vastly* better than doing a "focus group" or a survey of our friends. Why? Because when people read about this in the newspaper or on a flier, their decision either to continue reading or to ignore it is made *on impulse*. They don't sit and ponder it. The decision to click on a link is equally impulsive.

3. This is a *great* way to come up with titles for magazine articles, white papers, books, and names for new products. And believe me, the votes you get will

surprise you. What you *think* sounds cool is probably not what your customers think is relevant.

You can use this exact method to test the marketability of almost *any* idea you have. You can take it a step further than I did—bringing visitors to your own website and further testing their response to different offers.

HOW TO BE SURE THERE'S A MORE PROFITABLE MARKET FOR YOUR IDEA, BY DEVELOPING A PRODUCT *AFTER* YOUR CUSTOMERS TELL YOU WHAT THEY WANT

Let's say you're thinking about writing a software program for doing automotive repairs. It's for do-it-yourself car enthusiasts, and it does engine diagnostics that help increase your fuel efficiency by five miles per gallon.

If a guy bought your software (which you haven't written yet), he could buy a cable at Radio Shack, take his computer into his garage, hook it up to his car, and your software would collect a load of data and display it on the screen. Your program would then tell the guy what to tweak in his engine.

Sounds like a great idea. But how do you know there's a market for this?

You can find out if there's water in the swimming pool before you dive in. You certainly don't want to spend weeks writing software if nobody's going to buy it. So here's what you do:

1. *Write an e-book, white paper, or guide.* Call it "How to Use Engine Diagnostics to Improve Your Car's Fuel Efficiency by Five Miles per Gallon." In it you tell people how to do it the *hard way.* The whole routine that takes you three days, including the spreadsheet and the connector from Radio Shack. (I have a free email course on writing white papers at www.perrymarshall.com/whitepapers).

2. *Head over to Google and bid on starter keywords.* Find all of the major terms related to engine diagnostics.

3. *Post an ad* like this:

   DIY Engine Diagnostics
   Simple Procedure Improves
   Your Car—5 MPG or Better
   www.AutoDiag.com

On your landing page, you have a sales letter that tells them about your e-book. You can also follow up with a series of emails that talk more about this.

1. *Get ideas and feedback from your readers.*
2. *Sell the e-book.* Or even give it away for free. But not without a plan. While you're marketing your e-book, you're going to take the next step with your buyers.
3. *Test your customers' response to your actual product idea.* What do they say back to you? Are they interested? Do they pester you to find out when this will be available? Do they offer to pay you for it now, hoping to get first dibs on it when it comes out? If so, you know you've got a winner.
4. *Sell your product,* and the dollars will come rolling in.
5. You've listened to your customers, you've put together a product in line with what they ask you for, and you've proven to yourself that they're interested. Now when you give them exactly what they want, you'll make the cash register ring.

WHAT YOU LEARN WHEN THIS DOESN'T WORK THE FIRST TIME OUT

Now what happens if it's a flop?

Don't cry in your milk—learn your lesson and get on with something else. You can come up with a new idea and test it for no great sum of money.

And what if the idea is only marginal?

Play with it. Change your ad, change your landing page, fiddle with the title of your report or e-book, adjust the price if you sell it, give visitors incentives in exchange for lots of feedback, and try again. If it won't work, then move on. If you can clear out the bugs, then run like the wind.

Did you know that infomercials also run on this same premise? It costs $50,000–$100,000 to produce an infomercial and run it for a few days. If the producer can get 80 percent return on investment (i.e., only lose 20 percent) the first time out, he won't scrap the project. He'll play with the offer, the upsells, the testimonials, and the other ingredients until he gets it above his break-even point. And he's not afraid to cut his losses if he has to.

When you test ideas that don't work, *fail fast.* Get it over with as quickly as possible. Spend the money, get the results, cut your losses, and move on.

"Wait a minute," you might be thinking, "I don't have hundreds of dollars to blow on pre-testing. I can't afford to do that."

The reality is, you can't afford *not* to. Spending those dollars and going into the red now could save you *thousands* of dollars later in botched advertising and mediocre returns, and can prevent you from having to start again from scratch.

BRYAN TODD

The Insights You Get When Customers Vomit All Over You

I spent more than four years in Mainland China, during which time I went from not even knowing how to say "hello" to becoming conversationally fluent in the language. It saddened me as I watched many of my westerner friends there struggling with the language and getting nowhere.

I learned through trial and error a host of practical, working methods for acquiring the language. Multiple times during my stay there my American and European friends would tell me, "Wow—you need to share your whole method with me, because whatever it is, it's obviously working."

So I listened. And after returning to the United States I sat down to write a book that would teach other English speakers to do just what I did.

I then decided to take our marketing advice: I wrote a series of autoresponder emails and bought Google traffic *first,* planning to sell the book to customers later.

I was a newbie at the time. I set up my Google campaign, sent traffic to my new website and let it go.

And here are two of the responses I got:

> You have shown me absolutely nothing. You have wasted my time and paper printing off your worthless emails. I learned more in five minutes from a Chinese business website than I could ever expect to learn from your time-wasting activities.
>
> D.M.

> You have not provided me with any practice Mandarin lessons, which is what I wanted. Instead you provided generic information, as a "carrot" to buy your course. This is a scam.
>
> F.P.

Oh, crap! Here I am in the middle of writing a book about learning the language living in China, while these people are in their home country looking for simple online lessons.

Thank God I hadn't created a whole product yet.

But get this: They *did* tell me exactly what they were looking for. The first guy above left me the URL of the Chinese business site he had mentioned, so I could go and compare. The second guy told me specifically that he wanted "practice Mandarin lessons." Others weighed in, too.

These people wanted online lessons. I didn't have the resources to put something like that together at the time. But I logged it away to pursue in the future.

Now what about my e-book? Should I cancel the project?

No. I *knew* from experience with friends that I had something of tremendous value. But how was I going to find the folks who really needed it?

I finished the book and set my ads to show only in Taiwan and Mainland China—not even in Hong Kong, where Cantonese and English are more common than Mandarin. I turned on the traffic again.

When Your Machine Finally Kicks In

And that's when the positive emails started pouring in. Grateful readers who had moved to China and Taiwan from the U.S., Israel, Germany, Australia, the UK, New Zealand, India, and from all over the globe wrote in to tell me that they were finding my email course to be helpful and relevant.

More importantly, *they were buying the book* and telling me that they were using it. I even found myself doing late-night telephone consultations to Beijing with my customers now, helping them improve their Chinese-learning strategy even further.

In reality, the book is an invaluable resource regardless of what language a person is learning. The principles are universal and apply anywhere in the world. Still, focusing on China and Taiwan paid off.

One buyer sent me this:

> At about midnight last night, I paid for and downloaded your products. I thought I would take a quick glance before going to bed.

It is now five o'clock on Sunday afternoon, and I haven't been to bed yet. I read the entire document twice; your bonus article three times. During this time, I experienced a gamut of emotions; everything from the knowing smile, kissing the computer screen, wildly punching the air, and dancing around the room.

Your product is excellent, Bryan, and worth every cent I paid for it. For the price, I could not have had a better night! Don't even think about returning my money, as I love your work, and I am looking forward to any stuff you do in the future.

—Andrew V.

When you find your market, *boy, do you ever find them!* Giving people exactly what they need and then having them turn around and thank you for it is the true joy of marketing.

The market spoke. The book sold. I made a profit. People like Andrew wrote testimonials, which in turn sold more books.

When Your Market Speaks and You Respond, It's Money in the Bank

Start small with Google, and when your market talks, listen. You'll knock your head against a few walls in the early going, but there's no better education to be had.

In fact, behind every angry rant you hear is someone who didn't get what they really wanted. Go with what your prospects tell you they want. And don't ever stop asking. Especially when your *existing customers* talk. That's as good as money in the bank.

Since I lived in China for four years, I listened for *four years* as friends and acquaintances complained about their struggles in learning the language. That taught me *what* I need to create for people.

Then I spent two weeks listening to my Google visitors in order to discover *where* I needed to market it.

Then Andrew used the book. It improved his Chinese. He wrote back to tell me about it. His testimonial resulted in more sales. He went on and told friends and coworkers. Word traveled around. More people bought.

That's exactly what people will do for you when you hit their sweet spot.

Uncle Claude Sez

Almost any questions can be answered, cheaply, quickly and finally, by a test campaign. That is the way to answer them, not by arguments around a table. Go to the court of last resort: the buyers of your product . . .

We establish averages on a small scale, and those averages always hold. We know our cost, we know our sale, and we know our profit and loss. We know how soon our cost comes back. Before we spread out, we prove our undertaking absolutely safe.

The Most-Ignored Secret Behind the Most Profitable Marketing Campaigns in the World

This could be the most important chapter in the whole book because this ingredient in marketing trumps all others.

■ ■ ■

With this ingredient, *everything* in marketing gets easy.

Without it, people wander around in an aimless stupor for years. They spend buckets of money on ads and get nowhere.

What's this "thing," this magic ingredient?

It's having a good answer to the following question:

Why should I do business with you, instead of any and every other option available to me, including the option of doing absolutely nothing at all?

Another way of asking the same question is:

What do you uniquely guarantee?

When you have a really powerful answer to these two questions, your ads practically write themselves. When you have a really powerful answer to these questions, people will line up to buy from you.

When your business possesses a simple, unmistakable mission, it stands out in an age of obfuscated marketing messages and Byzantine corporate speak.

Your answer to this question is your *unique selling proposition:* A statement of value that's so clear and focused it's almost impossible to *mis*-understand it.

Less is more. Your business will grow, the world will sit up and take notice, and even your Google ads will write themselves when you stand out from the crowd with a clear, simple, and utterly unique message.

WHAT IS A USP?

Your USP is that one thing special about you that your customer can't find anyplace else. It's your *unique selling proposition.* It's what you bring to the table that no other business does, or even can.

Your USP is about the uniqueness of your product, and it's more than that. It's your whole argument for not only your product but also its accompanying services, why it's necessary in the first place, and the timing of getting the product and seeing your problem solved now, rather than later.

A lot of the difficulties people have with Google come not from doing Google AdWords wrong per se, but from having a USP that isn't clear or maybe isn't even unique in the first place.

If you have this right upfront, everything from the keywords and ads to the price of your product—all that falls into place.

HOW TO IDENTIFY YOUR USP

Your first step is to answer these four questions:

1. Why should I read or listen to you?
2. Why should I believe what you have to say?
3. Why should I do anything about what you're offering?
4. Why should I act now?

In fact, these are powerful guidelines for what to include in your Google ad *and* on your web page when folks click through. Answer them, and you've taken your message and made it that much more compelling.

We've all fallen on our faces attempting to be all things to all people. *You can't please everybody.* If your purpose is murky and if your sense of identity is vague, it confuses your customers and robs you of time and energy.

Perhaps the most famous USP of all is from Domino's Pizza:

Fresh, hot pizza delivered to your door in 30 minutes or less, guaranteed.

This isn't unique now, but in the early days of Domino's, it most definitely was. A multibillion-dollar business was built from this very unique, simple statement of value.

Just look at what a focused USP does in streamlining the daily Domino's work routine:

- *Fresh:* The stores don't have to keep freezers full of prepared inventory. They keep all of the needed ingredients on hand, along with adequate staff to prepare the orders. And the pizza doesn't even have to taste good (although they're allegedly working on this now).
- *Hot:* They keep a disciplined time schedule, getting the pizzas into the oven in time with orders that come in. They keep the right containers on hand and the delivery guys make sure the pizzas are well packed.
- *Pizza:* No spaghetti. No lasagna. No fine wines. No burgers.
- *Delivered:* This isn't an eat-in joint. No servers or extra busboys, no extra chairs or tables.
- *In 30 minutes or less:* Everyone works fast.
- *Guaranteed:* When the customer hears this, he sits up and pays attention. And the manager has financial incentive to keep the operation moving.

When you have this message defined and focused, it will *liberate* you. You become the specialist. People ask you to solve problems that you're not geared to deal with, and you simply refer them elsewhere. Nobody expects you to be an expert on anything other than your one niche.

You can certainly expand into other areas, and many businesses have multiple USPs. Every product in a retail store has its own USP. But in each case it needs to be unique, and it needs to be clear.

A good USP will fit in a Google ad—or at least the most important part of it will. Here's an ad that turned up on a search for "pizza delivery":

1-800 PIES 2 GO
Great Pizza Delivered to your Door
Free call Fast Delivery Great Pizza
www.1-800Pies2Go.com

SAY IT IN JUST ONE SENTENCE: YOUR ELEVATOR SPEECH

You'll arrest the rabid interest of people in seconds with a good USP. When a guy asks you in the elevator what you do and you've got 14 seconds before you get off at the next floor, this is your answer. It's your "elevator speech." Craft it right, and the guy will probably perk up and ask for your business card and website.

Here are some great examples:

> I sell the world's best comprehensive health insurance plan
> to businesses with ten employees or less.

Google Ad

Health Insurance
www.SmallBizHealthInsurance.com/10
Comprehensive Health Plans for
Businesses with 10 Employees or Less

> I help high-tech companies grow sales and eliminate waste
> with highly targeted web traffic, marketing, and publicity.

Generate Leads
www.PerryMarshall.com

Make Customers Call You First
Don't Sell Harder—Market Smarter

B2B Guerrilla Marketing
www.PerryMarshall.com

Eliminate Cold Calls & Ad Waste
Instant Web Traffic & Free Publicity

> I teach you how to find the love of your life in 90 days or less.

Find Love in 90 Days
www.90DayMatch.com

Discover Your True Love & Life Partner.
Based On 30 Years of Research.

Imagine how people will take notice of you when you have a quick answer like that. We're all drawn to a simple, clearly defined, gutsy message. Hammer out your own, and you've got a verbal business card that's irresistible.

YOUR USP MAKES A GREAT GOOGLE AD

A couple summers ago I went searching for a solution to my increasingly slow computer. I typed "my computer is slow" into Google, and this surprising ad popped up:

> ### Slow Computer?
> www.RegistryFix.com
> The Problem is Registry Errors.
> Scan Your PC Now—Free Trial

Registry errors are a common problem with Windows. Software that repairs these errors is available all over the place. But no advertisers that I've seen are as clear and gutsy as the guy who wrote this simple ad.

It got my attention. So I clicked. As did thousands of others.

This advertiser sells software to fix registry errors. That's it. The diagnosis is uncomplicated, the offer is compelling—a free and quick, no-obligation registry scan—and the result is a faster computer.

Can't beat that for clarity.

Can you take your message and whittle it down to one short sentence, enough to fit in a Google ad? Can you restate your USP to diagnose a problem, and position yourself as the solution? It's amazing to us how many advertisers could, but don't.

Be different. You'll get the clicks.

BIG ASS. BIG ASS FANS. HOW TO BUILD AN UNFORGETTABLE PERSONALITY AROUND YOUR USP

It was of the funniest ads I've ever seen.

The naked truth? It could easily be knocked off. But it gets love letters. It gets hate mail. And all the while this company has created a product with broad appeal and an incredibly unique identity in the marketplace. This is its amazing story.

The company started in Lexington, Kentucky, as the HVLS Fan Company. It manufactured large, slow-moving fans for giant spaces like warehouses, dairies, and factories. Those initials stand for *high volume, low speed*. But it changed its name, and now most folks know the company as Big Ass Fans. And it took its world by storm with some of the savviest guerrilla marketing we've ever seen.

You read it right—it sells fans. Great big ones. Fans with blades literally wider than your house. Factory-sized fans, fans that take your breath away.

But Big Ass Fans' marketing is not just "cute." Its growth literally jumped to the *triple digits*. In a lousy economy where titans like Allen-Bradley and ABB were having their worst stretch in decades, Big Ass Fans found itself rising like a rocket.

It isn't a terribly exciting product. It's not a magic portable DVD player. It's not some satellite receiver with built-in GPS. It's just a fan.

But Big Ass Fans has created a personality around this product so powerful that it grabs people's attention immediately and *catapults* its advertising effectiveness into the stratosphere. With its trademark image of Fanny the Donkey, Big Ass Fans is now a permanently recognizable brand.

More importantly, there's a real economic argument here.

Let's say you've got a warehouse equipped with a standard fan, circulating air at 10,000 cfm (cubic feet per minute). Run it for one hour, and it would cost you 5.6 cents.

But suppose that you needed to circulate 125,000 cfm of air—13 times that amount. Using 13 standard fans would cost you 75 cents an hour. Run those 24 hours and you've got a one-day electric bill of $18.00.

But run just one Big Ass Fan, and you'll circulate the same amount of air and do it for $0.88 a day. Sound like a good deal?

Here's how it breaks down over time:

	1 Day	1 Week	1 Month	1 Year
13 Standard Fans	$18.00	$126.00	$540.00	$6,570.00
1 Big Ass Fan	$0.88	$6.16	$29.12	$321.00

This is now part of Big Ass Fans' USP. It doesn't just shock you into buying its product. It *proves* that this is an investment. The question now becomes, can your warehouse afford *not* to put in a Big Ass Fan?

In that industry, folks think it's a crime to stand out, to look different, conspicuous. Advertisers in industry magazines and trade journals work hard to keep their own ads looking just like everyone else's ads.

Which, of course, is marketing suicide.

We talked with the company's marketing manager on the phone about this very question. "Most folks look at my ad," he explained, "and they think to themselves, 'Whoa—if I wrote ads like that, they would look totally different from everyone else's.'" His reaction? "*Of course* your ads should look different from everyone else's. How else will they get noticed? That's the whole *point!*"

Want to dominate your market? Take your USP, add some serious chutzpah, and give it an unforgettable delivery.

WHY A GOOD USP MAY SAVE YOUR LIFE, LITERALLY

In her landmark book *Nickeled and Dimed: On (Not) Getting By in America*, daring journalist Barbara Ehrenreich tells of a risky personal experiment she undertook: abandoning her city, her identity, her education, and her professional qualifications for three months, she attempted to live on $6 per hour working as a Walmart employee, waitress, and maid in an unfamiliar city.

Ehrenreich discovered how it's barely possible to survive on those wages. She had to work two jobs, she constantly lived on the verge of homelessness, with no insurance and no safety net. And, not surprisingly, she was treated with little respect. She experienced the worst of everything.

While Ehrenreich has shown great insight into the daily grind of America's "working poor," she has offered little in the way of answers or solutions, other than a poignant appreciation of the hard-working waitress who pours your coffee at Denny's and the goodness of leaving a generous tip.

You see, here's the real problem:

How is it that a person can go to school for 13 years, graduate with a diploma, and be qualified for nothing more than waiting tables or stocking shelves at Walmart? Is $6 an hour all the value that a person gets from a modern high school education?

Sadly, that seems to be the case. There is a missing ingredient, however.

If you have a USP to offer the world, you're not a commodity anymore. The book *Nickeled and Dimed* is not just about low wages but also about being a commodity. One hundred twenty-five pounds of "human capital." An awful state to live in.

One of Ehrenreich's jobs was working as a maid. In that industry if you want to be a bona fide cleaner of homes or businesses, you have to get bonded, and there are a number of hurdles you have to overcome. But what would prevent that same person from creating a clever USP, printing up a compelling flier, distributing it, and getting five or six families to employ her directly—for $20 per hour instead of $7—without having to go through the official hurdles?

It's a free country, after all.

Aristotle Onassis once said, "The secret of business is to know something that nobody else knows." Don't let yourself become a commodity. Discover how to do something valuable that few others can do. That's not something you learn in a classroom of 30 kids. And the funny thing is, while you *will* learn that in a marketing seminar, unlike a traditional education, nobody can give you your answer, your USP, on a platter. Your challenge is to identify it for yourself.

The lesson in all of this? The concept of a *unique selling proposition* is not merely a marketing technique, but in fact is a fundamental life skill, an essential ingredient in all human endeavors. It's as important as reading, writing, and 'rithmetic.

And it's your ticket out of the rat race.

THE NUMBER-ONE SYMPTOM OF A BAD USP IS . . .

You try for hours to write an interesting ad, and you can't come up with anything.

A product with a great USP is easy to write an ad for. For example, how hard would it be to write an ad for an Apple iPad?

> This thing fits in your purse, and it's like a computer with built-in internet everywhere you go. You can Facebook, you can Tweet, you can blog, you can watch movies in an airplane, you can download thousands of apps, and you can surf the web, and its battery lasts ten hours.

Easy. Because it's got a great USP.

What if you're writing an ad for a packet of bland-tasting instant coffee?

> You can stir this in hot water, and you have bland-tasting coffee in about 30 seconds. I don't really know why you'd want to drink it, though. It sure ain't Starbucks.

A GREAT USP IS ALWAYS A WORK IN PROGRESS

Your number-one mission in marketing—especially online marketing, where uniqueness is the name of the game—is to constantly upgrade and refine your USP. Nobody gets to sit still. And when you have a great USP, you're like Apple. People anxiously await new products and line up to buy them.

Uncle Claude Sez

A person who desires to make an impression must stand out in some way. Being eccentric, being abnormal is not a distinction to covet. But doing admirable things in a different way gives one a great advantage. So with salesmen, in person or in print . . . .

There is refreshing uniqueness, which enhances, which we welcome and remember. Fortunate is the salesman who has it.

How Email Transforms Those Expensive Clicks into Long-Term, Profitable Customers

No discussion about Google AdWords would be complete if I didn't show you how to turn that expensive split-second click into a long-term relationship. When someone clicks on your ad, Google charges you 50 cents regardless of what happens next. If the guy leaves after five seconds, he's gone, and you'll probably never get him back without paying *again*.

■ ■ ■

Fifty cents for five seconds of someone's attention—dang, that's $600 an hour! Kind of depressing if you look at it that way.

On the other hand, if that person gives you his email address, you can communicate with him on a regular basis for little or no cost.

If you're trying to sell a $1,000 product, which is easier to get from your prospects—a $1,000 order or an email address?

The more complex your sales process, the more important it is to break it up into bite-sized steps. That is why the main Google AdWords page at www.perrymarshall. com/google is an email opt-in page:

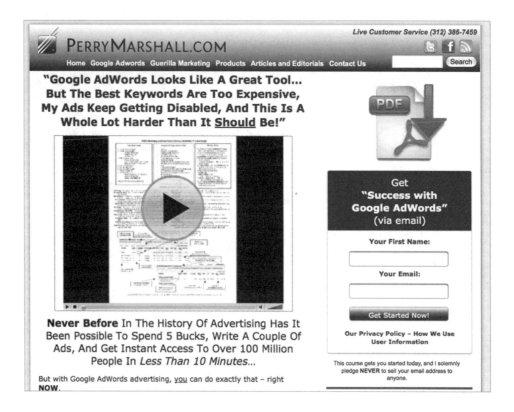

Visitors can either opt-in to take our free cheat sheet and email course or leave. I figure if a person's really interested in Google AdWords—that is, likely to buy my *Definitive Guide to Google AdWords*—she'll at least give her email address first.

This is better than only getting email addresses from people who buy the book on the first visit. And it's better than having only one shot at selling people our services.

HOW TO PUT PERSONALITY AND PIZZAZZ INTO YOUR EMAIL MARKETING

In a day when much of the manufacturing industry is downsizing, cutting management, laying off employees right and left, and moving in a panic to India and China, B&B Electronics in Ottawa, Illinois, has been setting growth records.

It had to hire more staff to handle its growing number of incoming catalog orders and mounting list of willing buyers.

Most people would never think to utter the phrase "infectious personality" and "electronics manufacturing company" in the same breath, but B&B is both.

It refuses to surrender to the dull, corporate geek stereotype. Instead it has loads of fun with the stereotype. B&B regularly courts its growing customer list's inboxes with witty, lively messages that celebrate the stale, geek image of the Dilbert-cubicle engineer. Marketing director Mike Fahrion graces customers with his regular "Mike's Politically Incorrect Newsletter" rant column.

A techie's girlfriend recently wrote B&B to thank it for turning the engineer stereotype on its head:

Hey Mike,

This is the hapless girlfriend who shares an email account with a techie who subscribes to your newsletter.

The amount of dry, poopey emails that we get in our inbox is criminal, and it's pathetic that the other electronic types are perpetrating the geek image that's out there by sending those incredibly boring messages.

I mean, come on! "All you've ever wanted to learn about C++, Extensive Layer Management Plug-In for mental ray Pipeline"? BRUTAL!

Thank you for the sense of humor in your newsletters.

Mike—I think you need to start a "How to Write a Cheese-Free Newsletter" course. I can think of many companies that need your help!

Signed,

Disgruntled Dish

Does B&B owe its stellar growth in a stagnant industry all to its email? No, but it's a vital ingredient of its carefully thought-out marketing strategy.

> Use email correctly, and your customers will stick around three times longer. It's the most personal online medium there is. With it you can sell to your customers again and again by building trust and creating an entire business around your own unique personality.

Mike understands this. (Which is why he originally hired Perry to ghostwrite his "Politically Incorrect Newsletter.")

Whether you're B&B Electronics or Martha Stewart, capturing a person's email address turns a one-time click into an opportunity to build a relationship that can work for you again and again and again.

Buying Google traffic is only the first of many important steps in our marketing process. If we had to credit our own success to just one thing, it would be the use of email and autoresponders.

POWER IN THE PERSONAL: SIX KEYS TO EMAIL MARKETING SUCCESS

Run-of-the-mill advertisers have little respect for the personal nature of email. They don't realize how easy it is to turn off otherwise receptive prospects to their message, just by violating that.

You need to write to the person as one person. Unless the person you're writing to is part of a group where he or she personally knows each of the other members, then the last thing you want to do is write as though you're talking to a crowd.

This is you, an individual, talking to your customer, an individual.

1. A "From" Field that Shows You're a Real Person

So if that's the case for the actual text of your email messages, chances are that same principle will apply to other details in your email. Such as your "from" field, for example. Consider the different impressions these "from" lines create:

> Bill Kastl
> William Kastl
> William D. Kastl
> Nakatomi Corporation
> William D. Kastl, Nakatomi Corporation
> Nakatomi Sales Department
> Bill Kastl, Nakatomi Sales

You want to be warm and personal without looking like spam. This is a challenge because spammers are themselves always trying to make their messages look like they're from some forgotten friend. The key is to say something that is so specific to readers' particular interests they know no spammer would ever come up with it.

Pick a "from" field that your customers will understand, and stick with it.

2. A Provocative Subject Line

The most important thing about email is that its success or failure is all about *context*. Email subject lines work *not because they follow standard copywriting formulas* but because *they tap into what specific people are interested in at a particular time*.

If I showed you generic examples of email subject lines, it would be almost impossible for them to not sound like spam.

So let's take examples from a specific context that *you* understand: Google AdWords. Here are the subject lines of some of the emails I've sent out to my Google AdWords customer list:

· When Google is NOT the Best Way to Get a Customer
· Are Google Employees Spying on You?
· Google's 'Don't Be Evil' and all that
· Five Insidious Lies About Selling on the Web
· Fistfight at the Board of Directors Meeting

These headlines do not assault the reader with cheesy-sounding promos, but they do hint very strongly at a story. They provoke curiosity rather than scaring people off.

3. Everybody Loves a Good Story

B&B Electronics sells industrial communication hardware via catalog and the web. A "boring" geek business if there ever were one. But when Perry writes its monthly newsletter, he turns that dull, geek image on its head and interrupts a dreary day of engineering with wry humor.

His method? Storytelling.

Subject: **ZIGBEE AND THE GEEKS' REVENGE**

Leslye was the girl who made my heart go pitter-patter in junior high school.

I was always sure to take the long way to Social Studies, down the stairs to first floor, past her locker, then back up to 2nd. Just checkin' up.

I was not the boy who made her heart go pitter-patter. She liked Sam, and maybe Rodney too. She wasn't interested in me. And she never discovered that I liked her. It was my little secret.

Now maybe you didn't run the sound system in Junior High like I did. Maybe you ran the film projector instead. Maybe you programmed Apple II computers in BASIC and belonged to Chess Club.

Still, you and I were geeks, and the pretty girls took no notice of us.

But it's 2009 now, and we geeks rule the world. We're the people who really know what's going on. All the pretty boys and their material girls have viruses on their computers and they can't function without us. They're at our mercy.

And the latest Geek Revenge these days is . . .

ZigBee.

ZigBee is sort of like wireless instant messaging for sensors and smart devices. You drop ZigBee nodes wherever you want, no cables necessary, and the more nodes you have, the more communication paths there are and the more reliable your system is . . . .

It's a little wonky. It doesn't surrender to the stereotype that engineers are dull, lifeless geeks who only understand ones and zeros. No. It *celebrates* it. It turns it into the central message. It plays with the concept and has no end of fun with it.

More importantly, though, while it celebrates the engineer stereotype, at the same time it smashes it to pieces.

Engineers make buying decisions on emotion no differently than the rest of us do.

Storytelling *does* work when marketing to them, no differently than people in any other profession. Plus, every geek out there has suffered the heartache of unrequited love.

Every time B&B sends out an email blast, it gets emails from customers saying, "Your newsletter is the only one I read every time it comes" and "I always look forward to getting emails from you guys."

Why We Chose Engineers as an Example for Email Marketing

Most people stubbornly insist you can't use storytelling and humor to sell to "logical" people like engineers and scientists. Most people also think that business-to-business marketing has to be dreadfully serious.

This campaign shoots holes in both beliefs because we're doing both at the same time here—using emotional, human-touch email marketing to sell business-to-business products to engineers and scientists.

Does this work in other markets? You bet it does. Bryan sold more books on learning Chinese and ignited more feedback and fan mail through this one message than anything else he sent out:

Subject: **WOMEN WHO HOLD HANDS; MEN WHO HUG**

William kept brushing against me as we walked down the street.

Now I'm a guy like he is—and I'm straight, too—and I found this a little unnerving. This was back during my first month living in mainland China, William was my new friend, and he had some habits that were awfully strange.

And when we'd go out walking somewhere, he always rubbed his shoulders up against me. I kept thinking I was crowding him, so I'd move to the right. Then he'd move right too, get closer and rub up against me again.

Sooner or later I figured out that this was just his way of being friendly. No, not "friendly," just friendly—you know, normal, nice-guy friendly.

It's that classic issue of personal space. Every culture has different rules. My Chinese guy friends rubbed shoulders with each other, and with me, as they walked down the street.

Americans don't do that, unless they're in a relationship.

Younger women in China hold hands.
Sometimes regardless of age. Arm in arm, hand in hand, they saunter together down the street.

Ah, but do they HUG you?

None of my friends ever did.

At least, not until I was with a couple of guys being visited by a lady pal of theirs from Shanghai . . . .

This email was part of Bryan's regular timed-email autoresponder series, and didn't even explicitly promote his book. But it got a *reaction* from people. Still does. It turns the spotlight in a sensitive yet eminently funny subject.

It paints Bryan as completely and totally human. Not a peddler, not a salesman, not a pushy marketer, but as a regular guy whose experiences his mainland or Taiwan-based readers all share.

Most importantly, this approach *trains* people to read your emails by convincing them that you've always got something interesting to say.

4. People Can't Forget You When They Hear from You Often

Get an autoresponder series going and you can win the hearts of customers for life:

1. We like five-day sequences. Five is a good number. Prime numbers like 3, 5, and 7 are good.
2. After that five-day sequence is done, keep in touch at a slower rate. In our "The Nine Great-Lies of Sales & Marketing" e-course (www.PerryMarshall.com/9), messages continue every few days and taper out for more than two years afterward. (You read it right: two years.)
3. Your unsubscribe rate should be 3 to 10 percent. If it's more than that, your message isn't matching your market. (If it's less, you may not be edgy enough.)
4. Want to squash refunds and returns? After people buy from you, send them a series of messages that show them how to use your product more effectively and shares features they might have missed.
5. When people complain that they've missed a day or two from you, it's a sign that your content is good *and* that the spam filters are doing their job.

5. If You Violate the Expectation of Relevance, You Damage Your List

Let's say you're a chiropractor and you've just launched a new herbal remedy. It's a fantastic product, and you want to tell your customers. What should you do? Should you blast your entire list with it?

Odds are, you could maximize your sales total for that day by doing so.

But you're going to pay a price. All the people on your list who aren't interested in herbal stuff are now going to be *less responsive* to everything else you do—even if they don't unsubscribe. You've just taught them that you like to send out emails about stuff they're not interested in.

Which means they're that much less likely to read your next email.

It's a nasty mistake to treat everyone on your list the same, unless they really are. If you've got a back pain newsletter, it's likely only a few people on that list would ever be interested in a knee pain newsletter.

The typical marketer will treat everyone the same and when he gets a back pain subscriber, he'll also send knee pain stuff, neck pain stuff, herbal stuff, environmental stuff, whatever.

The smart marketer will not. The smart marketer will have different lists for each topic—different sublists.

So if you're the chiropractor, you build an herbal sublist, and then sell the herbal remedies just to those folks. That way you maximize the value of every single list you have.

In email—and by extension, direct mail and other forms of communication—that means that some of your prospects and customers don't ever want to hear from you (the bottom 5 to 10 percent). They, of course, do not matter. They can unsubscribe. But for the people who do:

- Some of them (maybe 50 percent) would like to hear from you no more than a few times a year.
- Some of them (20 percent) would like to get your three-, five-, or seven-day auto-responder sequence for a few days, then only hear from you if something really important happens.
- Some (5 to 10 percent) would like to get all your newsletters, and if you have email lists for six different problems or products, they'll want to be on every single one.
- Some (1 to 2 percent) would like to hear from you every day.
- A tiny handful (less than 1 percent) would literally read ten emails from you every day, if you were willing to send them.

6. The Human Touch Sells

Don't hide behind your email. Use it to express more of yourself. You're not a faceless corporation; you're a person. Show that side of you, and people will remember you. And buy. And tell others about you.

Express a personality that people can instantly recognize. This is free branding. When you introduce new products or make changes in your marketing program or message, now you can attach those to a name—your name or another person that your business is known for—and now your name itself has even more meaning and credibility.

A MEDIUM THAT WILL NEVER GO AWAY

When you communicate with your customers in multiple media rather than just one, it greatly solidifies your power in the marketplace.

There's power for you in adding offline marketing to your arsenal. Communicating with your customers via direct mail (or even fax) takes you out of the ephemeral, fly-by-night online world and plugs them into you by an entirely new medium—a medium that is harder to break into but potentially more rewarding and enduring.

You can bank on the fact that the guy in the blue-grey uniform who comes to your house every day is going to *continue* coming to your house every day pretty much as long as the earth keeps rotating on its axis (or as long as politicians depend on him to deliver their campaign mailings).

A customer who finds you offline and goes to you online is usually more valuable to you than a customer who knows you only online. In the same way, a customer who knows you offline through physical mailings and physical products as well as online is going to be a much more valuable customer than one who only knows you online.

OPT-INS: MORE THAN JUST AN EMAIL ADDRESS?

Most opt-in pages only ask for a name and email address, but is that all the information you want? Many, if not most, businesses should also collect physical addresses and fax numbers. Asking for this information, even requiring it, makes your database much more valuable.

It also gives you a valuable communication medium besides just email. What if you accidentally get on a spam blacklist, if your email service goes belly up, or email suddenly gets a lot more expensive? It's a mistake to rely solely on email.

THEY CAN KNOCK OFF YOUR PRODUCT, BUT THEY CAN'T KNOCK OFF *YOU*

Anybody can have a TV talk show, but there's only one Oprah. Anybody can rant about the Democrats, but there's only one Rush Limbaugh. Products can be replicated and ideas can be stolen, but personalities cannot be duplicated.

Use email to express your own personality and you'll have a unique bond with your customers that nobody can take from you.

Uncle Claude Sez

A person who desires to make an impression must stand out in some way. Being eccentric, being abnormal is not a distinction to covet. But doing admirable things in a different way gives one a great advantage.

That's why we have signed ads sometimes—to give them a personal authority. A man is talking—a man who takes pride in his accomplishments—not a "soulless corporation." Whenever possible we introduce a personality into our ads. By making a man famous we make his product famous. When we claim an improvement, naming the man who made it adds effect.

Chapter 21

The One Magic Number That Defines the Power of Your Website

Every business and every industry has a basic measure of success. For example, retail is real estate. The real estate in your local mall is leased on a square-footage basis, so in retail sales the measure of the store's success is sales per square foot.

■ ■ ■

On Google, traffic is charged for on the basis of dollars per visitor. So success is also measured in dollars per visitor. If 100 people come to your site and you get $200 of sales, then your *value per visitor* (VPV) is $2.00.

There are other metrics you track to measure your website's success. But this is as fundamental as any of them. How would your strategy change if you made it your mission to have a high VPV, or *visitor value*?

If you have a high visitor value, you'll be like the hottest and most fashionable spots at a highbrow mall: Nordstrom, Lord & Taylor, Starbucks, Saks Fifth Avenue, and Macy's.

If you have a low visitor value, you're destined to be like the strip-mall stores: Dollar General, T.J. Maxx, Piercing Pagoda, and the like.

If your visitor value is even lower than that, you're on the slagheap, eeking out a meager existence at a flea market, or hawking your excess inventory on eBay.

> The marketers who make the real bucks are the ones whose websites have the highest visitor value, which is the average sales value of each click they buy. When you grow your visitor value, it means more money deposited into your bank account. Plus it means more affiliates and joint venture partners will come seek you out, because you can advertise more aggressively and pay more money to everyone.

Profit is your goal. That's why you're in business in the first place. But your profit alone doesn't tell you how sleek and effective your sales process is. You might just be getting lucky with unusually cheap click prices.

Visitor value is a powerful measure of what your clicks are actually worth. It's a measure of how smart your website is, how effective your sales copy is, how powerful your offer is.

How do you calculate visitor value? Simple:

Visitor Value = (Your Total Sales Value) ÷ (Your Number of Clicks)

So if you make 50 percent margin on a $1,000 product and one out of every 100 visitors buys, then your visitor value is $10.00 and in theory you can spend up to $5.00 per visitor to buy the traffic and still break even.

If one out of every 1,000 visitors buys, then your visitor value is $1.00 and in theory you can spend up to $0.50 to buy the traffic.

We know this is an oversimplification of what margins are and how they work. But the point is the same: visitor value tells you what your clicks are worth and what you need to do about it.

DOLLARS MEAN MORE THAN PERCENTAGES

Let's say you sell a widget online, and you've got two prices: your budget version for $9.00 and your deluxe version for $29.00. At the end of August you make some tweaks in your sales page, and then you watch your numbers through September. Here's what you find if you just measure percentages of sales:

	Clicks	Number of Sales	Percent Conversion	Sales Amount
August	3,447	45	1.3%	$1,241
September	3,921	82	2.1%	$1,260

Hey, this is great! You had more clicks, you sold almost twice as many widgets, your conversion rate jumped up, and your sales dollars in September improved over August, right?

Wait a minute.

This isn't an improvement at all. Your tweaked sales letter actually hurt your cause. Now visitors are spending less money, and your clicks are worth less than before:

	Clicks	Number of Sales	Percent Conversion	Sales Amount	Visitor Value
August	3,447	45	1.3%	$1,241	$0.36
September	3,921	82	2.1%	$1,260	$0.32

Your conversion percentage went up, but people are just buying your cheaper version now. Now your sales process is less profitable than before, and you're less attractive to affiliates because they'll now make less money sending visitors to you.

Don't miss this: When you're split testing landing pages, opt-ins, and sales, you're not just going after high percentages. It's the *dollars* you care about.

That percentage thing is a one-dimensional view of your traffic.

Visitor value reduces a *multidimensional* process to a single number. When you try things, you learn those kinds of secrets, combining percentages with dollar values to establish how much you can bid for your clicks. Once that's settled, you move on to adjust for your own ultimate big number: your net profit.

Heck, you could *double* the value of your clicks just by offering similar products at higher price points. This is something sales percentages alone don't tell you.

Buying web traffic reduces a complex process to a simple question: *How much can you afford to pay for a visitor and still make a profit?* At first, you may not know how many visitors you need to make a sale. But you can find out pretty fast: Just buy traffic and test it. Check out the checklist on the next page.

HOW TO USE SPLIT TESTING TO BOOST YOUR VISITOR VALUE

Google AdWords is so revolutionary because it has made split testing unbelievably easy. Now you can test two or more ads against each other and systematically beef up your

QUICK AND DIRTY CHECKLIST FOR IMPROVING YOUR VISITOR VALUE

An effective sales page follows the time-honored classic formula:

1. An attention-getting, benefit-driven headline
2. A statement of unique value
3. An unbeatable offer
4. A clear and specific call to action
5. An easy way to respond

So in order to have your sales page produce the results you desire, you need to:

❏ Continually test new headlines.

Headlines have the biggest influence on whether your visitors continue to read or not, and will make the biggest difference in your sales.

❏ Offer something clear and specific on the landing page.

Tell visitors where to go, what to do, and why it will help them. A site full of pretty images and polite puffery won't sell nearly as well as a simple, clearly written page that tells people what they'll get if they respond today. Most of the main pages on the website www.perrymarshall.com have a specific offer and call to action.

❏ Continually change your offer, to test response.

You may well find that by changing the payment terms, including a free bonus gift, offering free delivery, or adding an option to gift-wrap the item, you double your sales!

❏ Add an opportunity for your visitors to opt-in.

Offer a report, coupon, discount, white paper, e-book, book, CD, software, consultation, or problem-solving tool in exchange for their name and email address.

click-through rates over time. The process is simple, the numbers are easy to read and understand, and winners and losers are clear.

But this can also be applied to your entire sales process. You can split test two similar landing pages, two sales letters, two different email series, two purchase pages, two thank-you pages—everything.

This testing will multiply your sales and exponentially increase your profitability.

Google's Website Optimizer (www.google.com/websiteoptimizer) lets you do this testing automatically with your web pages. And there's a host of online services and downloadable programs that you can use to run tests like these from outside your website, but which give you all the numbers and data you need to win the game of visitor value.

One such tool we've been using successfully for years is Hypertracker. We put together a video tutorial at http://video.hypertracker.net that shows you how to set up this type of account to split test and track multiple sales pages, multiple opt-in pages, and more.

The best part is, if you have multiple price points for certain products, that's not a problem at all. In fact, that's the *strength* of this kind of tracking and testing. Hypertracker and other services like it can track and measure sales of different products and different dollar values, and then give you the figures you need in order to discover the visitor value of your Google campaigns.

PERRY MARSHALL

The Greatest Asset You Can Have Is a Marketing Machine You Can Turn On at Will That Continually Spits Out Money

My first successful sales letter was for a training program called "DeviceNet Boot Camp." Engineers would come to our training class for $1,500 and we would teach them how to use a new technology.

That sales letter sold a quarter million dollars of training in a year and a half.

Dang, that felt good! Every time we mailed out a couple thousand of those letters, we would get $10,000 to $20,000 in training revenue. Plus, about half the time we sent out mailers for the class, we would also get requests for custom, on-site classes.

Not only did this become a profit center for our company, it positioned us above all our competitors as experts, because we offered specialized training.

All from a four-page, folded self-mailer sales letter. We got $8.00 of registration money for every $1.00 we spent sending out those letters:

Is that a great asset or what?

When you have three, four, five assets like that—especially a combination of Google campaigns, e-mail promotions, teleseminars, and direct-mail pieces, you have the most liberating, profit-producing thing a business owner could hope for.

Uncle Claude Sez

A rapid stream ran by the writer's boyhood home. The stream turned a wooden wheel and the wheel ran a mill. Under that primitive method, all but a fraction of the stream's potentiality went to waste.

Then someone applied scientific methods to that stream—put in a turbine and dynamos. Now, with no more water, no more power, it runs a large manufacturing plant.

Advertisers will multiply when they see that advertising can be safe and sure. Small expenditures made on a guess will grow to big ones on a certainty.

Chapter 22

Maintaining Your Edge: How to Consistently Stay Ahead of Your Competition in Google AdWords

Two essential factors determine whether you win, or your competitor does:

1. precision targeting, and

2. eliminating slop.

■ ■ ■

Most people don't have any idea how much data Google sifts through just to generate one search result. It's truly mind-boggling.

I have a friend who built a search engine some years ago, and he was astounded at how much bot-generated spam there was. He told me, "90 percent of the internet is spam!" The fact that Google not only hides that garbage from you but often gives you exactly what you want based on your search history, your location, and even with misspelled words is incredible.

As an advertiser, your job is to take advantage of as much of Google's capability as is reasonably possible. This chapter is a checklist of ways you can squeeze every drop of juice out of the orange. How many of these capabilities are you using?

Remember: You can combine levels of specificity to get extreme precision targeting that your competitors are almost always too lazy to execute. Better yet, it's almost impossible for them to reverse engineer what you are doing.

For example, you could target men between ages 35 and 45, living in London. You can choose to have your ads show from 5:00 P.M. to 8:00 P.M. on weeknights only on smartphones. Or, your ads only show on web pages about model airplanes. You could pile more levels of specificity than that, too. As many as you want.

I'm going to quickly summarize Google's capabilities here, with some useful tips.

CUSTOM GEO TARGETING

Custom Geo Targeting is potentially a hugely profitable way to target your customers. Most national advertisers have gaping holes because they have huge geographical biases in regard to who buys from them and who doesn't, *but they don't know it.*

Below is a heat map of the Chicago suburbs. The dark areas are suburbs where I tend to get customers. The white areas are suburbs where I get almost no customers.

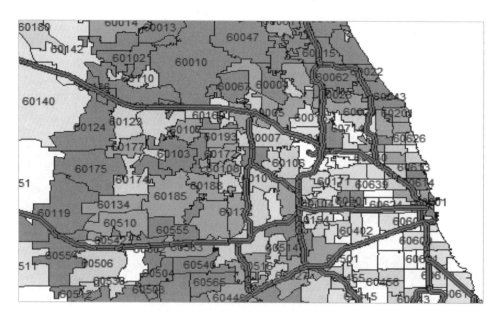

This map is very, very different from population density. Some of the white areas, especially in the city of Chicago, have huge numbers of people—even people who search for what I sell—but no buyers!

I hired Ben Morris of Kristalytics (www.kristalytics.com/) to analyze my customer database. Ben determined that I'm 25 times more likely to get a customer from the affluent suburb of Hinsdale than from the somewhat blighted suburb of Maywood or the Chicago neighborhood of Austin. Traffic from Hinsdale converts *much* better than Maywood and Austin.

This is a major problem, especially for national advertisers. And it's epidemic. If you're bidding the same amount for the entire United States (90 percent of national Google advertisers do), then if there is a hot local market for what you sell in Los Angeles, your ads are probably underwater in Los Angeles. Nobody's seeing your ads there at all!

On the other hand, Lubbock, Texas, could be a lousy market for you but your ads are showing up in the premium listings there. You're paying top dollar for crappy clicks.

> Many national advertisers are committing the Google equivalent of being completely absent from an upscale shopping mall in Beverly Hills while spending all their money to be in a low-rent strip mall in Gary, Indiana.

This is a very expensive mistake. So some combination of any of the following geographic options may be right for you:

· City
· State/Region
· Latitude/Longitude
· Postal Code
· Country
· Combinations of all the above
· Custom messaging to chosen segments

If you have enough customers, it's possible to create a custom geographic profile and target only the postal codes or metro areas that have your kind of customers.

This is not a magic pill—sometimes it doesn't work all that well; it depends on how niche your product is. But I can tell you that some of my clients who advertise nationally have increased the return on investment of their AdWords campaigns by 30 to 200 percent by using carefully crafted geo-targeting profiles—and eliminating literally three-fourths of the country entirely.

Ben Morris of Kristalytics offers a free initial evaluation. You can contact him at ben@texas.net.

OTHER WAYS TO PRECISION TARGET

There are a number of options I don't discuss in the list below, but what you see here covers 95 percent of your selective power on AdWords. Custom Geo Targeting, when done right, is among the most powerful waste-eliminating methods of all.

Conversion Tracking: It's a must!

Networks:
Search (Google only)
Search Partners
Display Network

Languages: You can target Spanish-speaking people living in the United States; you can target Dutch-speaking people living in England.

Keywords:
Synonyms
Words from thesaurus
Words from a book index
Words you or competitors are search engine optimizing for
Model and part numbers

The "See Search Terms" is extremely valuable for adding missing keywords to your list and also for identifying negative keywords.

Keyword match types: Broad, phrase, exact, modified broad

Negative keywords: Broad, phrase, exact

Display Network targeting:
Keyword targeting
Site targeting
Topic targeting
Negative sites

Bid Types:
Cost Per Click
Cost Per Impression
Cost Per Action

A presentation on CPA bidding—paying for leads instead of click or impressions—is available from CPA expert David Rothwell at www.perrymarshall.com/supplement/. Many times you can gain an advantage just by using a different bidding method than everyone else.

Daily Budget. You should only set it low if you're deliberately conserving expenses for an experiment. Otherwise you should normally use bid prices to throttle your spend. If Google normally sends you $100 of traffic per day and you set your budget to $100, Google will give you less impression share than you want. If you can, set your budget to two to three times your typical daily spend.

Day Parting. This feature is not used nearly as often as it could be. Many times customers are predisposed to search at certain times of the day or week. The best way to start is to see if there's a time of day or week that gets you *bad* traffic and eliminate bidding during that time.

Campaign Start and End. Again, seldom used but obviously useful.

Campaign and Ad Group Segregation. You can create about as many campaigns as you want. The problem with dividing things too finely is that no single campaign gets enough traffic to get statistically significant results. Every ad group ought to at least get enough traffic to perform a valid split test every couple of months. Otherwise you're splitting things up too much.

Devices:
  Desktops
  Smartphones
  Tablets

Remember that many people search for things on their phones and then finish the purchase on the phone or on their computer. If in doubt, include the device.

Text Ads. Numbers, word pictures, free offers, locations, rhythm, people, brands, visual, auditory, kinesthetic, friends, enemies, desires, fears, capabilities, direct marketing offers, prices, slang.

Ad Extensions. Phone numbers, tracking phone numbers, Sitelinks, User ratings ("stars").

Special buttons. The +1 Button and the Google Checkout Button.

Image Ads:
  Sizes
  Colors

Fonts

Objects

People

Images that look like text

Texture

Focus

Animation

Display URL:

Split-testing multiple domain names (easier to do on Yahoo/Bing than Google)

Subdomains

Subdirectories

Frequency Capping. This prevents the same person from seeing your ad 100 times in one day. Typical frequency caps are 3 to 15 impressions per day.

Remarketing. Visitors who came to your site and didn't buy will see your ads in the days, weeks, and months following their visit. Your ads "follow them around" and, if done tastefully, can recover other lost business. See Chapter 26.

Demographics available on the Display Network. Think of these as a way to eliminate portions of the population who are not going to buy from you:

Male

Female

Age Ranges

REALITY CHECK

The 80/20 Rule is ALWAYS at work. The way you win is by getting 80 percent of your traffic from 20 percent of

· Ads

· Ad Groups

· Geographical targets

· Age ranges

· Times of day or week

· Keywords

· Devices

· Ad sizes

You don't have to slice your campaigns into a million pieces. You just need to make sure the most important pieces are laser targeted to exactly the customer you want.

WHY I LOVE ADWORDS!

You can never run out of things to improve, ways to outsmart the other guy. No other advertising medium even comes close to Google AdWords in its razor precision. This is one of the reasons I love Google AdWords so much—because it's so incredibly powerful.

Far from being a stupid bidding war where the guy with the deepest pockets always wins, AdWords is truly a fight for the intelligent and savvy. If you dial down with enough precision, you can unseat almost any competitor.

Persuasive Ad Copy:
The Ultimate Silver Bullet
How to Mint Money with the Printed Word

When I left the Dilbert Cube in 2001 and hung out my shingle, my copywriting skills were more than adequate for corporate client work—writing press releases, product descriptions, and magazine articles. However I wanted to sell information: toolkits, books, e-books, and the like. I wanted a sales-on-autopilot business, not a consulting project business.

■ ■ ■

That kind of business required far greater copywriting and persuasion skills. My skills were not up to the task. I needed a mentor.

I hooked up with the legendary copywriter John Carlton. He would rip my pages apart and bust my chops. Then he'd bandage my damaged body parts with some words of encouragement and instruct me on how to re-assemble my message for killer persuasion power.

Then . . . the first letter he made me rewrite went from 1 percent response (not quite breaking even) to 2 percent (solidly profitable). I was elated!

John's guidance got me over the hump. I can attribute my business "escape velocity" to his tutelage. His help was essential to moving my rocket ship from launch pad to orbit.

So I asked John to contribute a chapter to this book. He's taught more people to successfully sell in print than almost anyone alive, so pay close attention.

The dirty little secrets behind effortless selling . . .

YOUR FIRST ROOKIE LESSON IN CLASSIC SALESMANSHIP

Here's your launching pad to finally transform your ability to persuade, close deals, and earn the Big Bucks . . . with the time-tested fundamentals of getting your sales message across that nobody told you about.

By John Carlton
(The most respected, ripped-off rabble-rousing marketing expert alive)

Is it OK if I teach you three super-simple secrets—right now, today, right here—that will systematically transform your ability to:

- ✓ Get the undivided attention of your best prospects . . .
- ✓ Convince them to listen to what you have to say . . .
- ✓ Earn their sincere respect . . .
- ✓ And turn them into buying customers.

And to do all this whether you're speaking directly to a prospect . . . or reaching him through an ad or website or email or TV commercial or any other media?

Is this something you feel could affect your bottom line?

It is? OK then. Let's get going.

First, let's do a little "spot check" on your current Sales IQ, with a sneaky question: What is the *single most important thing* you need in your personal "tool kit" to become independent . . . wealthy . . . respected . . . and happy?

Go on, think about your answer for a few moments. The single most important thing. Most folks get it wildly wrong, including many entrepreneurs who should know better.

All right. What did you come up with?

If your answer included anything about brain power, or investors, or an MBA, or any kind of "advantage" you feel should give you a head-start on attaining independence, wealth, respect and happiness . . .

. . . please reconsider how you think about success.

Because the answer to this question is much more simple: **You need to learn how to *sell*.**

Oh, the shame of it all. The *horror* of resigning yourself to being "that guy" who has ulterior motives whenever he talks to you, because he wants to "sell" you something. That just can't be the answer. It's too . . . creepy.

So let's get straight on this basic secret of lasting, empowering success, right off the bat.

Consider this: Do you have a *great* product? Something that people can really use to improve their lives, save more time, save money, get better results? Do you run an ethical business that fulfills on all promises, and delivers exactly what you say you can deliver?

You do?

Then guess what.

If you have a product that your prospect needs . . . and can put to good use . . . especially if it's something that addresses a critical, life-changing situation he's in . . .

. . . and you can't *explain* this to him in a way that makes him realize that he needs to become a customer right now . . .

. . . then *shame on you*.

Because you are HIDING your product from people whose lives would be better if they knew you existed. And that you can deliver exactly what they need.

Salesmanship is nothing more than the ability to move past the natural (and very solid) resistance that people have to "being sold" . . . and help them get their hands on your product (which can change their lives in amazing ways).

It's what separates the failures in the business world from the folks who become successful. What kind of entrepreneur *are* you if you can't sell? The "Marketing Graveyard" is crammed to bursting with great products, really superior stuff . . . that *died* because no one figured out how to sell them.

Yes, you need all the other things that business experts and technology wizards insist you use in your marketing. All the software and equipment, the order-taking processes, the SEO, the traffic-capturing tactics, the auto-responders, all of it.

But you need to know how to sell FIRST.

All else is just a detail to getting your sales message out to the world.

Have you ever watched a YouTube video that made you laugh? That you wanted to show your friends? That you told others about?

After watching that video, did you then send a dollar to the person who posted it?

No, you didn't. Because no salesmanship took place.

Yet, this is how too many business owners run their operation—they believe that getting page hits, clicks, or opt-ins is important. And it's good to have those things . . .

. . . but they will do nothing for your bottom line if you *can't close the deal*. And make a sale happen.

Selling isn't magic. It's a very simple process most anyone can master. It's the essential element of all great marketing. However, it's also misunderstood and avoided.

So, first breakthrough: Stop pretending sales will happen because you have a great product, or you're a nice person, or you pump a lot of money into your business.

The fact is, a nearly broke entrepreneur at his kitchen table who knows how to sell can bring home a fortune . . . while even the biggest companies on the planet can crumble into dust if they ignore salesmanship.

It happens all the time. Many of the most famous success stories start with a lone person, lacking funds and connections and experience . . . but knowing how to sell . . . conquering the world.

This knowledge will be your secret weapon no matter what you do with your life. You will know how to close a deal, which is the prime talent of anyone who strives to be successful.

It's the Missing Link between having a dream . . .

. . . and making it a reality.

I am not a "natural born" salesman. I was clueless about business and selling until I was in my 30s . . . and only began my now-legendary career because I admitted that nothing good was going to happen to me "accidentally." And I needed to get busy learning how the world worked.

I made every mistake possible in my climb to success as a renowned copywriter and creator of ridiculously effective marketing campaigns. I blithely wandered down every blind alley, made every dumb decision, suffered all the consequences possible for a clueless dude out in the wilderness of advertising seeking clues.

However, I also hunted down the best mentors I could find, read voraciously and critically, and *applied* everything I learned to the harsh test of the real world.

And, I took notes. This is how I became a decent teacher. I made the blunders, fixed the damage, and forced my way into the party. I spent *decades* in the front trenches of the business world, watching businesses rise and fall and new businesses spring up from the ruins.

If something worked, I continued to use it.

If it didn't work—out there where you get zero credit for a "nice try"—I ditched it.

The advice I'm able to give, at this point in my long, battle-scarred career, has been proven over and over and over again.

You want theory, go somewhere else.

You want hard-core tactics and specific steps to take . . . keep reading.

Now, I am NOT going to teach you to write ads today. I'm also not going to teach you to be "creative."

Instead, I'm going to teach you the three simple fundamentals *behind* every great ad, and every great "creative" idea that actually produced sales.

These three tactics are lifted directly from my notorious "**Simple Writing System**" course, which Perry can get you a special deal on, just as soon as you're ready to rock and roll.

Relax. Even if you're terrified at the thought of having to write an ad, certain that you cannot possibly get up the nerve to actually ask another human being to buy what you offer . . .

. . . just get over your bad self.

With these same simple tactics I'm about to share with you, I've taught the most stubborn, self-sabotaging scaredy-cats you've ever met to get past their fears . . .

. . . and start selling stuff like crazy. Using every type of advertising media out there.

This stuff works in spite of your effort to ignore it. It's only 1/10th of one percent of everything I have to offer you . . . but it's easily enough to help you transform your ability to persuade and close the deal. Just play along.

Here is Simple Selling Tactic #1: **What are you *really* selling in your business?**

Think about this for a moment. Write down your answer here. I'll even help you get started:

"I sell _____

_____

_____

_____

_____

_____."

Just fill in the blank.

When I do this exercise at seminars, the most common answers I hear are "I sell a book on making more money," or "We sell the finest equipment in the industry," or "We sell a proven way to do xyz."

I also hear a number of people insist they sell "hope." Or "the opportunity to succeed."

All are wrong.

Most entrepreneurs and business owners are NOT selling what they THINK they're selling. You're not selling a book, or a service, or a consultation, or widget, or a new life.

No.

Rather, what you are selling . . .

. . . is what your book, service, widget, or claims of spiritual rejuvenation . . .

. . . *DOES for your prospect.*

It's not the "thing." **It's the RESULT.**

I don't want your book. I want, instead, what *happens* to me as a result of reading your book.

If there was a magic way to get that result *without* reading your book . . . I'd do that.

This is what trips up so many marketers. You get caught up in the weight, heft, bulk, the "thingness" of what you offer.

But it's just a thing. A DELIVERY SYSTEM for what I really want. And I want results.

So get clear on this: If you, or your competition, come up with an even simpler, easier, faster, tidier, and cheaper way to get what I want . . .

. . . like freedom, wealth, happiness, fun, revenge, health, beauty, another chance at life . . .

. . . then I'll go do that instead.

Don't get trapped in admiring the "thingness" of what you offer. What really matters is what your prospect believes he can GET from it.

As Perry likes to say, "Nobody who bought a drill wanted a drill. They wanted a hole."

See? That wasn't so hard to understand, was it? And yet, it's one of the fundamentals of persuading people to buy that is commonly ignored (or never realized) by biz owners frustrated at their lack of sales.

Let's go to Simple Selling Tactic #2: **"The Elevator Chat"**

This tactic can change your life, right now.

Consider this scene: You step into an elevator with another person . . .

. . . who just happens to be your perfect prospect. They're in dire need of what you offer, but you don't know this yet.

They politely ask you what you do for a living.

And what do you say?

If you cannot explain to a total stranger who you are and what you offer . . . in the time it takes an elevator to go from the 9th floor to the lobby . . .

. . . in a way that instantly alerts your perfect prospect to your value in their lives . . .

. . . then you do not have a sales message at all.

This is where many biz owners stumble. Standing right next to someone who should go goggle-eyed at meeting you . . . because they desperately need exactly what you're offering . . . you cannot clearly and succinctly tell your story.

It doesn't matter how "hot" this prospect is. Most of your prospects out there don't know who you are. They don't know what you offer, or what you do.

No matter how they got to your website, or your ad, or in front of you . . .

. . . you're just a cipher to them. They're distracted, uninterested in hearing a stranger mumble about his business, and SKEPTICAL of anything you say that smacks of ego, or confusing detail, or (worst of all) a long story that you can't seem to spit out.

Your perfect prospect has a problem or situation that requires a *solution*. And if you cannot deliver your credibility at providing this solution simply and concisely . . . they will move on. And you've lost any chance at a sale.

It's the same face-to-face as it is online, or in a magazine, or on television. You get one brief moment to capture her attention and get her interested in what you offer.

So here's how the Elevator Chat formula works: You must be able to fill out this template (or something similar):

"We help [this group of people] . . . do or get [this benefit] . . . [better, cheaper, faster, easier] . . . even if [worst-case believable scenario]."

That's it. That's the "starter kit" for an elevator chat that will get the attention of a perfect prospect.

Want some examples? Here is my own elevator chat:

"I help small biz owners and entrepreneurs . . . create their first killer sales messages that bring in the Big Bucks . . . even if you flunked English or are scared to death of writing."

Another one, from a former client:

"We help golfers with huge handicaps . . . to immediately start hitting long, straight, gorgeous tee shots, and score so low they win all the money from their buddies . . . even if you've been slicing, hooking, skulling, hacking, and putting like a baboon your entire life."

For an accountant:

"We help understaffed biz owners grossing one to ten million a year . . . to pay the least amount of taxes legally owed each year . . . without adding a minute of extra work to your day . . . even if your bookkeeping is a total disaster zone right now."

For a financial advisor specializing in debt restructuring:

"We help broke people buried in debt . . . to get *out* of debt within a short time . . . and have more money in your pocket without taking on another job, or borrowing. Works best if you have no understanding of finances or economics whatsoever."

For a weight-loss product:

"We help overweight people . . . to lose 15 to 30 pounds of body fat within one month . . . without ever feeling hungry or deprived or sweaty from exercise. Works even if every diet you've ever tried before has failed for you."

Can you see how quickly telling the story of what you do for people, in ways that directly address the needs of your prospect, can help you position your business in their eyes as a positive solution to their situation?

This process is, more or less, the lazy man's way to find your "unique selling position" . . . that particular story about who you are and what you offer . . . which is the foundation of persuasion.

This is Simple Selling Tactic #3: **"Why You, Why This Product, Why Now?"**

Your prospect needs information before she can make a satisfying decision to buy anything. She lacks knowledge about the quality of competing products out there . . . she is not on the "inside" of your market and so doesn't know if your price is high, low, or outright theft . . . and she has no clear criteria to help her make a good decision, most of the time. Even if she's familiar with the products available, and has experience with the market.

Even worse, she has to sometimes answer to the skeptical people in her life *after* making a buying decision. The nosy neighbor next door who loves to make her feel like she got ripped off, her spouse who is aghast that she's bought this particular product, her friends who are highly critical of everything.

So it's your job to help her make a good decision. To answer the fundamental questions: "Why should she deal with you and your company . . . why should she buy this particular product . . . and why should she buy it now?"

The way to do this is to position your product against all the competing products out there . . .

. . . uniquely . . .

. . . in order to sell.

All long-time salesmen know that it's often easy to get someone to agree with you that, yes, that is a mighty fine product you have there. It certainly seems to address the solution she's looking for. And it's priced attractively.

And, yes, at some point down the road, she thinks she may indeed decide to maybe buy it.

This is called "not closing the sale." A recipe for a starving salesman with skinny kids.

Instead, give her all the "ammo" she needs, in simple sound bites, to help her feel secure she is making the right decision to buy now . . . and has answers to the skeptics in her life, should they start harping.

You help her see how your product is—for example—a better overall value (if you're priced higher than the competition) . . . or a genuine bargain (if you're priced similarly). It is unique, because it's easier to use . . . works faster . . . is bigger or smaller or more substantial . . . or whatever it is that sets your product apart.

Most of all, you help her overcome her natural tendency to *put off* making a final decision . . . by pointing out the urgency of the deal, the temporary opportunity presented right now, the extra goodies available in this version, or whatever helps you to seal the deal NOW.

The basic formula for this (no matter what you're selling) is:

✓ Here's who I am.
✓ Here's what I've got for you.
✓ Here's what it will do for you.
✓ And here's what to do now.

This is the essence of good advertising and selling. It's the building blocks of a sales message that addresses your credibility (who you are) . . . the nature of what you're offering (what you've got) . . . the results that make this product a solution (what it does) . . .

. . . and, most important for your bottom line . . .

. . . how to OWN this product right now. Tell her precisely what to do next in order to have this product start doing its thang in her life.

This is why entrepreneurs and biz owners who know how to sell succeed, where others fail. Your sales message must be clear, concise, and targeted at the "sweet spot" of need in your prospect . . .

. . . while educating her on all the reasons this purchase is a great idea . . . and should be completed right now.

Face-to-face, it's easy to see why this process can work. Poor salesmen wait for prospects to ask questions, and leave it up to them to figure out whether to buy or not.

But the world-class salesman becomes an *advocate* for the prospect—explaining precisely why this product is the best choice (or even a good choice), among all the other choices available . . .

. . . and why making a decision now is the right move to make.

There's more to all this, of course. You cannot argue your way to a sale—you must *persuade*. And you must know your competition as well as a spy would . . . so you can speak knowledgeably about the uniqueness of your product, and why it's a bargain (even if it's priced higher . . . not all prospects are looking for the cheapest option, especially when their ideal solution is critical to their survival and happiness).

However, this is a good overview of how a solid, built-for-success sales message is constructed.

And here's the main thing for entrepreneurs: Once you understand how a good sales message is created . . .

. . . you can use the exact same process to create ALL of your advertising and marketing needs.

Spoken, this sales message will persuade prospects face-to-face. Written out, it will be the best ad you ever create (either for printed ads, or for websites). It will be the fuel for your video sales letters, your radio spots, your television segments, your email campaigns, your product launches . . .

. . . everything you do to get your message out there.

A great sales message can be used with any media you choose, to reach your best prospects, and to persuade them to buy from you.

If this little primer on sales messages has helped you . . . and you would like to learn even more proven, time-tested ways to make your selling abilities sizzle . . .

. . . then listen to my interview with Perry here:

www.perrymarshall.com/copywriting/

This is the very simple, do-it-yourself-quickly track that has helped transform thousands of entrepreneurs, business owners, professionals, and even rookie marketers . . .

. . . into sales-generating monsters. And it doesn't matter whether you've ever sold anything before or not, or where you're at with your career, or even if you previously failed at biz.

There you'll also get access to a special deal on my Simple Writing System.

The process of acquiring, and using, the best salesmanship tactics in the world is not brain surgery. It's actually very simple and straightforward . . .

. . . and once you learn it, the skills are yours forever.

Having a great product is one part of the equation. Having all the gizmos and technical wizardry is another part.

However, the KEY to making any business work . . . will forever be your ability to persuade someone to buy what you offer. It's the foundation for true independence, legitimate access to wealth streams, and the chance to fulfill your dreams.

I hope this has helped. Now go get 'em.

Uncle Claude Sez

Many of the best accounts in agencies are the accounts developed from small beginnings. Often much is at stake on these advertising possibilities. A mistake may ruin a fine prospect. Mediocre service may result in a small account where a big one might have been. That is why competent ad writers are paid such large incomes.

Chapter 24

So You Have a Killer Sales Machine. Now What?

The New Army of Generation-X Marketers

A new breed of direct marketer is emerging: the one that's learned from the firsthand experience of split testing rather than the secondhand tutelage of gurus. And these marketers learn fast, too, because with Google and the internet the answers are all but instantaneous.

■ ■ ■

When you start to join this new and elite crowd, you'll find paybacks on a level you'd never have imagined.

This can create unexpected problems sometimes. Conrad Feagin, one of our coaching students, grew his business from $7,000 a month to over $100,000 a month in 12 months. A couple of months after that I got this email from him:

Hey Perry,

I have been dealing with my merchant account provider for the last 2 days.
The Bad News: They are tying up some of our funds.
The Good News: We apparently "broke the bank," so to speak.
We went from $103,000 in February to $175,000 and counting in March.
Should end up around $190,000 or so.
This is all a little scary. Hopefully I will not have any problems but, needless to say, I am applying for another account at another provider.
Thanks for all the help!

I love getting emails from people who have problems like this! It proves that the commies haven't killed the entrepreneurial spirit in America yet.

And this guy is no old-school copywriter. I doubt he even knew what copywriting was a few years ago. He got these enormous results by steadily testing and improving his website.

Most niche marketers don't have big enough numbers to easily test lots of stuff, and they certainly don't have a whole staff of bean counters to help them do it. So they rely heavily on gurus, "best practices," and copywriting courses and seminars.

And many of the best niche copywriters I know, people like John Carlton, the late Gary Halbert, and Scott Haines, haven't had tons of their stuff split tested the way we're talking about today.

Their craft is really the result of lots of experience and intuition. These guys are good enough that most of the time they can crank out a winner the first time out.

Internet marketers who split test are mastering their trade faster than ever, and the best marketers discover what works by a combination of old-school tutelage and constant testing. The ultimate answer to every marketing question is *test it*. Answers have never been so easily within your grasp.

Now hang on, because the power of this is even greater than it appears. It's *exponential*.

THE IMPROVEMENTS DON'T JUST ADD UP, THEY MULTIPLY!

How to Get Massive Compound Interest on Sales and Profits

If internet marketing is some kind of magic show, I'm about to reveal to you the secret trick of the whole thing. This is what's truly important! Let's say your sales process looks like this:

1. Your AdWords ad
2. A landing page that offers a free video or white paper, a software trial, or access to video materials in exchange for name and email address

3. A sales letter

4. Your order entry page, or "action form"

We want to split test each of these four steps. We not only test the AdWords ads, we split test two different landing pages, two different sales letters, and two different order forms. What happens when we do this?

2 AdWords ads > 2 Opt-in Pages > 2 Sales Letters > 2 Order Forms

A challenging goal would be to double the effectiveness of each step. This is *not* impossible. And you don't have to be a genius—you just need to try some sensible things.

So if we double the CTR of the AdWords ad, and the landing page, and the sales letter, and the order form, our improvement is

$$2 \times 2 \times 2 \times 2 = 16X$$

A 16-fold improvement! Notice that the improvements multiply, cascading from beginning to end. Every improvement is magnified in the end result.

If you go into a competitive market on Google—such as anything computer related, weight loss, martial arts, web hosting—these are hyper-competitive categories that are very hard to win in.

It's not unusual to start out losing money at a 4:1 ratio—i.e., for every $4 you give Google, you only make $1 in gross profit. Not fun.

But now you double each of these four steps—and you improve your numbers by 16X—now you're making $4 of profit for every $1 you give Google. That's pretty amazing. Continuous split testing unlocks the whole thing like the key to a safe.

And like I said, let's take a common scenario—a threefold improvement on AdWords, a threefold improvement in your opt-in page, a twofold improvement in your sales letter, and a mere 50 percent improvement in your order page (order pages are extremely sensitive to small changes—that sale hangs by a thin thread!)—now you've got as much as a 27X improvement in conversion over what you started with.

What you've done so far would have been very hard to do in the offline world—and ten years ago not a whole lot easier in the online world—because there was never a consistent, controllable source of traffic. Pay-per-click traffic, however, is fairly consistent, and it's always 100 percent controllable. Within two to three months (as opposed to two to three years), you've tested several dozen variables and eliminated all but the best. You've polished a sales process to the point where it delivers killer results.

You're making a killer ROI on your sales process. And because you're so effective at turning visitors into dollars, you can afford to pay more for your traffic than all your competitors. You're getting unstoppable.

What now?

Now we go out with our growing war chest and buy all the traffic we can get, using the Expanding Universe Theory of internet marketing.

You've started out with Google AdWords and refined your marketing machine. Now you take the same messages and sales process, and roll out your product in this order:

1. Google AdWords
2. Search Engine Optimization
3. Other PPCs such as Yahoo/Bing and Facebook ads
4. Email promotions
5. Affiliates
6. Banner ads, advertising networks such as Advertising.com
7. Social media (Facebook status updates, Twitter)
8. Press releases
9. Direct mail
10. Print advertising

Items 2 through 10 are more expensive and less controllable than Google. Get it right with Google first, where you have total control, then do email.

Then get help from affiliates. Don't let any of these other things or people be your guinea pig. If it works on Google AdWords first, then you can invest in these other things and be fairly certain it will work.

I can't overemphasize how powerful this is. Usually search engine traffic represents only a tiny percentage of the people who are potential customers for you.

When you roll out items 2 through 9, you may make 5 to 50 times as much money as you were making with AdWords. And remember, no longer is it necessary to risk more than a few hundred dollars on a marketing campaign!

EXPANDING INTO OTHER MEDIA: PROFITING FROM THE WINNER-TAKE-ALL PHENOMENON

The top dog has a disproportionate advantage over the others. The top three players in any market get more business than all the rest combined. This is true on Google as well, and there's a snowball effect.

You enter a market, you start split testing right away, and you use sound marketing techniques, copywriting, and all of the tools at your disposal.

How fast can you go from zero to dominating a market? Answer: As fast as you can split test.

AFFILIATES: THE MOMENTUM KICKS IN

Affiliates want to make money, and the Holy Grail for an affiliate is a program that consistently sends it very good dollars in exchange for its traffic. You never want your affiliates to be blind test subjects for your experiments.

Friends come and go, but enemies accumulate!

Do your experiments with PPC traffic first. Then verify it with email promotions and inclusions in e-zines. Now that you have rock-solid numbers, take it to your affiliates.

Everybody's trying to turn traffic into dollars. Affiliate marketing is what MLM was in the early 1990s—a craze. (It also works better.)

You'll never read about this in *The Wall Street Journal,* but anywhere from 10 to 30 percent of all internet traffic is driven by affiliates. It's an invisible empire.

If you're the guy with the content and the efficient sales process that spins off dollar bills, the world's your oyster.

Good affiliate relationships are extremely profitable. And more affiliates breed more affiliates. The snowball effect multiplies, and you eventually hit the point where you're getting so much traffic you can't make it stop.

HOW TO GRIND DOWN YOUR COMPETITION: A GOOGLE LESSON FROM HAN SOLO

Harrison Ford, aka "Han Solo" and "Indiana Jones," was working odd jobs back in the mid-1970s when he was asked by George Lucas to fill in doing readings for the part of Han Solo for *Star Wars.*

Ford wasn't even being considered for the part. Lucas actually had his eye on Nick Nolte. Kurt Russell and Christopher Walken were prime candidates for the role as well.

But during these test readings Lucas realized that the man perfect for the role was right under his nose. Harrison Ford was in the right place at the right time. George Lucas decided he wanted him for the part, and the rest is *Star Wars* history.

Did he just get lucky? Ford told *Us* magazine back in 1981:

Right from the beginning, I believed that staying on course was what counted. The sheer process of attrition would wear others down. Them that stuck it out was them that won. That was my belief then. It still is.

According to Ford it was *attrition* that was the key to landing the big roles. Celebrity status and million-dollar title roles came his way because he hung in there long after other actors had given up and gone back home. Movie history vindicated his decision.

> Sometimes the secret to success is grinding your competitors down, making incremental improvements over time until you're ahead of them.

The secret to staying power, the secret to long-term sales numbers that your competitors will never beat, starts with always testing two ads against each other, two opt-in pages, two sales letters, deleting the losers, and beating the winners.

BRYAN TODD

Split-Testing + Attrition = Success: Brian K. Wins by Attrition and Surprises Even Himself

Some time back a gentleman named Brian, who had a website that sold custom gift products for children, joined our Bobsled Run personal AdWords coaching program (www.BobsledRun.com). He and I had several productive one-on-one sessions together where we examined every element of his whole sales process and suggested changes and new approaches and small tweaks here and there.

A few weeks into the process Brian was on the verge of giving up the ghost simply because of the amount of work involved in keeping his whole operation running, along with his perception that there were no significant changes that he could ever make that would push this site over the top into serious profitability.

Perry and I managed to talk him out of quitting.

Several months later we had Brian on a group call again. He raised an innocent question about conversion rates on websites, not realizing how far out of everyone's league he had actually progressed: "I'm averaging maybe a 5 percent clicks-to-sales ratio on my whole website. I feel like I could do a lot better and wonder if anyone else on the call struggles with this too."

There was silence on the line.

"Uh, did you say *5 percent?*" one of the callers asked.

"Yes, that's right. Why? Is that kind of low?"

More silence. Perry piped up: "Five percent is really, *really* good!"

One in every 20 of Brian's visitors was saying yes and buying his physical product from him. Just a few months before, Brian had been averaging less than 2 percent—one in 50. What made the difference? There was no point where Perry or Bryan or Howie gave some single Eureka-moment piece of insight that allowed Brian to make the leap from two up to five of every hundred visitors buying.

No, rather it was Brian's very calculated, systematic, methodical approach of simply split testing our new ideas against his existing old ones and keeping the one that worked better. He did this tirelessly over the course of six months and *more than doubled* the response on his website.

To Brian, this seemed totally commonplace, simply because the process had been so gradual. So unremarkable.

And it really is not rocket science. Of all the secrets that Brian and others in our Mastermind Club learn, this is the least glamorous, and yet the single most profitable. You can do this with any sales process, and every piece of it, and see gradual, unmistakable improvements over time. The answer lies in *split testing.*

Google Makes It So Easy

What makes Google so elegant is your ability to do such painlessly easy, real-time split testing of different ads. Take an ad that's getting a CTR of 1.1 percent, write a second one with smarter copy, and run it live against the first one, and discover after a few days or weeks that you've now got a CTR of 1.4 percent. Then delete the old ad and try another copy idea to run against the new winner. That one gets you a CTR of 1.6 percent.

You repeat this process over and over again, and find that you're eventually, after several weeks or months, pushing CTRs as high as 2.5 percent or better. Maybe even close to 3 percent.

Are you patient enough to do this? I'd virtually guarantee that most—not all—of your competitors are not. They're eventually going to tire of split testing, if they haven't already, and conclude that what they've got going is adequate.

> If you are patient enough, you can do what Brian did. He was ready to throw in the towel in March but by September had doubled his traffic, simply through his patient, methodical, can-do mindset of never giving up while making just the slightest incremental steps forward.
>
> When you combine the power of split testing with the force of attrition, you'll come out the winner.

NOUVEAUX SKIN CARE COMPANY GETS AN UNEXPECTED TURN IN ADVERTISING

Julie Brumlik, who sold an exotic skin care product using Google, happened to have a huge advantage coming into the game: Her product had already proven itself and she had been able to get celebrity endorsements, even winding up on Oprah's show.

When she joined our Bobsled Run program, we advised her to use her keywords in her ads—especially the headlines. This was based on good experience; she tried it and did fine. But split testing new ideas all the time will sometimes bring you new insights that even beat otherwise sound advice.

Julie followed her hunches and tried a different approach:

<u>Wrinkles Instantly Vanish</u>
www.celebritybeautysecret.com
Oprah, Melanie, Goldie, Demi, Nora,
Beyonce, Marisa and Dr. Weil Agree
2.0% CTR

<u>As seen on *Oprah*</u>
www.celebritybeautysecret.com
Age-Defying natural product line
for skin care. Erases wrinkles!
2.2% CTR

10 percent improvement. Not bad.

Don't miss this though: Julie tried this new "As Seen on *Oprah*" headline and it worked for *some* of her keywords. But not for all of them. The only way to know was to split test in each ad group and see where it worked and where it didn't.

It's no exaggeration to say that *every keyword literally represents a different market.* Julie's approach appealed to women who respect Oprah. In a number of cases it worked but not in all. And eventually the Oprah empire stepped in and demanded that she no longer use Oprah's name in her ads. Julie had no choice but to comply.

Some keywords represented markets where the headline appeal to Oprah turned the trick. In other cases it was a flop. That's the real world for you.

AMERICA'S SECOND HARVEST WINS BY ATTRITION AND WE DONATE TO HURRICANE KATRINA VICTIMS

Our business supports micro-enterprises and AIDS orphans in impoverished countries, from Haiti to Africa. Need knows no political boundaries.

One U.S. organization stood out from the crowd, however, and I parted with a donation based solely on its brilliant marketing approach. America's Second Harvest has an ingeniously simple message: It purchases un-bought groceries from supermarkets before the products reach expiration and distributes them to the needy.

Its costs of doing this are ridiculously low, and it hits you with a clear and simple claim:

> Every $1.00 you give provides four bags of groceries!

How could you not give to a cause like this, when you know your dollar is stretching that far?

I gave once and continued to receive mailings. It doesn't just send plain, dreary letters begging for money every time. Actually, no two mailings ever look alike.

Each one comes in a different shape and size. One is a large, lumpy, clear package. Another is a postmarked lunch sack. Still another is a full-color brochure on how to volunteer with the needy in your local community.

Always full of pictures, always interesting, always fresh. At Thanksgiving in November it wowed me with a matching promotion offer to buy 300 Thanksgiving meals for just $20.00.

How could I not give?

When Hurricane Katrina devastated the Louisiana Gulf Coast in late 2005, we were bombarded left and right with requests from all across the United States to donate.

Even though I had prioritized giving to third-world causes, sure enough, a letter came—from America's Second Harvest, saying that it was in the thick of feeding hurricane victims through its program, and would I please contribute.

It was a no-brainer. By this time the ASH letters were a welcome and regular part of every week, and I trusted them. My first gift to Second Harvest had been small, but it kept at me. So when disaster struck and it was there again like a familiar visitor, I gave big this time.

The people behind the ASH effort are no slackers. They understand that you win by attrition. Others drop off the radar, but you stand strong—and you win. You always win. This is true with Google; this is true with any marketing effort you put forth.

Harrison Ford landed the part of Han Solo through attrition and a fair share of luck. For you it doesn't need to be luck at all. You've got Google's outstanding system for split testing and the flow of traffic from all over the world to vet your sales funnel.

Uncle Claude Sez

Advertising and merchandising become exact sciences. Every course is charted. The compass of accurate knowledge directs the shortest, safest, cheapest course to any destination. We learn the principles and prove them by repeated tests. . . . We compare one way with many others, backward and forward, and record the results.

When one method invariably proves best, that method becomes a fixed principle. . . . One ad compared to another, one method with another. Headlines, settings, sizes, arguments and pictures are compared. . . . So no guesswork is permitted.

. . . We test everything pertaining to advertising. We answer nearly every possible question by multitudinous traced returns. Some things we learn in this way apply only to particular lines. . . . Others apply to all lines. They become fundamentals for advertising in general. They are universally applied. No wise advertiser will ever depart from those unvarying laws.

Chapter 25

How to Get High Rankings in Google's Organic (Non-PPC) Search Results

Pay-per-click traffic is great, and you have 100 percent control of it. However, if you have a listing on the *left* side of Google instead of the right side, it'll often generate at least twice as much traffic, and sometimes *better* traffic. Plus that traffic is free.

■ ■ ■

Getting to the left side of the page is often a function of Search Engine Optimization. SEO can really pay off big-time. Ignore it at your peril!

Before doing SEO, you need to pick your battles. Your PPC work tells you which keywords are valuable and how valuable they are; now you can selectively choose keywords to optimize.

Sometimes in super-competitive markets, PPC expenses generate a negative ROI and your actual profit comes from SEO traffic. But you would never have gotten SEO without the PPC intelligence. The two work together. You dollar-cost-average all your traffic sources. In combination, they gain you new customers profitably.

The rest of this chapter is by Stephen Mahaney and Kristi Hagen of Planet Ocean. I read their Search Engine Newsletter every month as soon as it comes out. From the beautiful state of Hawaii, here are Stephen and Kristi with a brief but highly relevant tutorial on Search Engine Optimization.

SEARCH ENGINE OPTIMIZATION

by Stephen Mahaney and Kristi Hagen of Planet Ocean

Years of experience and research have taught us a simple truth. (It's the reason Perry Marshall invited us to contribute a chapter to this book.) That truth is:

> True online success comes from blending the most effective marketing strategies to create that complete online presence to put your business in front of as many people as possible—getting you the most conversions.

Perry and his team know the importance of balancing your marketing efforts, and how powerful the combination of PPC and SEO can be. We're going to show you how the PPC knowledge you already have can be applied to optimize your site for the search engines, making it work double-time for you.

Before you even think about doing any actual site optimization, you need to know how to pick your battles. All of your work and research within the PPC industry puts you far ahead of most beginners. You already know one of the top three aspects of SEO—how to research and find the best keywords. Now you can apply that same knowledge and selectively choose the right keywords to optimize.

Believe it or not, the secret to building a high-ranking website can be boiled down to three simple steps:

1. Build a site that's easy for search engines to find and index.
2. Make proper use of the keywords that customers use when searching for your product or service.
3. Locate the so-called "important" websites that are similar in topic to your own and get them to link to your site.

Although Search Engine Optimization (SEO) can seem mysterious, especially if you're just starting out, 90 percent of it is really just focused on finding ways to achieve the above three simple steps.

Of course, while these steps may be easy to understand, they can be a bit more challenging to accomplish. That's why many of the best marketers start out using PPC to test the effectiveness of their site's landing pages and keywords. Then, once they know they have a site with a low bounce rate and high conversions, they branch out into organic search because, after all, those clicks are technically free.

In other words, if your system is working in AdWords, it's also very likely to be profitable in organic search as well. The big catch is that scoring at, or near, the top of the organic search results can take time and patience. On the other hand, a well-run AdWords campaign can drive traffic to your site almost instantaneously. So if you're new to SEO, then keep in mind that a good organic search campaign takes time to build.

In any case, by understanding the fundamental building blocks of SEO, you'll be better able to avoid wasting time and energy on strategies that have no effect, or worse, could even harm your page's position in the organic search results.

HOW TO GET STARTED WITH SEO

First off, your web pages have to be easy for search engines to find and process. Seems easy enough, but you would be surprised to know how many people are completely unaware that their web pages are configured to be difficult or *even impossible* for search engines to index. They come to us baffled—asking how and why their site isn't doing better in the search results.

Some of the most common reasons are:

· long and difficult to crawl dynamic URLs
· poor use of page redirection
· pages that use images when they should be using text
· over-reliance on Flash and JavaScript

The good news, ironically, is that while there are many ways to kill a site's ability to be indexed by search engines, they're all relatively easy to avoid.

The technical details for dealing with each of these could fill a book, but you'll be pleased to know that Google offers a service called *Google Webmaster Tools*. One of the many great tools featured there is a site-map tool designed to make sure your pages get into Google's index. You can find this at: www.google.com/webmasters/tools.

For a more in-depth analysis of how to fix the technical glitches that scare off search engines, check out a good SEO manual like Planet Ocean's *UnFair Advantage Search Engine Book* and its monthly publication Search Engine News (www. PlanetOceanNewsletter.com).

It's also important to know that making your site search engine friendly, by itself, won't propel you to the top of the rankings. It's really more about avoiding the mistakes that will *damage* your search engine rankings. To achieve that top spot, you need to take the next step and understand the essential role that keywords and inbound links play.

What will get your site to rank at the top of the results for your chosen keywords is leveraging the following two truths:

1. *Keywords tell search engines what your page is about.*
2. *Inbound links tell search engines that your page is important.*

It may surprise you to know that, although keywords are a critical part of search engine optimization, inbound links—and the keywords found within those links—actually have a far greater effect on ranking than the keywords found on the web page itself. In fact, we've seen cases where high ranking pages didn't even contain the keyword that they were ranking for. Instead, in every such case, the page had inbound links that displayed the keyword in the visible text of the link (also known as the *anchor text*).

Of course, similar to AdWords, finding the *right keywords* plays a crucial role in letting a search engine know what search queries your pages should be displayed for. Once found, your best keywords should then be placed into your web page's viewable content. However, strictly from a ranking perspective, you'll find that *building quality incoming links to your site* is the single most effective approach you can take when it comes to ranking well over the long run. In fact,

> *A link to your page from an important site that uses your keywords in the anchor (or viewable) text of the link will likely produce a more positive ranking effect than all of your other ranking efforts combined!*

That's why link building is the most important component to getting your web pages ranked highly in the search engines.

BE REALISTIC IN YOUR TIME-FRAME EXPECTATIONS

Getting to the top of the search engine results for popular keywords is a gradual process. Chances are some of your competitors may already have a fairly robust SEO program up and running. It's also possible they've been on the web for a long time, and these days, *time* is a search engine optimizer's greatest friend—or worst enemy, depending on your perspective. If a search engine has already determined that your competitor is the most relevant site for a particular keyword, then you should expect that it will take some time and effort to make that search engine change its mind.

Achieving top listings for a competitive keyword can often take six months to a year or more. Focus on gradually adding more and more relevant links while improving the overall quality of your site and you will reach the top of the search results. If you're building a top-quality site with great inbound links, your hard work will pay off. For competitive keywords, that's the only way it can be done. This is a fact that can make life difficult for professional SEOs, since so many clients unrealistically expect immediate results.

Again, that's why so many professional online marketing specialists use pay-per-click (AdWords) to gain the immediate traffic they need to test their systems and juice their profits. This buys you time while your organic search strategies are allowed to grow, mature, and ultimately blossom into top rankings.

Provided that your SEO strategies are focused on creating valuable content and getting links from important, topically related sites, your top-ranking website can become a cost-effective *money making machine*.

KEYWORD SELECTION FOR ORGANIC SEARCH RANKING SUCCESS

If you have experience in keyword selection for an AdWords campaign, you'll find there are many similarities that transfer nicely to search engine optimization. For example, an AdWords campaign might focus on finding overlooked and underutilized keywords in order to get clicks for cheap.

In SEO, pages can be built around the concept that these overlooked keywords will also be easier to rank in the organic search results, especially in the beginning stages of optimization. The *Google Keyword Tool* is a great way to find these bargain keywords, just as in pay-per-click keyword selection: adwords.google.com/select/KeywordToolExternal.

Planet Ocean's *UnFair Advantage Search Engine Book* devotes an entire section to keyword selection strategies. There you can learn how to find the right keywords that allow you to get easy customer traffic from niches that your competition has overlooked.

Just remember that if you're competing only in popular keyword searches *where the majority of your competition is focusing their efforts*, you'll need lots of really good links to get to the top of the organic search results. By no means is that impossible—it just takes time.

KEYWORD PLACEMENT FOR ORGANIC SEARCH RANKING SUCCESS

To succeed in the organic search results over the long term, it's important to get your best keywords inserted into the appropriate places. Clearly there are on-page keyword placement locations, but there are also off-page locations that are extremely effective.

On-page locations include:

· Title tag

- Meta description tag
- Headline tags (H1, H2, H3...)
- Body copy

These are the most critical placements. In addition there is the element of *proximity* to consider. This is especially true when optimizing for two or more combined keywords that make up a keyphrase. It's better to place the keywords that make up a keyphrase *close* to each other. Also, it's better when the keywords appear early in the page's content. Usually, you can just keep in mind—the earlier the better.

Off-page locations include:

- The *anchor text* of your incoming links
- The domain name and file name

Having your keywords in the actual link that points to your page is very, very important. Having the keyword in the URL also tells both the search engine and the potential site visitor that the page is relevant to the keyword being searched for.

For example: www.doghouses.com is the perfect URL if you want to rank for the keyword phrase "dog houses."

HOW TO GET NATURAL LOOKING LINKS FROM IMPORTANT PAGES

One of the trickiest aspects of SEO is the process of building high-quality incoming links. It's also the single most important thing you can do to improve your rankings.

The challenge for most sites is to accumulate enough incoming links to appear relevant to the engines *without* tripping any one of the many spam filters and penalties that are applied to sites that (in the eyes of Google) cheat. The secret to getting it right is to take the search engine's point of view when building your incoming link structure.

The key point to remember is that search engines prefer a natural link structure to an artificial link structure. Some of the qualities associated with an "artificial" link structure are:

- Most inbound anchor text is identical
- A site's inbound link count increases suddenly
- The site links out to link farms or web rings
- A high percentage of links are reciprocal

Here are some of the qualities associated with a "natural" link structure:

- Inbound anchor text varies
- Inbound link count increases gradually

- The site links out to only reputable pages
- Links are rarely reciprocal

From the search engine's point of view natural links vary in anchor text, whereas artificial links tend to be identical. Natural links increase gradually over time as other sites add links to your site one by one. Artificial links can sprout in great numbers all of a sudden. When they do, the search engine often suspects they are either purchased or artificially manipulated in some other way. This is especially true when they don't see corresponding traffic, social media, or search signals that correspond with a natural link boost, such as when a company is mentioned in the news.

Sites designed around natural links don't usually swap links, so their outgoing links tend to point to pages that are already known by the engine to be in good standing. Oftentimes, these pages have been indexed for many years and may even be white-listed—a term that identifies trusted sites that are somewhat impervious to penalty.

Artificial links, however, often rely heavily on link exchange tactics, in which the sole purpose of the link is reciprocity. These links have little or nothing to do with adding value for the site visitor by way of linking to worthwhile content. Sites designed around artificial links will have outgoing links that point to pages that resemble link farms, web rings, or isolated nodes (i.e., groups of pages linking to each other but lacking inbound links from outside trusted sites).

Keeping these facts in mind, one should strive to build the most natural-looking incoming link structure possible. From the search engine's point of view, the best kinds of links are unsolicited ones. The engines are looking to bestow high rankings on only those pages that people voluntarily link to due to great content—not because some webmaster has spent a lot of time swapping links.

CHOOSE YOUR LINKS WISELY

Authoritative pages, those pages considered by search engines to be among the most important on the web, provide the very best links. One way to determine a page's authority is to use Google's PageRank scoring system, which you can access by downloading the Google Toolbar at: www.toolbar.google.com.

A simple rule of thumb is this: The higher the PageRank, the better the link. Of course, PageRank is not the only metric you should use in your site analysis, but it is an easy "quick and dirty" way to determine how important Google considers a web page.

Examples of authoritative directory sites include Yahoo's Directory and DMOZ, while extremely well-known sites like www.PBS.org, www.NationalGeographic.com, www.NASA.gov, www.CNN.com, and www.ZDNet.com would also be considered exceptionally authoritative.

GET LINKS FROM TRUSTED PAGES THAT MATCH YOUR TOPIC

Your next best option is to acquire links from sites that are trusted. Trusted sites are those that, while not necessarily top authorities themselves, are linked to from sites that are authorities. Trusted sites generally have been around for a few years, have lots of great content, and have established themselves as a credible online resource.

It helps even more if the pages linking to you from these trusted sites are on-topic—i.e., they match the topic of your page. Links from on-topic trusted pages can give you a significant boost in rankings, and can be an exceptional source of direct referrals as well.

COUNT THE NUMBER OF LINKS ON THE REFERRING PAGE

Another point to remember is the fewer the number of links on the referring page, the better. Ideally, the referring page would have only one link and it would be to your page. Of course, that's rarely the case. However, having your link on a page with 100 other links is much less effective because the value of your link will be divided by the number of links on the page—a condition we call *link dilution*.

While easier said than done, try to get your incoming links from popular, on-topic, high-PageRank pages that have few outgoing links and are found on trusted sites. And if you can control how those links are formatted (in terms of your keywords appearing in the anchor text), you'll be in even better shape.

AVOID GETTING INVOLVED WITH RUN-OF-THE-SITE LINKS

Run-of-the-site links are when every page of a site links to you. Many times you will see these links appearing in the footer of a site. When you have 1,000 incoming links all originating from the same site, it appears to search engines that your link count is artificially inflated. This is because when people buy links from other sites, those paid links are often run-of-site. Thus, search engines have come to view such links with great suspicion.

MAINTAIN CONSISTENCY IN THE FORMAT OF YOUR INCOMING LINK URLS

You may not be aware of the fact that the following pages are viewed by the search engines as four different URLs, in spite of the fact that each of them will land the site visitor on the same page.

· http://your-site.com
· http://your-site.com/index.html

· www.your-site.com
· www.your-site.com/index.html

If your incoming links are all pointed to these four different URL formats, then your page's link popularity is being diluted by a factor of four. This is not good!

Therefore, do everything in your power to standardize your incoming link URLs in order to consolidate your page's link popularity (i.e., PageRank). Doing this simple thing will produce the maximum boost possible from your incoming links.

GET YOUR KEYWORDS INTO YOUR ANCHOR TEXT

It's very important that you get your main keywords into the visible text of the link (anchor text) that other sites are using to point visitors your way. The boost in keyword relevancy is significant enough that it's worthwhile to contact everyone who is linking to you with a specific request regarding the text being used in your link.

For example: If you happen to be selling model airplanes, then anchor text such as *airplane models* or *model airplanes* will be infinitely more valuable to your relevance efforts than anchor text simply saying *click here*. From the search engine's point of view, the former states the topic of your page while the latter tells them nothing. This strategy alone can make a *huge* difference. Generally speaking, the search engines consider the *anchor text* as one of the largest influences in determining the topic of your web page.

A word of caution: It will look more natural to the search engines if the text used within the links pointing to your site is not all identical. Strive to maintain slight variations, as would occur if the sites that are maintaining those links were generating the anchor text independent of your influence.

GO FOR DEEP LINKS

Be sure that some of your links are deep links—i.e., links to pages within your site other than your homepage. Again, this makes your inbound links more natural. It also tells search engines that you have valuable content on your site, since those other sites are linking directly to your content pages rather than pointing all their links directly at your homepage. Getting deep links is especially important on large sites, such as an ecommerce site with thousands of product pages.

BEWARE OF THE "NOFOLLOW" TAG

See to it that your incoming links do not include the rel="nofollow" attribute within the source code of the link. Nofollow renders the link useless to your ranking efforts because Google doesn't credit your page for that incoming link.

BE CAREFUL WHO YOU LINK TO!

Avoid anything that looks like *an artificial effort to manipulate the engines*. That includes trading links with questionable or topically unrelated sites. Linking to these sort of unnatural linking structures can get you penalized, so always be very careful about whom you link to.

Here are three cautionary steps you should take before linking to another site:

1. Search for their domain name on Google and Bing. If they are not listed on at least one of the engines, that's a very bad sign. However, if they *are* listed, you can proceed to step two.

2. Determine who is already linking to them and how many of those are unique domains. The number of incoming links they have from the most diverse number of unique domains, the better. This means it's typically far more important to have 1,000 links from 100 unique domains than 1,000 links from 10 unique domains. And the more authoritative the sites are that link to them are—the better. Their PageRank score is one indicator of how important Google thinks the site is.

   Planet Ocean's *Site Strength Indicator* (SSI) tool (available to SearchEngineNews. com members) can be used to determine who is linking to *you, your competition,* or *any other site.* This is a great tool to use when *analyzing the competitive ranking strength of sites* or *for prospecting for good link partners.* It's located at: www.SSITool.com.

   Beware of linking to sites or pages that have a PageRank = 0. This could mean that Google has penalized them. Granted, this may not apply to very new sites that haven't earned any PageRank yet, and occasionally the Toolbar PageRank information may be messed up at the time you looked. However, if a site has been around for a while and lacks PageRank, then you be wary of linking to it.

3. Avoid linking to sites with controversial topics. Good examples of such sites would include gambling, adult, pharmacy, or loan/debt sites (unless you happen to be in one of these industries and the topic matches the content of your page).

Remember: You can definitely be hurt by who you link to, so choose your link partners carefully.

TRAIN YOUR EYE ON THE PRIMARY GOAL—PROFITS!

Of course, our biggest assumption is that you're optimizing your site with profits in mind. That being the case, you'll want to always focus your efforts on strategies and relationships that will generate the most revenue relative to effort. Therefore, you want to look for link relationships that will produce the type of traffic that fits the profile of your customer market.

While it's true that incoming links from just about any legitimate site provide a slight boost to your rankings, such links all too often fail to produce targeted traffic, which is what you really should be looking for. This is one of the many reasons a link from a topic-related site is immeasurably better than a link from an off-topic site. That on-topic traffic also generates very good signals that we want the engines to see, such as low bounce rates, high time on site, and ideally repeat visits.

THE BEST PLACE TO START GETTING LINKS

Rather than swapping links (which is arguably the most difficult and least productive link-building strategy), consider some of your alternative options for acquiring incoming links. Probably the best place to start is by submitting your site to web directories. Besides the two heavyweights—Yahoo Directory and DMOZ—there are others that come and go. Refer to Planet Ocean's "Ultimate Directory List" at: http://budurl.com/directorychart. There you can see which ones are currently worth your time and effort to submit to.

Some of these directories are free and some charge a fee which, when considering the value of your time, might be worth it to get a new site's foot in the link-popularity door. To add your site, look around on the directory's main page for a link that says something like "Add URL," "Suggest URL," "Add Your Site," or "Suggest a Site." Follow that link to get details on exactly how to add your site to its directory.

By the way, to avoid unnecessary delays in getting listed, be sure to submit your site to the *proper category* within each directory. Submitting your site to the wrong category can result in a ridiculously long delay, getting listed in a category that isn't getting indexed by the engines, or simply not getting listed at all. Remember that the directory editors receive an enormous number of site submissions, so save yourself some grief by carefully considering exactly which category your site belongs in *before* submitting. You should also verify that your chosen category is in a search engines index. Go to both Google and Bing and type in: *www.directoryname.com/category/you/want/* to see if the category page is even indexed. If it's not in the index, getting listed there will do you no good.

Also, when getting listed in directories, be sure they provide a direct, static link to your site. Some directories will send your link through a script running on their own servers so they can track who clicked on the link and then send the link on to your site. This is called a redirected link and is useless for boosting search rank. Although this may add to your traffic count, it does nothing to help your search engine ranking efforts. This is because engines fail to see the connection between the redirected link and your site's actual URL.

LINK OUTSIDE THE BOX

Deciding where to get your incoming links from is like solving a puzzle. It takes a little creativity coupled with various formulas and patterns. The following are several of our favorite strategies for building quality inbound links.

First, ask yourself: Who else has a site that might benefit from linking to me? Suppliers you do business with or professional organizations you're involved in might be willing to list you on their referrals page. Legal advisors, accountants, or financiers you do business with might also like to list you as a client or maybe showcase your business in their online portfolio. Your employees may have blogs or personal homepages that could link to you, and so forth.

Article Marketing

Many online business owners write articles about topics related to their site. They then offer to let other sites publish the articles in exchange for a link back to their site. You are probably an expert in the business you're in and therefore an authority on certain subjects that may lend themselves to interesting reading.

Look for compatible (but not competing) businesses, and then form a partnership where you link to each other actively through mutual promotion. The best partnerships come from websites that are useful to your customers and whose customers will find your site useful as well. Not only can this bring in new traffic and boost your PageRank, but you may also develop important business relationships this way.

Press Releases

Press releases are also an excellent way to gain relevant links to your company's site. Again, be creative—chances are that there's a number of reasons (product launches, staff additions, promotions, partnerships, new services, etc.) you can find to release news about your company to the press. The engines quickly pick up press releases and the links contained within them are typically trusted. They also tend to remain on the web for a good long time. Here's a great resource on optimizing your press releases for today's markets: http://budurl.com/optimizingpr.

Testimonials

Another interesting way to promote your own site is to submit testimonials to other sites about products they offer that you are really enthusiastic about. If the testimonial is well written, companies will often post it on their site. Ask them to include a link back to your site with your testimonial. Often they will if you ask.

Here's one of the most potentially productive tips: **Find out who's linking to your competitors and convince them to link to you instead.** To find out who's linking to your competition, enter their URL into Planet Ocean's *Site Strength Indicator* tool at: www. SSITool.com/.

Bear in mind that whenever you're successful in getting someone to switch their link to you, you gain twice: Once for gaining a new link and a second time for reducing the incoming link count of your competitor.

By using your imagination and dovetailing the nuances of your own business into the mix, you'll no doubt discover a plethora of opportunities for gaining legitimate incoming links.

THE PROBLEM WITH RECIPROCAL LINKS

Your best strategy in terms of *reciprocal links* as a link-building tactic is to *be conservative*. This is because when done badly in the eyes of Google, it is viewed as an artificial linking pattern—something that search engines are getting increasingly sophisticated about detecting.

When you think about it, it makes sense that having a high percentage of reciprocal links would look like an artificial linking pattern because natural links are not typically reciprocal. If Yahoo lists a site in its directory, that site doesn't routinely link back to Yahoo; that's one of the reasons a link coming from Yahoo looks "natural" to Google.

Of course there are plenty of exceptions, but, regardless, the engines are looking for pages that rank well due to popularity based on content, all while avoiding sites where it appears the site owners (or hired SEOs) have put a lot of effort into swapping links.

So, look at your incoming links from the search engine's point of view. If CNN runs an article about how great your company is, and your company's site links back to the CNN article, does that look normal? . . . sure it does. Besides, CNN is an authoritative, important site. This specific link exchange looks natural and your site's page can expect a substantial boost in rankings.

On the other hand, if your site (with its PageRank=4 or 5) is linked to by Joe Blow's homepage (with a PR=1, 2, or 3) and you link back to Joe's page, you shouldn't expect any boost in your rankings. In fact, it's entirely possible the two links are discounting each other based on an assumed link exchange arrangement that looks contrived because the search engines view neither page as "authoritative."

On the other hand, if you had 50 similar link arrangements with all the links being on-topic, and none of the pages involved had tripped the spam filters, then your page should get a reasonable boost in rankings. Still, you'd fare better by simply getting a single link from an authoritative site like CNN, Yahoo Directory, DMOZ, ZDNet, and so forth.

A good rule of thumb to use for links is to ask yourself a simple question: Will real people actually click on this link and visit the page? If you can honestly answer that question with a "Yes," then it's probably going to be a positive signal for the search engines. Great content that is valuable to people naturally acquires links over a long term and the engines can detect this. Great content is something people share and will link to.

CREATING AND PROMOTING *BUZZ* TO TURBO-CHARGE YOUR WEBSITE RANKINGS!

One of the most powerful ways to *quickly* build inbound links is to create a useful tool, video, or comprehensive written resource designed to spread across the web via word-of-mouth—*viral marketing*. SEO's often refer to such content as *linkbait*, since you're creating highly useful or entertaining content with the goal of compelling bloggers and other website owners to link to it (i.e., take the bait).

Often the easiest and most effective linkbait comes in the form of a detailed list with a catchy headline. We recommend making a list of topics your customers are interested in and then start cranking out articles that are loosely focused on your niche, featuring titles that begin like:

- 100 Tools and Resources for . . .
- 50 Tips to . . .
- 100+ Resources to Help You . . .
- 75 Online Resources for . . .
- 30+ Simple Things You Can Do to . . .
- 25 Ways to . . .

At its simplest, an article can be *"100 Resources for . . ."* followed by whatever your niche is, with a list of 100 sites, tools, and articles you've found online related to that topic and a short summary of each. You'll be pleasantly surprised to learn how many people will link to such articles and resource lists. By promoting this kind of content on social media sites like www.Digg.com, www.StumbleUpon.com, and www.Delicious.com, you can quickly reach a large audience of people who are very likely to link to your content.

DON'T SWEAT THE SMALL STUFF

You can't always control who links to you, so if you have a few low-quality or off-topic links pointing at your site, don't stress. Every site has a few off-topic links pointing to it. In fact, a small number of off-topic links makes your link structure appear even more natural. However, you should strive to make the bulk of your incoming links come from topically relevant sources.

CATCHING THE LOCAL SEARCH TIDAL WAVE

We've discussed the details of keyword placement and link building, but businesses with a brick-and-mortar presence targeting a regional audience should also be aware of the ever increasing importance of local search. Perry and Bryan have discussed using local targeting in AdWords to reach prospects via pay-per-click. However, you may not know that Google does something very similar in the organic search results too!

While the intricacies of *listing your business in Google's local search results* could fill a book by itself, you'll be pleased to know that Planet Ocean also offers a great guide to local search that you can find here: www.LocalSearchManual.com.

If your business has a physical location that directly services walk-in customers, then we can't stress enough the importance of creating a Google Place Page account and adding your business, or claiming your business if it's already listed.

WHAT REALLY SMART ONLINE MARKETERS DO

Smart online marketing professionals are multidimensional in their strategies. They seldom put all of their eggs in a single basket. This is especially true in regards to pay-per-click and organic search marketing efforts. Because so many aspects of the two strategies run parallel to each other, it makes good sense to understand how both work. This allows you to employ them in unison so your efforts work double-duty and your results are exponentially multiplied.

As you test your keywords, benefits, and features to learn what's working in your AdWords campaigns, it just makes sense to redeploy your successes along organic search as well. Failing to do so means you are probably leaving easy money on the table! Sometimes a LOT of money! We know of instances where successful AdWords campaigns have laid the groundwork for enormously successful and very long running organic search marketing campaigns—and at a fraction of the overall cost of maintaining the initial pay-per-click campaign.

As mentioned, success in the organic search results takes some time and patience. AdWords is quicker in the near term but arguably more expensive. (Note: PPC is not always more expensive than SEO!) However, by using AdWords to help you test and map out your organic strategies, it's possible to build a long-term cash cow with the potential for success that can run indefinitely and at a cost so low it's borderline free in the long run.

Bear in mind that this chapter is merely an organic SEO strategy primer. Therefore we will close by highly recommending the following resources since this is where we've obtained all of the info within this chapter—reprinted with permission, of course—as a sampling of Planet Ocean's in-depth research and useful resources:

- *The UnFair Advantage Book on Winning The Search Engine Wars*—http://Advantage. PlanetOceanNewsletter.com
- Planet Ocean's Members-Only Monthly Publication—SearchEngineNews.com, www.PlanetOceanNewsletter.com
- Get on the Map! Complete Guide to Getting Your Local Business Online, www. LocalSearchManual.com

Planet Ocean has been specializing in teaching people how to rank their sites at the top of the organic search results since 1997. It is the pioneer in the field and remains one of the foremost authorities on the subject—a trusted source for solid, long-term SEO strategy. It is the resource we use when mapping out our own organic search marketing strategies.

Chapter 26

Introduction to Remarketing

By Jeff Martyka, Neckties Inc.

Last summer my nephew told me he was going to get a new bike for his birthday. I asked him how he planned on convincing his parents to buy it for him. "Easy," he said. "They'll ask me, and I'll tell them what I want."

■ ■ ■

I realized he had made the same strategic error that many businesses make. He was going to take one shot, and one shot only, at closing the deal with Mom and Dad. No further followup, no method to ensure they bought him the model he wanted—nothing.

Most buying decisions aren't made easily, whether you're a parent deciding what to buy your son for his birthday, or making other, more weighty purchasing choices.

In the case of my nephew, he needed a way to "remarket" to his parents! So let's reframe the situation: We have a nephew (website) that has been asked by his parents (shoppers) what he wants for his birthday. He says he wants a bike (landing page). Does he get the bike with this minimal a marketing plan? Maybe . . . maybe not.

To help my nephew out I developed a "remarketing campaign" to get repeated "impressions" in front of his parents so they would be more likely to buy him the exact bike he wanted. He drew pictures of himself with a giant grin and put them in his parents' cars so they might take and display them at work. He cut out ads from the newspaper showing the bike he wanted and taped them to his parents' bathroom mirrors. He found articles about how children in the United States are obese and need exercise, and he taped those to the refrigerator. And while his dad was out in the driveway washing the car, he pulled his own (old) bike out of the garage and washed it right there in Dad's full view.

This is what remarketing is all about. You find highly targeted traffic that visits your internet property and redeliver messages to those prospects on the various sites where they spend time. That's how you get more sales . . . or in my nephew's case, a new bicycle.

Remarketing is a technology for showing ads to people that in some way big or small you've already interacted with. It's not necessarily a new concept; businesses have been collecting targeted leads for years by asking for names and phone numbers or addresses. Remarketing on the web is the same idea; it just uses more modern technology to track a person's activity on his or her web browser.

The best leads are people who were "warm" enough to visit your site once. Remarketing is just another method to encourage them to come back. It follows the principles of Perry's Tactical Triangle—traffic, conversion, and economics, all obeying the 80/20 principle—but its primary focus is conversion.

Privacy is a very real concern with remarketing. People bristle at the thought that they're being "tracked" or "followed" around the internet with a particular advertiser's ads. Google's remarketing tool does not track individuals; in only tracks specific web browsers on specific devices that access the internet.

It's important that your visitors be made aware that their browser can be tracked, and be informed of how to remove the tracking should they wish to do so. Incognito windows or Private Browsing windows can be created by most major web browsers that will prevent such tracking. And Google of course requires that you address this issue in your privacy policy. More on that in a bit.

Remarketing is more about gaining (and regaining) eyeballs and mind share than perhaps any other advertising platform within Google AdWords because it is focused on acquiring a conversion from someone who has already visited and taken action on your website.

Is Remarketing for Me?

Remarketing may be the most difficult feature within AdWords to measure in hard numbers. It doesn't give you the immediate feedback that Google Search does. It's not like posting an ad for "red wagon" where you get the click, sell the wagon, and call it good. Rather, you create leads. They're only mildly warm at first. But they do grow hotter the more contact you have with them.

You probably wouldn't walk into a car dealership for the first time and drive off in a new car an hour later. More than likely, you'd go online to search out the car that best meets your needs. Then you might go to an auto show. You might drive up to an hour one way to see the offers at all the dealers in your area.

Don't forget this: You are being bombarded the whole time with billboards and magazine ads. All of these are designed to get you constantly thinking about that brand.

Remarketing is no different. A person visits your site and Google marks his or her web browser so that targeted ads can be served to it. Those are warm leads that you'll want to return to you. Unless your site already converts nearly everyone who visits (and few sites do!), you're a good candidate for remarketing.

TERMINOLOGY

Here are a few remarketing terms you'll want to become familiar with:

- *Audience.* An audience is a collection of web browsers through which your site has been visited. You can define an audience: It might be comprised of everyone who visited a particular page or it could be people who made a specific purchase.
- *Combination.* A collection of audiences or conversions.
- *Retargeting.* This is just a synonym for remarketing. Many large organizations that specialize in this form of advertising call it "retargeting."
- *Privacy policy.* Your privacy policy will need to be updated so that your visitors are aware that you will be using cookies stored on their browsers and serving ads based upon their behaviors. They'll need a way to "opt out" of your advertising as well. That's a strict Google requirement if you plan to remarket.

Google's explanation of their privacy policy and its requirements can be found here: www.google.com/privacy/ads/.

HOW DO I KNOW IF MY REMARKETING IS WORKING?

Blind advertising is wasteful. Before launching any remarketing campaign you need to be sure your conversion tracking is set up properly, as that's your single best indicator of success.

WHAT REMARKETING INDICATORS DO I NEED TO PAY ATTENTION TO?

Some of the things you want to look at to determine the health of a remarketing campaign are:

- Direct conversions
- View-through conversions
- Path length and time lag
- Changes to domain name searches
- New vs. returning visitors

Direct Conversions

Within your campaign you'll be able to see which ads got clicks and conversions, just as with any other form of display advertising. After running remarketing for long periods of time, accounts typically end up breaking even on expenditure vs. sales.

View-Through Conversions

"View-through conversions" are the statistic used most often to determine the effectiveness of remarketing campaigns. A view-through conversion simply means a person saw your remarketing ad and eventually found his or her way to a page that had AdWords conversion tracking on it. This metric can be found in your AdWords account at the campaign or ad group level of your remarketing image ad campaign. (Note that text ads are not tracked for the purpose of view-through conversions.)

The art of view-through conversions lies in determining how to actually count them. Twenty-five percent is a good safe number to use when determining the success of a remarketing campaign.

To properly calculate this, multiply the attributed view-through conversion number by your average sale for returning visitors (a metric you can find within Google Analytics). Compare this with your spending on remarketing campaigns to get a ratio of cost to sales.

That may sound a bit confusing, so let me walk you through an example.

Let's say you have an account that has 723 view-through conversions in a given time period, at a cost of $1,446.12. And let's say that we find the average sale for returning visitors to be $43.18 over that same stretch of time.

The "sales/cost" column shows you how many dollars in sales these marketing efforts are bringing back to you, for every dollar you spend on advertising. (You'll also need to factor in the initial amount it cost to get the visitor to your site the first time.)

Attributed Percentage	View-Through Conversions	Average Sale	Remarketing Sales	Sales: Cost
10.00%	723	$43.18	$3,108.96	2.15:1
25.00%	723	$43.18	$7,772.40	5.37:1
33.00%	723	$43.18	$10,276.84	7.10:1
50.00%	723	$43.18	$15,587.98	10.77:1

Path Length

Path length tells you how many impressions or clicks it took before a visitor made a purchase. People are often surprised at how long it takes for purchases to occur. Sure, some visitors convert quickly. But you'll find that most folks who visit your site aren't immediately plopping down their credit card to make a purchase.

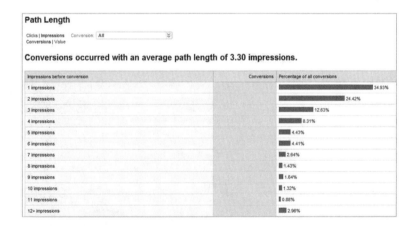

The Path Length and Time Lag reports can be found in your AdWords account by looking at the menu item "Tools and Analysis -> Conversions" and then choosing "Search Funnels" on the left. Note that these reports only give data for search ads running on Google.com. The path length and time lag are great to look at for trends but are not direct indicators of any impact of your remarketing campaigns.

Time Lag

Time lag from first impression again shows you why remarketing is so vital. While some sales occur immediately, compare the number of unique visitors to your site to the number that didn't make an immediate purchase. You'll find that there a lots of first-time visitors who require a good deal of wooing before they buy.

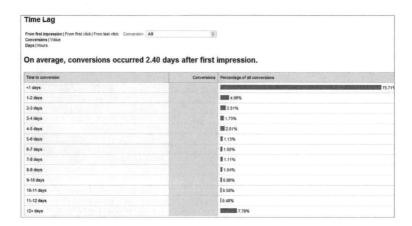

This report can be found in AdWords by going to "Tools and Analysis -> Conversions" and choosing Search Funnels on the left.

WHAT ARE SOME GOOGLE ANALYTICS REMARKETING INDICATORS?

If you are tracking your website performance with Google Analytics, there are a few more statistics you'll find valuable.

New vs. Returning Visitors

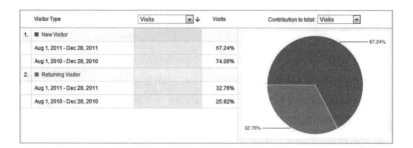

The Google Analytics report found under "Audience—>Behavior—>New vs Returning" is among the most telling reports. You're not after the total number of visits here—that number would increase simply by you creating more AdWords campaigns. Rather, what you're after here is your *percentage of returning visitors*. If you have a good remarketing campaign, that number should increase *significantly*.

Are More People Looking for You?

One good effect of a solid remarketing campaign is an increase in direct traffic. That specifically means more people typing your domain name in their address bar, or searching for your domain on Google. You can see these trends in Google Analytics by looking under "Traffic Sources—>Sources—>Direct" and "Traffic Sources—>Sources —>Organic," filtering to show just your domain name, and comparing a time period before you launched your remarketing campaign with an equivalent time period afterward.

ENOUGH TALK! LET'S CREATE SOME AUDIENCES

To create an audience, you'll need to be clear on three basic components:

- · The size of your audience
- · Combinations
- · Segmenting time

Size of Audience

An audience within Google AdWords must have at least 100 members. If you only get 100 visitors per year to an individual page, remarketing is probably not a good strategy for that page, unless you have an extremely long sales funnel or you sell a product that's purchased over some regular interval.

Audiences are accessed in your AdWords account below the campaign list on the left, under "Shared Library."

For your first audience, I suggest creating one called "Every Page." Leave the rest of the settings alone. (You can change the duration later by editing the "Membership duration" field for your list of audiences.)

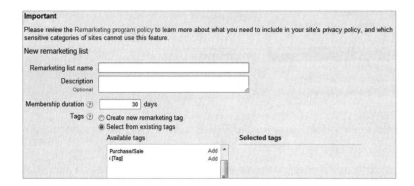

Once you've created this first audience you'll need to click on the tag. This will open a popup window containing the code you need to place on your website. It will also provide you a link to tips on how to correctly place that code on your site.

One consideration to be aware of is the security level of the page you're retargeting for. HTTP is the default. You should be sure that any conversion tags are set to the HTTPS security level. This is done by selecting the tag within the Shared Audiences and changing the Page security level setting.

Once that code is in place, you may not see any entries under the "Number of users" column for up to two days. That's a number that gets updated just once per day. It will show as few as one tagged user.

Next you want to create an audience for any conversions that occur. Again, you'll choose to add a new remarketing list, but this time choose "Select from existing tags." You'll see what conversion tracking you have in place. Those items will not have a [Tag] marker after them. Select the conversion tracking to create this audience.

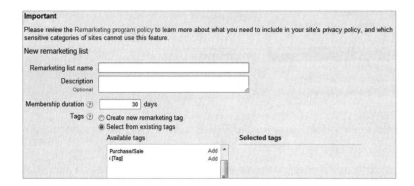

Combinations

A combination is a group of multiple audiences or conversions. You will most likely start with a combination list of everyone who has visited your site but didn't make a purchase.

The ability to manipulate this set is at the core of some very powerful advanced strategies.

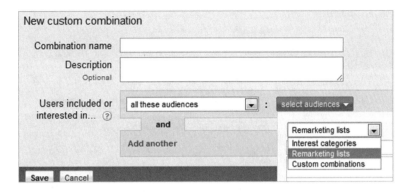

A basic combination you may want to create is "Users who visited a page but did not convert." To do so click on "New audience" again, but this time choose "Custom Combination."

To set the rules for this combination, we want to specify all of the people who visited a page but none of the ones who converted. That will be configured like this:

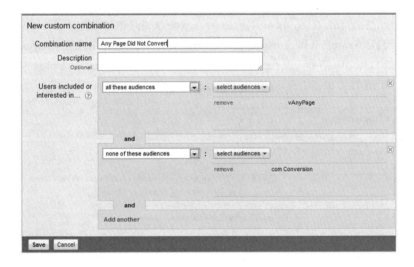

Segmenting Time

The same tag can be used multiple times. Place the tag on your site once and set it for different membership durations. For example, you might set this just to show people who visited your site 30 to 90 days ago.

In that case you would create your audience with a duration of 30 days. Then create an audience specifying the same tag and set the duration to 90 days.

You now have the basic components and are ready to create some campaigns.

CREATING REMARKETING CAMPAIGNS IN ADWORDS

The best practice structure is to create two campaigns: one for text ads and one for image ads. This structure allows you to control impressions per day by ad type. I would name my two campaigns "Remarketing Image" and "Remarketing Text."

In your campaign's settings under the "Networks and devices" section you'll want to turn off Google Search. The ads you're creating will only run on the Display Network. (You may also choose to target certain devices separately, such as Androids or iPads, just as you would with your other ad campaigns.)

HOW SHOULD I BID ON REMARKETING CAMPAIGNS?

Your bidding options are CPC or CPM. Each one has its advantages and disadvantages. I'll explain those here.

CPC

Cost-per-click bidding is what most people are used to. It can also be effective in remarketing. Generally you'll want to bid three to four times the amount you would normally bid per click on the Display Network, in order to get a substantial amount of impressions for your remarketing campaign. That might make you twitch a bit, but remember: People who return to your site through your remarketing efforts are *far more likely* to make a purchase.

CPM

Cost-per-thousand-impressions (CPM) bidding aligns very well with remarketing. Remember that the goal of remarketing is to buy eyeballs, and to gain mind share with your prospects.

I suggest starting out at a $2.00 CPM in order to gain some initial traction. More if you're in a pricey market.

You can then determine how many people are in your target audience and how many impressions *per day* you want them to receive. (You certainly don't want to overwhelm your prospects.) For example, if you have 1,000 people in your target audience and would like to display five ads to them per day, your maximum impressions would be set at 5,000. (In practice you might receive only 10 percent of that number.)

So Which is Better—CPM or CPC?

This depends on what your goals are. And it's something you may just need to test over time. For me, CPM bidding has usually resulted in lower total costs per click and higher numbers of impressions.

In this scenario, your cost per conversion will be higher than you're accustomed to. But that's OK, because you have a more immediate goal: impressions. The purpose of remarketing is to get your ads in front of more eyeballs.

Google directly controls how many impressions you get, which makes this bidding method more predictable for your purposes than just paying for clicks. That means you have a clearer sense of exactly what you're going to get for each dollar you spend. With CPM bidding you know you're going to get a solid and even distribution of impressions across your audience.

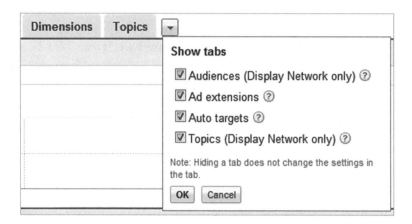

Keeping Your Audience Happy by Carefully Controlling Impressions

When doing remarketing there can be a fine line between respectful advertising and outright stalking.

I once went into a campaign that was set to show each of my ads up to five times a day per person and, without thinking about it, added 40 new ads to one of the ad groups in it. My customers suddenly got deluged with my ads on nearly every internet site they visited. I received some rather unhappy feedback from them for doing that.

Generally, 5 to 15 impressions per day work well. This is something you adjust under Advanced Settings.

The Lesson: Be *extremely* careful in choosing this number, unless you want lots of angry phone calls from lots of angry prospects. Any time you add new ads, consider this setting, and calculate how many impressions per day a user will be receiving.

Save this campaign to move on to ad groups.

ADD ADS

Next you'll want to create ads for your ad groups. Do not add any keywords, placements, or anything else that Google may offer at this point. You can work with those later, but for an initial remarketing campaign they'll only hinder your performance.

You'll save your initial ad group. Then and only then do you choose the Audiences tab. If you don't see this option in your interface, look over on the right for a dropdown arrow at the end of the row that lets you add the tab to your view.

Next you'll choose the "Custom Combinations" tab to find the combination we created earlier. Add that and save it.

You now have everything set up to run a basic remarketing campaign.

Ad Design Tips

The advertising message needs to match your customer's key desire and follow that through logically to the landing page. Your ad should be designed in such a way to make it clear that the ad is for your specific site. Use a graphical theme that's unique to you. Make use of your own colors or fonts, or images of your product. Your goal is to remind people again of a site they've visited but perhaps forgotten about.

Landing Pages

Remember: The visitors you're targeting have already been to your site. Give careful consideration to the landing pages you choose to send your remarketing traffic to.

Why didn't they make a purchase the first time? Did they have a trust issue? If you suspect that's the case, test sending them to a testimonial landing page. Were they uncertain about your shipping options? Try sending them to a landing page that contains clear and understandable shipping information, or even a special discounted or free shipping offer that persuades them to make the final purchase.

Do whatever you need to do to ensure that they land on a page that meets their need and convinces them that now is the time to buy.

Chapter 27

Place Pages:
Google's Gold Mine
for Local Business

By Dave Jabas

Dave Jabas is a longtime Planet Perry member, expert AdWords practitioner, and e-commerce veteran. Listen up while he talks about Google Place Pages and local search.

—Perry Marshall

■ ■ ■

"97 percent of all consumers use the internet to research products and services in their local area."

—The Kelsey Group

Most brick-and-mortar businesses don't realize the incredible opportunity available to them for free by combining the power of local search marketing and online reviews. This is one of the greatest, most profitable marketing frontiers.

Google has processed so many searches over the years that it has an excellent idea of how people make buying decisions and where an individual searcher is in the buying process. Because of this, the search engine can figure out whether a searcher is likely looking for information or to buy something locally.

Studies have shown that people searching Google to make buying decisions are commonly in the final stage before making a purchase. These users are also commonly more affluent and have higher incomes.

This means with just a few pieces of information in your back pocket and a little bit of work, your local business can finally compete with the large corporations for targeted customers. Not only that, but you can also completely dominate your in-town competition and gather the lion's share of local customers for yourself. In this chapter, we'll show you exactly how to do that.

RANKING ON PAGE ONE OF GOOGLE USED TO BE TOUGH FOR LOCAL BUSINESSES

In the early days of the internet, the majority of online searches were looking primarily for information, including information on particular products. Large corporations with generous marketing budgets could afford to build big expensive websites detailing their products, and they were able to ship their merchandise easily.

Remember, these were the days when even a modest website could cost five figures. It was extremely difficult for a local business to land on the first page of Google ahead of bigger companies.

BUT THAT'S ALL CHANGED

The internet is growing up and our search behavior has changed dramatically. A few years ago, Google started dedicating a certain portion of the search results to local businesses. Since then most people have started using Google like a phone book. In 2011, approximately 25 percent of all searches on Google had local intent, and that number is growing dramatically as more and more people buy smartphones with internet access.

Google's goal is to constantly provide the most relevant search results available. Thanks to improvements in search technology, that now includes local businesses.

It might seem a little unnerving, but based on a searcher's IP address, Google knows your geographic location. It knows if you're searching from your home, from a hotel, or from your cell phone in a far-away city. Because it knows where you're searching from, it can easily provide local solutions to your query.

Looking for a Chinese restaurant, mountain bike, battery for your son's radio-controlled helicopter, or a plumber? Your first page results will show you the businesses nearest you that may have what you're searching for.

This is great news because now your local business is only competing against immediate local competitors for these searches. When the search is clearly of local intent, you no longer have to worry about national companies hogging the first page of the search results. All you have to do is know how to get on the first page. So keep reading.

HERE'S YOUR FREE KEY TO THE FRONT PAGE OF GOOGLE

Google's response to all of the searches with local intent was to create what's called a "Place Page." Whether you know it or not, chances are Google has already given you one. You just have to optimize it correctly to turn it into a Google goldmine.

Most Place Pages are automatically generated based on information Google finds from multiple sources across the internet, including online phone books, directories, and websites.

Unfortunately, Google is relying on nearly two decades of often conflicting data. So very often there are glaring mistakes on an auto-generated Place Page. Sometimes there are even multiple pages for the same business.

Every local business needs to find and claim its Google's Place Page, and make sure all the information presented is correct and up-to-date.

To find your page, just search in Google for your business name along with your city, state, and zip code. If you are unable to find your Google Place Page, you can create one if your local business meets Google's guidelines for local search. That's the first step. Normally, it only takes a few minutes to do. Then you need to integrate your Place Page with your website and optimize it to rank highly for local search.

An example of such a Place Page is given below:

HOW TO OPTIMIZE YOUR PLACE PAGE FOR HIGH RANKINGS

Your Place Page contains all sorts of information designed to help the searcher choose you over other businesses that may also show up. You can list details like your hours, directions, payment accepted, or whether you have onsite parking.

Plus, you can add photos, videos, and coupons to your Place Page to make your business a more attractive choice. Part of optimizing your Place Page means filling out your page 100 percent. Every field should be filled out, including all the photo and video slots, and your hours.

REVIEWS ARE YOUR MOST POWERFUL ONLINE CREDIBILITY TOOL

One of the most important factors in optimizing your Place Page to appear on page one (and to get the click!) is stars. Customer reviews. You need to have a steady stream of positive reviews on your Place Page—it's not optional. Here's why: People now make choices based on the recommendations of others, even total strangers.

We live in the Recommendation Age, and we trust what other people say about a business more than we trust what a business says about itself. Studies show as many as 70 percent of us will trust what a perfect stranger says about a company.

Marketing experts are always talking about word-of-mouth marketing and how important a referral is. A review is permanent word-of-mouth. When the review is on Google, it has maximum value because it's available to searchers when they're closest to the end of the purchasing decision. They are using the review to affirm their decision based on the collaborative opinions of others who have bought from your company before.

So, positive reviews on your page will go a long way toward convincing someone to visit your establishment instead of your competitors.

REACH FOR THE STARS

Once you start getting reviews on your Google Place Page, you will start earning star ratings. Ideally, you want a five-star rating with consistent fresh reviews. Five stars are natural click-magnets, and Google now integrates and shows your five-star rating within your AdWords listings, at their discretion.

Having the five-star rating as part of your AdWords campaign can increase your click-through rate substantially (sometimes 50 percent or more), giving you greater impact with your marketing campaign and reducing your cost-per-click. (Please note that reviews and stars can come from many sources. You can make efforts to improve your ratings, but you should never expect to exercise total control over them.)

Star ratings can go up and down depending on how many reviews you have, how fresh they are, how positive they are, and how well your competitors are keeping up with you.

Just because you have five stars now doesn't mean you'll keep them forever. So to take full advantage of the power of local search marketing, you need to integrate some sort of system into your daily operations that will generate consistent reviews from your customers.

It also means you should monitor the reviews on your Place Pages on a weekly basis. This task needs to be assigned to someone and can never be put on the back burner or allowed to fall through the cracks. Just one negative review can mean an 80 percent drop in new business you might otherwise receive from local search. That's huge!

HOW TO HANDLE A NEGATIVE REVIEW

It's true you can't please all the people, all the time. But considering that anyone can say anything about your business on the internet and get away with it, customer service and conflict resolution are more important than ever.

If you receive a negative review online, it's almost impossible to get it removed. Google just isn't interested in getting involved in a spat between you and a customer. It has bigger things to worry about. So what do you do?

The best thing you can do to minimize the effects of a negative review is to have a constant flow of fresh good reviews. For most businesses, this means that the most recent review should never be more than seven days old. This is a general rule of thumb, and of course there are exceptions to every rule.

But let's say you're searching online, and you see one business has ongoing weekly reviews and another business's most recent review is two or three months old. Which would you choose? The obvious answer is the one with the most current reviews. Also, the one with the weekly reviews more than likely will also have a greater total of reviews.

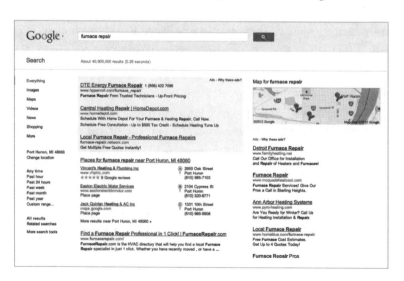

All things being equal, humans trust and are more inclined to choose the company with the highest star rating and the greater number of reviews. See how the five-star rating stands out from the rest.

Of course, the best way to deal with a negative review is not to get one in the first place. In today's Recommendation Age, it is really important that businesses acquire a new mind-set when dealing with an unhappy customer.

It is no longer a matter of whether the customer is right or wrong. The question now is, "What's the most cost-effective way to minimize the negative effect?"

If this customer were to post a negative review, it could have tens of thousands of dollars of negative impact for your business. Instead of allowing a customer to leave unhappy, pick a dollar amount that is an acceptable loss to minimize discussion and keep customers happy. Then give your staff permission to work within those parameters.

Your people must have your trust and the authority to use their best judgment and keep customers from posting negative reviews. If it will take a substantial amount of time or money to solve the problem, then make sure you have some process in place to handle the issue now.

Make sure your staff knows what to do. It's much better to solve the problem now than deal with the negative review later.

And by the way, yes, I know that feels like extortion. Sometimes it is. Our approach is to try to flag psychotic customers before they become customers. (There are usually warning signs.)

HERE'S YOUR SECRET WEAPON FOR COLLECTING STEADY ONLINE REVIEWS

You need to implement a proactive plan for asking your customers, patients, or clients for reviews. The best time to do this is when they've just completed their purchase, service, or treatment. Your good service is fresh in their mind; they are at their happiest point and pleased with the experience.

It's simple enough to say, "Hey, would you mind giving us a review?"

Most customers are agreeable. Most of your customers do, after all, like you. What's not so simple is to get them to actually DO it. They'll say "sure" and then move on with the rest of their busy day. They've forgotten about the review before they even leave the parking lot. It's frustrating!

However, there is a tool that allows your customers to provide a review right from their smartphones while they are still standing in your office or place of business. Customers can text, scan a QR code, or type in a URL and be instantly directed to your Google Place Page where they are walked through the review process. The system also prompts the reviewer with questions to help him or her provide a more relevant and positive review.

However, there is no coercion or obligation to write you a good review. People are free to say whatever they think so the review is not unfairly biased.

The feedback review tool at GoldStarFeedback.com also lets you offer an incentive like a coupon or extended warranty to any customer who provides a review. Here's an example of one review request sheet. If you like, you can test it yourself with your phone right now.

Users have reported increased business in as little as two to three weeks, and all it takes to get started is your business name and web address.

DOMINATE YOUR LOCAL MARKET STARTING TODAY

If you're using Google AdWords, a properly optimized Google Place Page, and a process for collecting ongoing fresh five-star reviews, you will have created an online marketing weapon—an effective way to boost your business with Google local search.

As a buyer of this book, you're entitled to a $100 discount. You can gain access at www.perrymarshall.com/supplement.

GOOGLE MAPS

Google Place Pages also have big impact on Google maps. In the screen shot below, notice the link to "Place Page" in each listing and how it corresponds to points on Google's map.

Your Place Page potentially impacts three pieces of real estate:

1. The local text listing
2. The map
3. The star rating in your Google ad (note the four stars for Zales in the ad on the right side.)

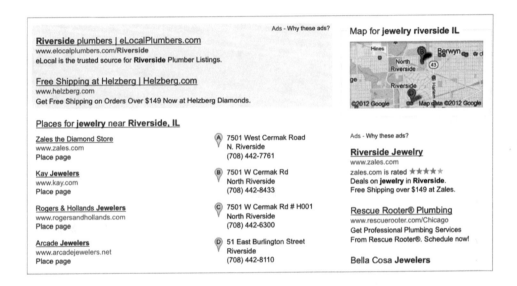

If you own a local business, you need to claim your Place Page. You also need a strategy for getting your customers to review your business—dollars depend on it. And if you're a local marketing consultant, you need to offer your clients a comprehensive service that includes both of these strategies.

■ ■ ■

Dave Jabas is the author of *How to Get Your Business on the First Page of Google: The Definitive Guide to Attracting More Customers by Tapping the Power of Google local search and mobile search.* He is also the CEO of GoldStarFeedback.com. You can reach him via email: Dave@GoldStarFeedback.com.

Chapter 28

17 Things Yo Momma Never Told You About Google

1. TEN THOUSAND HOURS

Malcolm Gladwell's book *Outliers* is all about his observation that the most talented boy-wonders of the world (people like Bill Gates, Steve Jobs, and the Beatles) were successful not because of innate talent but because they got a chance to invest 10,000 hours in their chosen profession and got their 10,000 hours in early.

I like the 10,000-hour theory and I talk about it myself from time to time.

Just the other day I was doing a phone consultation with a customer and he said, "If I were going to invest my 10,000 hours in pay-per-click, where would you suggest I focus my energy?"

I replied, "I'm not sure there's 10,000 hours worth of stuff to even *know* about pay-per-click. There's a keyword, there's an ad, there's a bid price. If you spent 10,000 hours studying that I'm not sure what all you would study."

"However," I added, "You can *most definitely* invest 10,000 in understanding what came before that click and what comes after that click. The story, the psychology, the progression of keywords from first inquiry to sale, the art of gently leading your customer where you want him to go."

Even as complex as AdWords can be, the AdWords machine is not 10,000 hours of complexity. You can master even advanced technical aspects of it in a year. It's the *psychology* of it that's tricky.

If you invest 10,000 hours (five years' worth of career time) aggressively honing your chops, you *will* be a master marketer, and you'll be in the driver's seat of one of the most lucrative careers in the world today.

2. THE "BEFORE" CIRCLE AND THE "AFTER" CIRCLE

Like I said, that click is just one event. The click is a bridge between two circles: the story the person is in before—and the story the person *wants* to be in after.

Before and After. That's the game.

Before the click she had a migraine headache. Not only that, she would experience mind-splitting, crushing headaches one to two times per week. Totally debilitating. She's short-tempered with her husband. She yells at her kids. When those headaches come, everyone knows to get out of harm's way.

She's so ashamed, and . . . on some days, so lonely.

She clicked on your ad and for the first time got a coherent explanation why she gets these headaches and why they refuse to go away. It wasn't just a doctor handing out pills; it was something she could sink her teeth into.

She purchased your program (she thought to herself, this had better work 'cuz if I don't find something that works I'm going to go out of my mind) and began following it religiously, day by day.

By week three she was down to one mild headache per week and by the fourth week she was completely free . . .

She's in a story. She wants her story to have a different ending. Your job is to enter into her story and change it. That's what she wants. She's dying for it.

The way you do your job is: You find out what conversation is going on inside her head; you step into it; then you change it.

3. THE PIE CHART OF DESIRES

Name a keyword. Name a market. What I'm about to describe applies to ALL keywords and markets. Let's say the keyword is "splitting headache." Now 100 people search "splitting headache," and you ask them this question: "What is the number-one thing you are looking for today?"

You ask 100 questions, and you get 100 answers. You lump similar answers together. The answers look like this:

· 36 percent have a headache right now and are looking for some action they can take to make their headache go away (i.e., what they're really looking for is a good tip—some kind of information);

· 27 percent have a headache right now and are looking for a medication they can buy online that will make their headache go away (i.e., they're OK waiting a day or two for a shipment).

· 19 percent suffer from migraines more than once a week.

· 12 percent have a friend, relative, or child who has a headache right now and they're looking for a solution.

· 4 percent suffer from migraines more than once a month.

· 2 percent took a medication that made their headache worse, not better and are looking for something different.

Total: 100 percent.

The pie chart looks like this:

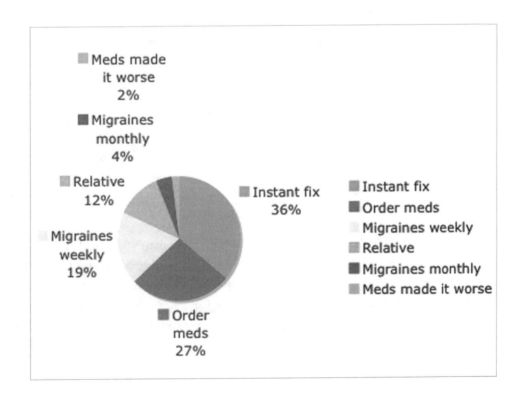

Now the obvious thing to do is write an ad that targets the biggest piece of the pie. But you may not want to do that. Why?

Because the slice of pie you can make the most money with is the question that they're having the hardest time answering.

That means if you're taking a survey, you need to add another question: "How hard has it been to find a solution to this problem?"

The problems where the answer is "very hard" are the ones you can most easily sell a solution to. These are also, by definition, the problems your competitors aren't addressing.

4. TELLTALE SIGNS OF MARKETS

Search for [keyword]. Google returns a result. *FREEZE.* Don't touch that keyboard.

What do you see? What comes up and why? There are many, many clues, and these clues tell you many things about the market that you are trying to compete in:

- · *Fewer than eight ads appear, only on the right.* This means this keyword is not very competitive and/or its market does not generate enough money to support very many advertisers. It's kind of like the Arctic tundra where few plants can grow.
- · *There are more than eight ads (there's a second page of results), but only eight ads appear on the first page of results.* Here, no advertiser is getting a high enough CTR/Quality Score to appear on the premium results. This usually means people who search this keyword have a huge range of desires and the market is very fragmented.

- *There are 9 to 11 ads on page one, including one to three ads across the top, and no second page of results.* This means a few advertisers are getting high CTRs and good Quality Scores, but most of the other advertisers are doing poorly. There is often a marked difference between the two kinds of advertisers. If you study the difference, you can tell what the market responds to.

- *There are 9 to 11 ads on page one, including one that threads across the top, and many pages of results, i.e., dozens of ads total.* This means the market is healthy and competitive, there is money in this market and some advertisers are successfully "nailing" their customers' sweet spot.

- *Many pages of advertisers but the advertisers change from one month to the next.* This means this market has a high churn rate with many advertisers entering and leaving the market all the time. This is a bad sign because it means nobody is making money. This is a very common occurrence in MLM and business opportunity keywords. Those businesses are a revolving door, and you should stay away unless you are a very experienced marketer with deep pockets and a better sales process than everyone else.

- *All the ads say fairly similar things.* This means most people searching this keyword want pretty much the same thing.

- *The ads are all over the place in terms of message.* This means that there is no one desire that this keyword represents. There is a whole pie chart of desires and there may be six to eight distinct desires in the market.

- *The lowest-ranking ads advertise sites like eBay, SuperPages, and ReachLocal.* This means you are in a market that is not very competitive and probably easy to win in. Often such markets don't have a great deal of traffic.

5. IMPRESSION SHARE

Most people don't realize this, but Google only shows most people's ads part of the time. When you're brand-new, they're probably only showing your ads 10 to 20 percent of the time. Your reports might tell you your ad got 2,236 impressions today, but you don't know that your keyword got searched more than 10,000 times.

Let's say you're bidding $1.00 per click and Google tells you, "First page minimum bid is $1.50." That doesn't really mean your ad is *never* seen on the first page. Rather, it means that your ad is probably only seen on the first page 5 to 10 percent of the time.

If you increase your bid, your impression share may grow to 25 percent, 50 percent, maybe even 100 percent. Google is serving up its inventory for maximum clicks. Google knows that people might search 5, 10, 15 times, and it knows if it keeps showing different advertisers, it can get more ads to get clicked on. This strategy is good because it is optimizing your CTR automatically.

But if you have a killer ad that gets a *great* CTR and if you have good Quality Scores, your Impression Share can approach 100 percent.

Something to be aware of: If you have a competitor who has excellent CTR and Quality Scores, Google may be showing its ad 100 percent of the time. If your CTR and QS are lower than its are, then increasing your bids to get 100 percent Impression Share may accomplish nothing more than spending lots of money.

Bottom line is, high CTR and Quality Score get your ads shown more often.

6. DOING ADWORDS FOR CLIENTS

All of the best AdWords practitioners I know developed most of their skills by managing campaigns for both themselves and clients—as well as masterminding with other AdWords experts. If you want to be an AdWords genius, these are my suggestions:

- *You should always have some project that is exclusively your own.* There is nothing like learning on your own dime. It teaches you more than anyone else. When there's money attached to it, the lessons are imprinted deep inside your mind.
- *You should always have some project that is not your own.* Other people's money. Other people's marketing results. I'll talk about how to get clients in a minute, but the reason this is so valuable is it extends your knowledge into markets you would otherwise have no experience with. If one of your markets is CRM software and another market is natural health supplements and another client sells management consulting, you develop a wide perspective that you would otherwise never get. You will also find yourself transferring ideas directly from one market to another. Not just AdWords ideas, but ideas for website design, landing pages, offers, email messages, and guarantees.
- *I did a special training program just for marketing consultants who want to generate clients, earn income and get paid to do what they love—sell stuff online.* It's called "Ready Fire Aim" and you can find out more at www.perrymarshall.com/readyfireaim.

How to Get Clients

Principle Numero Uno is to understand what you are selling when you are an AdWords consultant: You are selling dollars at a discount. What you are saying to your prospective client is:

> *Right now you are buying new 1,000 new customers per month for $10.00 each and this is costing you $10,000 per month. If you pay me $2,500 per month I'll get you 1,200 new customers for $6.00 each. Your AdWords spend will go from $10,000 per month to $7,200 per month; you'll get 200 more customers than you were getting before, and after you've paid me my fee you'll still be spending $300 per month less than you're paying now.*

So you can leave things the way they are now, or you can hire me and save $300 per month and get 200 new customers every month that you're not getting now.

Is that a good deal, or what?

Now in order to say this you have to do some research. You need to know how much it's costing them to get a new customer; you need to know what a customer is worth to them; you need to know what they're happy with and unhappy with. Bottom line is, you need to earn your keep.

7. HYPER-RESPONSIVE CUSTOMERS

There are three kinds of customers:

1. Customers who buy once and never come back again
2. Customers who buy from time to time, maybe for years
3. Customers who buy everything they possibly can from you

This last category is only about 5 percent of your customers, but these customers may bring you as much as 50 percent of your profit.

These are the people that you design your business for: The raving fans.

Let me restate that: You want to design your business such that "raving fans" are not only possible, but probable.

Some businesses could not possibly have raving fans even if someone was looking for a business to be a fan of, because everything is so mediocre. You need to be outstanding at *something.* Which is to say you need a powerful USP.

But once you have that USP, you want mechanisms (such as email/snail mail/ autoresponder follow-up, and customer appreciation events) that stimulate customers to come back, and come back, and come back for more. You brainstorm things that will re-ignite your old customers' interest.

If you do the math for a typical website, about one Google click in 2,000 represents a hyper-responsive buyer. That's right, about one person in 2,000 has a propensity to have this kind of buying behavior. These customers buy compulsively from other companies, and they'll buy compulsively from you if you have an appealing offering.

We all know people like this. You know people who are Apple fanatics and own five Apple computers and eight iPods. You know people who have dozens of pairs of shoes in their closets. You know people who constantly go to motivational seminars. You know people who buy and read every single Stephen King book.

Notice that this kind of buying behavior is personality driven. People love buying from personalities and companies who have a lot of personality. Don't be afraid to have personality.

8. INNOVATION AND THE HYPER-RESPONSIVE BUYER

Pinpoint a major keyword. It gets, say, 50,000 searches a month. Picture all the people who are searching for those keywords. Imagine, even, a person who searches for this not just for a few hours or a few days, but from time to time for months or even years.

That person is a true hyper-responsive buyer.

I have a question for you: What will get HIS attention?

I propose to you that this person is very jaded, has seen everything before, and is hard to impress.

But if you impress him, if you deliver something that is truly a breakthrough, he will tell all his friends; he'll give you a killer testimonial; and all his friends are hyper-responsive customers too.

You can "flip" an entire market just by winning the affections of that rabid 5 percent.

9. GOOGLE LACKEYS VS. REAL GOOGLE REPS

There are two kinds of Google reps:

1. *The rank-and-file AdWords person who replies to your Help Center inquiry.* This person typically knows very little about AdWords, and unless there is a simple obvious issue with your account (i.e., a basic problem like when your ad gets disapproved), he often won't know what the problem is.
2. *The professional Google account rep.* If you are a medium- or large-sized business that spends upwards of $100,000 per year, you'll likely be assigned a professional Google account rep. Sometimes these reps know the inside scoop about how Google's system works and the vagaries of Quality Scores, etc.

There *are* people at Google who know how the system works, but you generally have to be spending money to talk to them. Fortunately Google doesn't give big companies a special discount—the clicks themselves are a level playing field—but it does give them more information.

If you want to be on the leading edge of that kind of information, I have two suggestions for you: 1) Our Mastermind Club (www.perrymarshall.com/mastermind) members pool their experience and solve problems together. 2) AdGooRoo (www. AdGooRoo.com) collects data on hundreds of thousands of Google advertisers—as well as you—and provides competitive data on your ad positions, Impression Share, and budgets.

10. "WOULD I SEND GRANDMA TO THIS SITE?"

One of my colleagues was asked to help with a site that was severely "slapped"—had Quality Scores of 1. Because of his close relationship with Google, he was able to get a "real" Google rep to give him a "real" answer to why the site was slapped.

The answer: "I would not send my grandma to this site."

Yeah, I know, some people will retort, "What does YOUR GRANDMA have to do with anything?"

I looked at the site, and I would not send my grandma there either.

The person at Google didn't elaborate. So please permit me to elaborate.

This particular site was selling a specific business opportunity. The hype factor was through the roof. It was a pure "squeeze page" with nowhere else you could go to learn about the vendor. All the bullets were tease, and the claims were extraordinary.

It had a smarmy feel.

Google didn't like the site. So somewhere in the account, a Google reviewer punched in a low quality score, and all the keyword and SEO tweaks in the world won't change that.

I realize this is all totally subjective on Google's part. But it tells you a few interesting things:

· Google is NOT just run by robots. It's got more than enough money to put real people on the assignment, and it does.
· In my opinion grandma is a GREAT criteria. Grandma doesn't know nuthin' about the internet, so she trusts you to tell her who's OK to listen to. Should she sink her retirement money into that bizop? Well, in Google's opinion, if there's more than a 10 percent chance of her getting screwed, then . . . absolutely not. Remember: If grandma doesn't have a tech-savvy grandson, then she has to rely on Google.
· The site failed to prove what it was saying. Let's say this bizop was totally legit. If so, then it should be able to prove it. Names, cities, states, numbers. Qualifications, cautions, requirements.
· The site should have contact information, preferably including street address and phone number, and not appear to be some guy hiding behind his computer.

Might I suggest . . . add "Would a Google rep send her grandmother to this site" to your bag of tricks, and let's all do our best to make the internet a more trustworthy place.

11. EVERY MARKET HAS A HOLE

There is no such thing as a market where you cannot find a way to "chisel your way in." Even if it has 100 or 200 or 500 bidders, I can guarantee you at least a few of the top ten advertisers in that market still have a vulnerability.

That vulnerability can come in many forms, all of them boiling down to inability to convert visitors to sales. And the number-one factor in that is a need in the market (in the pie chart of desires) they are not meeting.

If you want to crack into a new market, the number-one question you need to ask is, "What unmet need in this market are people willing to pay money for?"

There is always some need that few if any of the competitors are addressing. That's your "in."

12. BOOTSTRAPPING VS. VENTURE CAPITAL

One time I was on the board of directors of an online startup company.

The president of this company had started four other companies. Two had failed, and two had gone public. That is a pretty impressive track record for startups.

His approach was "if you build it they will come." Raise venture capital or angel money from private investors faster than you "burn" the money, and eventually you get the attention of some big company who buys you out. Everyone breaks out the champagne and makes millions of dollars.

My approach was far less glamorous than that. My approach was: **"Make ONE dollar."**

In other words, do whatever you have to do, build whatever you have to build, to get to a point where you can predictably spend $1.00 on Google clicks and get $2.00 from paying customers.

Which is to say, it's OK if you have overhead and investment and everything else far in excess of that $1.00. Maybe you've invested thousands, tens of thousands, hundreds of thousands of dollars. But in the marketing department, you're making money at least on a small scale.

Once you're doing that you just scale up.

That's my approach. I have personally coached more than 500 businesses through this process in over 200 industries. It's basic, it's humble, most of the time it's done from a spare bedroom or basement office. But it works. It's made me and countless others literally millions of dollars.

When I joined this company, I was told that we were going to use a hybrid approach, that we were going to "make $1.00," but we were not in any way going to limit ourselves to the meager growth limits of a self-funded startup. We were going to raise money and scale this thing big and fast.

Gentlemen, start your engines.

So off we go. We built a Google campaign that acquired new members at an excellent low cost-per–acquisition, and we had tons of traffic to the site.

But for whatever confounded reason, I could not get the president of the company to make $1.00. I could not get him to sell something to these people.

At least not anything you could realistically make money on.

Yet every quarter at board of directors meetings, he would chide us for not bringing enough investors.

I finally resigned and sent them all a nasty email telling them that they were defrauding their shareholders because two years into it they still had no business plan that had any hope of making money.

This *could* have been a tremendous success. There was nothing wrong with growing a company fast on the shoulders of investors. But the investors were so distracted by the dog-and-pony show about how big this market was and how much money was in this market and all the grandiose promises that they never bothered to look into the core marketing DNA and sales story.

The DNA of any sales machine is real simple:

"What does it cost you to get a customer and how much money do you make on that customer in {1 day/1 month/1 year/1 lifetime}?"

If you do not have at least a partial answer to that question, you don't have a business. You have a pipe dream. Doesn't matter if you've got a $10 million building and a Startup of the Year award from *Inc.* magazine.

On the other hand, if you've got a Google account, a teeny, tiny little e-commerce store built on a free Blogspot site, and a Paypal account, and you're putting $1.00 in and getting $2.00 out, *you have a real business.*

13. JUST BUY THE STUFF AND SHIP IT

Notice that the DNA of a real sales machine is not having a manufacturing facility, ownership of the product, a flawless system for customer service, or anything else.

With that in mind, consider a contrarian, renegade approach to building that business.

If the DNA of a real sales machine is the ability to put $1.00 in and get $2.00 out, then you're off to a good start if you can put $1.00 in and get 80 cents out.

So if you're starting out, the FIRST thing you must do is simply prove that you can sell something.

That's it.

Just prove that you can sell something. Doesn't matter where you get it or how much it costs to obtain it.

So let's say that you want to sell some kind of high-end $1,500 bicycle, and it's going to cost you $250,000 to put them into production. You know that after you put them into production, it will cost $600 each to make them and you'll have a $900 gross margin.

Most people will put the bikes into production first, then try to sell them. Big mistake.

Let's say it costs you $5,000 to build them by hand.

Then what you should do is advertise your bikes for $1,500, take some orders, and THEN bite the bullet and build the first 10 bikes for five grand each.

Yes, I know you're sending out $3,500 with each shipment. Doesn't matter. It's still the lowest risk way to enter the market. It'll cost you $35,000 to sell the first 10 but it's better than spending $250,000 to sell zero!

Make sure there's water in the swimming pool before you jump off the diving board.

The same advice applies even if you're doing something as simple as selling hand soap. Get the orders first. Then if you have to, drive to Walmart, buy a case of hand soap, and sell it at a loss. But get the marketing and sales machine right before you hammer out the fulfillment issues.

14. ARTIFICIALLY HIGH BIDS IN A FEROCIOUSLY COMPETITIVE MARKET

I have a student who's in a particular segment of the printing industry, which is a fiercely competitive niche. Typically he's battling against 90 plus bidders in a price-sensitive commodity market.

He soundly established a presence on one keyword, and after several months of fine-tuning, he got his cost down to $2.00 per click.

He asked me what he should do next, and I said, "Knock yourself off. Create another brand with a different USP in the same market." So he did.

For the first week, his cost-per-click was $11.00.

OUCH.

He was real doubtful at first, but I told him to stay the course.

Sure enough, after some time went by, he "earned" Google's trust, and the cost-per-click dropped to $2.00.

What he had just encountered was Google's artificial barrier-to-entry for new advertisers.

It's daunting when you're new, but once you're established, it protects your territory from poachers.

Carefully follow the instructions in this book—and especially this chapter—and you'll be able to enter any market at will.

15. PERSONALITY VS. TRANSACTIONAL MARKETING

There are two kinds of approaches that are most often used in selling products, even physical ones: 1) institutional "brand" advertising and 2) personality-driven advertising.

Examples of the former are Tide laundry detergent, Crest toothpaste, Chevy trucks, and Harvard University.

Examples of the latter are George Foreman grills, Donald Trump's real estate properties, Wendy's Dave Thomas, and Video Professor training courses.

I submit to you that personality-driven advertising is easier to "pull off," happens faster, and costs less money than traditional brand advertising.

Here's a way to think about it:

Think of authors and radio/TV personalities such as Oprah, Dr. Phil, Rush Limbaugh, and Dr. Laura. Think of Roger Ebert and the late Paul Harvey. Consider how these folks deliver news, entertainment, and opinions to people who are, literally, "fans." Their job is to communicate their version of reality to a clearly identified audience.

The way you do personality marketing is, you add a bit of Oprah or Rush Limbaugh to your product. You take a very specific position, you have strong opinions, and you talk about a far wider range of topics than merely what you sell.

People like that.

Thus your website is a platform for you being you, not just a person who sells your product.

I've included a bonus chapter about personality marketing at www.perrymarshall.com/supplement/.

16. WHAT I LEARNED FROM INFOMERCIALS

Some people watch infomercials. Some who watch buy from them. Some don't.

I for one have never bought a single thing from an infomercial. I'm not "an infomercial buyer."

In general I don't even care to watch them all that much, even though they are extremely educational for salespeople. (TIP: If you want to see a sales pitch that has been scientifically proven to work, just watch an infomercial that's been on the air for three months. I can guarantee you it's making money. Take notes, and look for ideas you can borrow.)

But anyway, in 2002 when I first began using Google AdWords, I almost instantly knew how the entire AdWords market was going to develop. Even though it was virgin territory, it was undeveloped, and nobody understood it.

I foresaw that in 2010 and beyond, it would be a fiercely competitive, dog-eat-dog marketplace and there would be certain things you HAD to do in order to win. I knew that because I had **studied** infomercials.

What does Google AdWords have to do with infomercials?

Back in the '80s broadcasting laws changed, and it suddenly became possible for TV stations to sell extended slots to advertisers. You may recall that 30 years ago most TV stations went off the air at 1 A.M. or 2 A.M. They said, "We'll be back at 6 A.M. . . . "

So people started making 30-minute commercials.

I remember when I was a kid, turning on the TV one night and seeing an infomercial shot at a Holiday Inn meeting room. It was a single camera pointed at an overhead projector, and some guy was pitching information on how to get rich in real estate.

When infomercials were new, the airtime was incredibly cheap. You could actually shoot a cheap video at a seminar, air it, and make money.

Then companies started discovering that this worked. And the bid prices went up.

Today if you want to *test* an infomercial, you're going to spend a minimum of $75,000 to $100,000 to put a show in the can and test it in a few markets. It's going to have to be professionally produced and superbly scripted. Otherwise it doesn't even stand a chance.

Most of the players in the infomercial biz are companies that specialize in this area and do hundreds of millions of dollars of business. The largest such company is Guthy-Renker, whose sales are about $2 billion.

The barrier to entry is now very, very high.

I knew that AdWords would be a niche-market version of the same thing, just on the internet. And as the AdWords market matured, I always knew what was next. Because I knew history repeats itself, I studied history.

Here are some factoids about the similarities between infomercials and AdWords I would like you to think about:

- It used to be said that infomercials were the most competitive place you could possibly sell anything because the customer's hand is always on the remote control and she can change channels if she gets bored for two seconds. The same is true online: People have 12 windows open, and the entire internet is only a click away.
- Back end is everything. Real success is seldom achieved from a one-time sale. It has more to do with your ability to win a loyal customer who buys and buys again.
- Testing is essential. You have to test ads, landing pages, and offers in order to maximize your sales. The most successful advertisers will be those who test more than everyone else. Fortunately it's not hard to be that person.

17. "PICK THE CHICKEN CLEAN"

Economical cooks find ways to use ALL the parts of the chicken, not just parts of it. Similarly, you want to find ways to satisfy ALL your customers' needs, not just one. Ask yourself these questions:

- If you sell a $50 product, what could you possibly offer that would cost $500? What could you offer for $5,000? There is hardly a market where there is not an answer to this kind of question. There is always a small percentage of people who will spend lots of money to scratch an itch, and those people will contribute a large percentage of your profit.
- What related things do they buy?
- Can you get them to buy on a repeat basis, for example, a membership or monthly shipment?
- Do your competitors offer something that you can sell to your customers, such that you earn an affiliate commission? Your customers will probably buy from the competition anyway (it's not like you "own" them, after all), so you might as well get in on the action. Especially on the internet, you can't keep your customers from finding the other guy. Just decide to profit from the transaction instead.

HOW TO PICK THE CHICKEN CLEAN WITH CREATIVE GOOGLE ADS

A Google ad has 130 characters: 25 characters for the headline, and 35 characters for lines 2 and 3 and the Display URL.

What can you do with a measly 130 characters?

Consider this: If you take all the letters, numbers, characters, and spaces that are possible in a Google ad—just the ones on an English keyboard—there are 92 possible choices for 130 positions. That's 92^{130} combinations.

$$92^{130} \text{ is } 2 \times 10^{255}$$

The number "googol," which is where the name "Google" came from, is 10^{100}. It's the biggest number anyone even has use for. There are only 10^{80} particles in the whole universe.

So there is an inconceivably large number of things you can say in that tiny little Google ad.

Now I realize that an ad that says

```
tgQwqBIg)JCmisLfhx
NC5AwUS oRxXghe VZ<d MoX
CUppEdJo,urXcOeol07J"[Sg
jP6paH$k&Fp Fae laVselog
```

HOW TO PICK THE CHICKEN CLEAN, CONTINUED

is completely useless, and you can be sure that even a million monkeys typing for a million years could never fix it.

But even when you limit your choices to real words and sentences, there are VASTLY more things you can say than it seemed you had room for when you first started.

Those tiny little Google ads aren't so tiny. They're a vast universe. The ultimate ad might be a needle in a haystack, but that needle is worth finding. Fortunes lie inside that ad.

Uncle Claude Sez

I started with Lord & Thomas at $1,000 per week. But soon we agreed that the right plan was a commission basis. Then the agency paid me only for service which proved profitable to them. On the other hand, I received what I earned. Under that plan I earned in commissions as high as $185,000 in a year. All earned at a typewriter which I operated myself, without a clerk or secretary, and much of it earned in the woods.

Chapter 29

That Last Winner-Take-All Edge: Google's Tools for Smarter AdWords Results

Bruce Lee famously said, "I fear not the man who has practiced 10,000 kicks once. I fear the man who has practiced one kick 10,000 times."

Google provides a huge number of tools and features in every account that give you data sliced a thousand different ways. But no serious professional uses all of them all the time. The best of the best have a tiny handful of tools they wield consistently for top results.

■ ■ ■

In the words of Thomas Friedman, author of *The Lexus and the Olive Tree*, "The gap between first place and second place grows larger, and the gap between first place and last place becomes staggering. In many fields there is rarely one winner, but those near the top get a disproportionate share."

How would you like to be the winner who takes all? How would you like to have that disproportionate share?

> Here are the practices that the best AdWords managers follow consistently and the tools they use to get their best edge over competitors.
>
> This is not an exhaustive list of bells and whistles. This is a series of strategies; specifically, what we believe are the most important strategies you can put to use in your AdWords account once you've got the basics of ad writing and peel-and-stick under your belt.

THE BEST ADWORDS ADVERTISERS LIVE AND DIE BY ADWORDS EDITOR

I know of no AdWords account manager who does not swear by AdWords Editor as the fastest and easiest way to keep track of large volumes of campaigns, ad groups, ads, and keywords. It uses Google's API and allows you to download all necessary account information to your computer desktop, edit it there easily, and upload it back to your account.

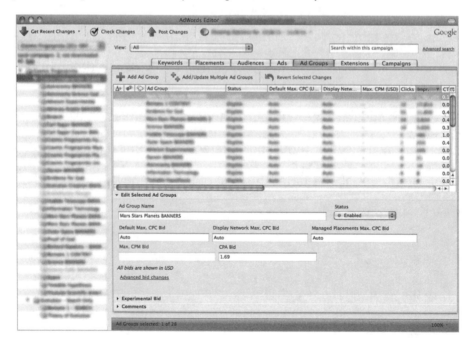

Yes, it has a brief learning curve. But once you're familiar with it, you will save lots of time. Every principle we teach is implemented faster and more easily with this tool.

And it's free. Download it at www.google.com/intl/en/adwordseditor/. You will thank us for this.

FOR BROAD- AND PHRASE-MATCHED KEYWORDS, KNOW PRECISELY WHAT YOUR VISITORS TYPED IN TO FIND YOU

This can go a long way toward cutting your spending and increasing both your click-through rate *and* your conversion rate.

With your broad- and phrase-matched keywords, Google shows you any and every conceivable related search that it can get clicks on. That means you're going to get a ton of clicks from search queries that are completely irrelevant to you.

So how can you know? Simple: Select a keyword in your list, and click the "See search terms" button above:

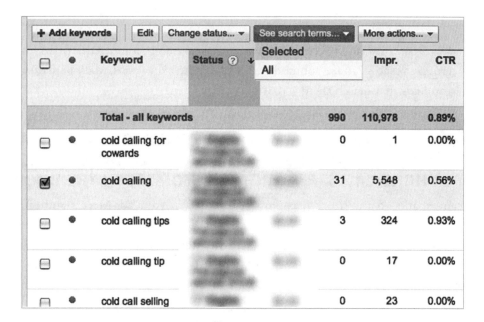

Google will then give you a listing of exact search terms people typed in to find you. You'll find two things in this list:

- *Search terms you should not be showing for.* Add them as negative keywords. In the example above I would add "telesales tips" and "cold war" as negative phrase-match keywords:

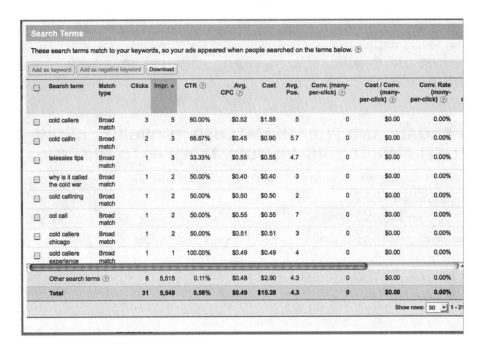

- *Search terms you haven't been bidding on, but should.* Add them into this or another ad group as exact-, phrase-, or modified-broad-match keywords. Make sure they have good ads that match them verbatim.

MORE THOROUGH AND SPECIFIC INFORMATION IN YOUR AD RESULTS IN MORE QUALIFIED CLICKS, MORE CONVERSIONS, MORE PHONE CALLS, AND MORE CUSTOMERS IN THE DOOR

You can expand on the three-lines-plus-URL model in your ad. Most significant for your clicks and conversions, we believe, are the additional clickable links and the phone number extensions you can include in your ads. All this is found under the "Ad extensions" tab in your interface. Once you've found the tab, click "New extension," and follow the simple directions there:

Sitelinks only show up when your ads are in the premium links in the colored space at the top of the page. They appear as clickable links immediately underneath your ad:

Having these topic- or product-specific links in your ad may get you a better click-through rate. But far more importantly, they stand to earn you a better *conversion* rate once people click to your site because they take visitors (if you set things up correctly) to the specific page relevant to the text in the link.

You can enter up to ten possible destination URLs and the link copy for each, and Google will show up to six of them at any given time.

Call Extensions let you include a phone number in your ad. That way you can track phone calls generated by Google clicks. This is especially useful if your customer or prospect is looking for you on a mobile device such as a Droid or iPhone.

This information is accessible under the "View" menu:

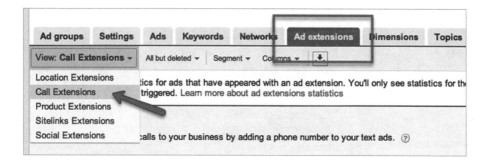

The first and simplest option here is to show your own phone number, and only on phones. The second option is to have Google generate a phone number and show it everywhere, on phones and desktop browsers alike.

Add call extension

Drive and measure phone calls to your business by adding a phone number to your text ads. ⑦

Country or territory	United States ▾
Phone number	(402)476-9211|

Phone number options ⑦ ⦿ Show my business phone number only on high end mobile phones (CPC)
○ Show a Google forwarding phone number on all eligible ads and devices

High-end mobile phone options ⦿ Allow click-to-call and clicks to your website
⑦ ○ Allow only clicks-to-call

This ad extension works with location extensions. Learn more

Save Cancel

Ads on desktop browsers show up with phone numbers you can call.

Farmers Insurance® 1 (855) 287 2149
www.farmers.com +1
Get an Online Auto & Home Quote Today & See How Much You Can Save!

Get a Quote   See How Much You Can Save
Find an Agent

Ads on mobile devices show up with a phone number you can click to call, or a link directly to the site.

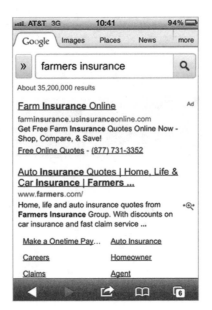

Either way, you can set it up, if you like, such that ads on mobile devices are click-to-call only. Touch the ad, and the phone makes a call. That's useful if you don't have a mobile-friendly version of your site up yet.

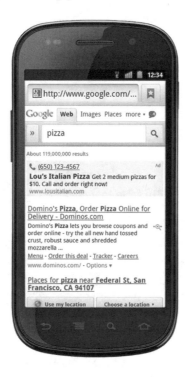

The easiest way to see your call numbers once you have this up and running is to add these metrics as additional columns in your interface:

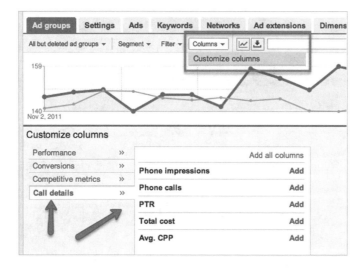

CUT COSTS AND EARN A BETTER QUALITY SCORE BY SLICING UP YOUR DATA IN NEW DIMENSIONS

The "Dimensions" tab enables you to quickly cut out huge amounts of unnecessary waste and pinpoint key shortcomings in your performance. It's at its most powerful when you're tracking large numbers of conversions, though it may also prove useful with CTR data.

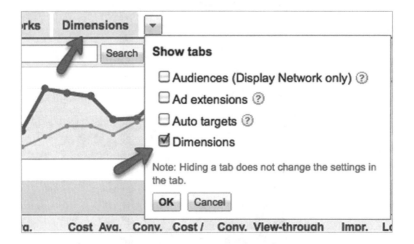

It gives you scores of ways to slice up your data, but we're going to show you the three that will make the biggest immediate difference.

To get started, rank everything in descending order by "cost" and look at just three "slices."

1. Geographics
2. Time > Hour of day
3. Time > Day of week

You can also rank in descending order by "cost-per-conversion." When you choose the "Geographic" option,

it lets you see in what states, provinces, or cities you're getting good click-through and conversion rates, and where you're not:

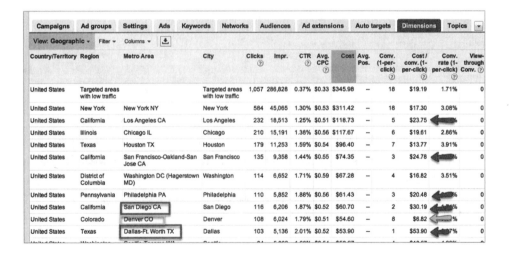

In your campaign settings you can then exclude the geographic areas where you're **not** converting well. When you choose the "Time > Day of the week" option,

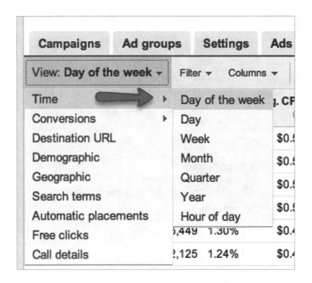

you now see on which days your performance is weakest:

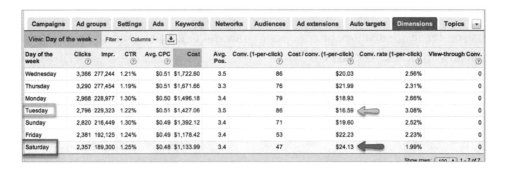

Run the same process with the "Hour of day" time option. You'll see which times of the day produce clicks that result in conversions and which don't. Now you can use Ad Scheduling from within your campaign settings to turn off traffic when it's bad and turn it on when it's good.

Fixing each of these types of shortfalls in your account will give you an immediate increase in quality score.

WHAT PERCENTAGE OF THE TIME ARE YOUR ADS ACTUALLY SHOWING?

A quick glance at one metric in your account can tell you volumes about how relevant Google thinks you are. That metric is impression share.

Another nice thing about the Dimensions tab is that it gives you ad-group-level access to data for your impression share, which is the percentage of the time that your ads actually show for the keywords you're bidding on. You may be surprised to know that it's rarely 100 percent.

Choose your preferred campaign or ad group and, with the Dimensions tab selected, click to open the "Customize columns" option and add the competitive metrics of impression share and the two types of "Lost IS":

Day	Clicks	Impr.	CTR	Avg. CPC	Cost	Avg. Pos.	Conv. (1-per-click)	Cost/conv. (1-per-click)	Conv. rate (1-per-click)	View-through Conv.	Impr. share	Exact match IS	Lost IS (budget)	Lost IS (rank)
	10	337	2.97%	$0.05	$0.53	2.8	0	$0.00	0.00%	0	31.24%	25.10%	19.98%	48.77%
	6	399	1.50%	$0.07	$0.40	2.6	0	$0.00	0.00%	0	40.06%	39.10%	0.09%	59.85%
	5	271	1.85%	$0.09	$0.46	3.2	0	$0.00	0.00%	0	32.99%	28.16%	17.63%	49.38%
	3	325	0.92%	$0.04	$0.13	2.4	0	$0.00	0.00%	0	45.11%	51.85%	1.96%	52.93%
	6	261	2.30%	$0.09	$0.55	3.1	0	$0.00	0.00%	0	33.62%	37.50%	11.08%	55.30%

This is the quickest way of telling if Google is punishing you for low CTRs or low Quality Score. If your daily budget is well above what you actually spend in a day and your impression shares are 80 percent or above, odds are pretty good that you're not being penalized at all. But if your budget is set high and your impression share is significantly lower than that, then the share you're losing will show up as "Lost IS (Rank)." This means that for the campaign or ad group you're looking at either your CTRs or your individual bid prices are too low.

A global summary of your impression share is also available from the "All online campaigns" view:

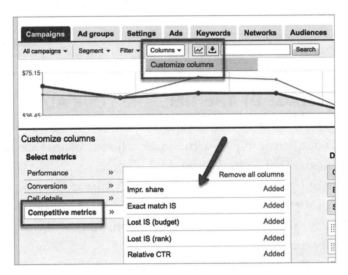

There's a way to know if you can make up that lost impression share by raising your bids: Use Google's bid simulator on individual keywords. When you're in an ad group with the keywords tab selected, a little tiny button that looks like a graph will appear next to each active keyword with history:

	Status ⑦	Max. CPC	Clicks	Impr.	
	💬 Eligible	$2.00 📈	25	1,628	1.
	💬 Eligible	$2.00 📈	8	1,164	0.
arshall	💬 Eligible	$2.00 📈	3	30	10.
	💬 Eligible	$2.00 📈	3	461	0.

Mouse over that and the bid simulator will pop up, telling you how many more impressions are available to you if you bid higher. That right there may be your "Aha!" moment because you finally see where your lost impressions are going.

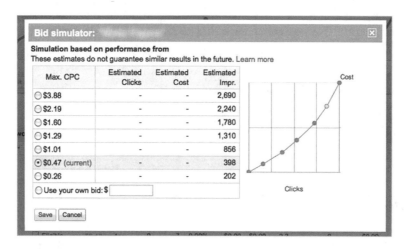

GOOGLE CONVERSION OPTIMIZER

This is the future of AdWords for a great many advertisers. With Conversion Optimizer, Google systematically identifies:

· which of your ads
· shown at which positions on the page
· for which specific search queries
· at which time of the day
· on which day of the week
· in which geographic locations

. . . result in the conversions you want at the price you've asked for.

To qualify for Conversion Optimizer, you need a campaign that's had 15 or more conversions over the last 30 days. If you have such a campaign, you can then go into its settings and set your bidding option to "Focus on conversions":

Google then watches user behavior and finds the traffic and the circumstances where you're most likely to get clicks that turn into conversions. It technically charges you for each click that comes in, but you bid with an average or maximum cost-per-action (CPA) in mind.

Let's talk about this. As our friend David Rothwell (www.DavidNRothwell.com) teaches, there's a three-stage strategy to making your campaigns work, and even in the best possible scenario, you're leaving Google Conversion Optimizer (GCO) off until half to two-thirds of the way through the process. The three stages are discover, optimize, and expand. Each one will require no less than 30 days.

For a special section and recording on Google Conversion Optimizer and cost-per-action (CPA) bidding, see www.perrymarshall.com/supplement/.

IMAGINE YOU'RE 15 YEARS OLD AGAIN

Would you get in a car you'd never driven before and drive it as fast as you could to your destination? No. You'd kill yourself—and likely others. Same with AdWords. Put $1,000 in the tank and go as fast as you can with broad-match keywords 24/7, and your money's going to go nowhere. You'll have a wreck.

So your first stage with new campaigns and a new account is always "Discovery." There are ways and places to buy the best traffic. You need to pinpoint the right keywords, match types, and ads, and see which networks, locations, and times give you the best results.

You might succeed in making a few sales at this point, but more importantly you're going to get data. As Google says, "Data beats opinion." The work you're doing in your campaigns at this point cannot and will not involve GCO.

Your goal is the perfect AdWords campaign, one that runs 24/7 and consistently gives you more money back than you put in.

The next stage is "Optimization." Do more of what's working once you've tested it and less of what isn't. What ads are you showing people, and for what keywords? What time of day and in what geographic area do you get the best conversions? You're aiming to create a working, profitable infrastructure. When you feel you have that, turn on GCO, and see what Google does from there.

Finally, you come to "Expand." Your campaign is up, you've trimmed your spending here and there, your match types are adjusted, your ads are written, and your landing pages are tracked and tested, adjusted, and fine-tuned. Does everything work? Is it predictable? Is it reliable? Good.

Now we want as much as we can get because we know it's safe. So now with GCO on and running, you're free to increase your *daily budget* without fear. And set your ad delivery to "accelerated."

Who Will GCO Work For?

Your conversion tracking has to be robust, reliable, set up correctly, tried, and tested. Your conversion event must take place online (as opposed to over the phone or in person). You need to know what the value of your conversion is because GCO is all driven by *your* numbers, not Google's.

GCO works best when it's aiming for a transaction of a single fixed dollar value, or at least a narrow range of values. If your products have wide price ranges (wedding rings, clothing, various services), then you have to account for that. Conversions must take place within 30 days of the initial click; that's set in concrete.

Bigger time delays between click and conversion make it more difficult for Google to make accurate predictions. Regardless, the more conversions you can get, the better, and the more consistent your conversions, the better.

You can read about Conversion Optimizer and get started by going to www.google.com/adwords/conversionoptimizer/.

For detailed info on Google Conversion Optimizer and cost-per-action (CPA) bidding, see www.perrymarshall.com/supplement/.

Know Who Your Visitors Are, Better than Anyone Else: Google Analytics

The "conversion tracking" that's built into Google AdWords gives you a skeletal view of how well your keywords are producing individual actions like opt-ins and sales. Google Analytics goes far deeper to connect those keywords to very specific visitor activity everywhere on your site.

Google gives you graphics and reports that tell you much more about who is finding you on the internet—and when, and where, and how, and how long. With Analytics you can know:

- · How many visits your site gets, daily and hourly
- · What websites your customers are coming from
- · Where your visitors are finding you around the world
- · How much time visitors spend on each of your pages
- · Where your potential customers are bailing out
- · What order they click from page to page
- · What browsers, platforms, screen sizes, connection speeds your visitors are using
- · And much more.

We highly recommend the Analytics learning materials and tools available from our friends over at www.ROIRevolution.com/blog/analytics.

SHARPENING YOUR EDGE

In the Google world (and the rest of the world, for that matter), the winner takes all. That last 1 percent of edge that this level of leverage gives you can mean the difference between your sitting at the top of a market, controlling it, or your competitor taking over. Which one will it be?

Google's pattern has *always* been to aggressively thin out everyone who is not a top performer. That's the only way its user's search experience continues to improve. It also puts more money in Google's pocket because that makes it more of a privilege to show up at the top.

Bruce Lee, Part 2

"I fear not the man who has practiced 10,000 kicks once. I fear the man who has practiced one kick 10,000 times."

There's another way in which this applies, and that's how you learn to be a great marketer in the first place.

I just went to YouTube and typed in "Marketing." I got the first page listing of 5.4 million videos.

As nice as this appears to be, and as good as some of those videos surely are, it's really a significant problem. Because most people in the 21st century learn how to be better marketers or guitar players or cooks or whatever by listening to 1,000 different dispensers of advice. What these people end up with is a patchwork of slightly incompatible ideas all thrown together in a stir-fry.

The symptom is marketing project after marketing project that *almost* works. "Ten minutes from triumph," and then something fizzles.

Frankly I've never seen this work.

What works is listening to a very small number of mentors (usually no more than one to three) and absorbing their formula for mastery. Learn to think like they think.

By this point in the book you know whether you like me or not. If what I say makes sense, then tune in to my webinars, emails, and events because there's much more where this came from. Offerings range from courses on a variety of topics like time management and Facebook ads to private coaching programs where entrepreneurs from all over the world gather three times a year behind closed doors.

Whether I'm the guy for you or not . . . find *someone* who knows what they're doing and watch his or her every move. You'll learn as much by watching what they do as from listening to what they say.

Chapter 30

FAQ: Answers to All Your Frequently Asked Questions

Answers to the questions asked most often by students in our Mastermind groups, Personal Coaching program, and roundtables.

■ ■ ■

Here are the topics you'll find covered in this section:

Organizing and Getting the Most from Your Keywords and Ads

- Why aren't my ads showing?
- How can I set up my new campaign in a way that will ensure that my keywords get the highest possible CTRs and convert traffic to sales?
- How do I find out in advance what it will cost to be in various positions on the page?
- Should I really have thousands of keywords in my ad groups?

- How many keywords should I have in my Display Network (GDN) ad groups?
- What do single keywords in quotes " " represent?
- What does "Bid is below first page bid estimate of $x.xx" mean?
- What can I do when Google says, "Bid is below first page bid estimate of $x.xx"?
- What should I bid for clicks on Google's Display Network (GDN)?
- What is Quality Score, and what is it based on?
- What's the best way to find the right keywords for my product?
- What do I do when healthy, active keywords are still deathly expensive?
- Does Google disable/deactivate ad groups, campaigns, or keywords?
- What does adding a "+" plus sign do to my keywords?

The Peel & Stick Method

- What is "Peel & Stick," and when do I use it?
- Google doesn't have a "Peel & Stick" feature. Do I have to do this manually?

Getting a Better Click-Through Rate

- What do you consider to be a good CTR?
- How exactly do I split test ads?
- How many impressions or clicks do I need before I declare a winner?
- Do you recommend clicking on your own Google ad a few times when you first post it, in order to start it off with a high click-through rate?
- What's the best way to manage my daily, weekly, and monthly AdWords costs?

Better Landing Pages

- I want to collect opt-ins on my landing page. What's a good structure?
- What's the advantage of sending someone to an opt-in page vs. sending them directly to a sales letter?
- I have a simple e-commerce site. Are opt-ins of any use to me?
- Should I have three different websites selling the same product, all bidding on the same keywords and advertising from different Google accounts?

Getting Your Customer to Talk to You

- I want to survey my visitors. What tools do you recommend?
- How do I survey people without making them angry or losing sales?
- Is live chat a good investment for my site?

Testing and Converting Your Traffic

· Do you recommend using Google's Conversion Tracker?

· What tool do you recommend for split testing landing pages?

· What do I do when I see that some of my keywords are converting to sales and some aren't?

· Do you recommend Google's Website Optimizer?

Using Special Tools

· How trustworthy is Google's Traffic Estimator?

· What exactly is that Dynamic Keyword Insertion feature with the squiggly brackets { }?

· If I'm in the United States and want to see how my Google ads look on searches from other countries, how can I do that?

· When is Ad Scheduling useful?

Where and When to Show Your Ads

· How do I get my ads into the "preferred listings"—those ultra-high-visibility sponsored positions on the top left of Google's search results?

· I have two ads, but Google doesn't show them evenly. Why is this?

· I've set it to show ads evenly, but my ads still don't get shown evenly. Sometimes it's 90 to 10 percent or worse. What's wrong?

· If I delete an underperforming ad and write a new one, how can I compare the performance of the two together?

· With Google AdWords is there a "sweet spot" for my ad to be in—first, third, fourth, or sixth position on a page?

· I hear the Display Network is lousy traffic. Should I advertise on it?

· Should I advertise on Yahoo/Bing or other PPC engines?

Working in Specialized Markets

· Does network marketing or MLM work on Google?

· How do I do affiliate marketing on Google?

· How do I market a high-dollar item effectively on Google?

· My niche is specialized, and I have found very few keywords that draw more than a few thousand requests per month. Is this still a good avenue for me?

Google's Regular Search Engine

· Does using Google AdWords improve your ranking on Google's regular organic search engine listings?

How to Become an Affiliate

· Do you have an affiliate program?

Answers begin below.

ORGANIZING AND GETTING THE MOST FROM YOUR KEYWORDS AND ADS

Q: Why aren't my ads showing?

1. Did you trust Google's Traffic Estimator when you set up your campaign? They say you'll be in third position from the top on such-and-such a price, when in reality you'll be back on page 3 or, more likely, showing only 20 percent of the time. Set your bids conservatively, and check back after your ads have run to see what average positions your keywords have been in. Then adjust them accordingly.

2. Check what countries you're showing in. Your ads may be in position 1 in the UK but position 20 in the United States (or vice versa), while Google tells you your average position is 3 or 4. (By the way, this same ranking problem can occur between large metro areas and rural areas in the United States. You can see different search results on Google just by changing the zip code of your location.)

3. Click the "search" button again, multiple times, to be sure.

4. Double-check the daily budget for the campaign you're in. Is it possible that you already hit the limit for the day, and Google is done showing your ads?

5. Understand that only a tiny percentage of advertisers in any market show up all the time, 100 percent, for all searches on a particular keyword. Those are the advertisers that get the most clicks, have the best Quality Score, and have been in the game the longest.

Q: How can I set up my new campaign in a way that will ensure that my keywords get the highest possible CTRs and convert traffic to sales?

First, wherever it's humanly possible, *only put keywords in an ad group that actually appear in the ad*—better still, in the ad's headline. If you've got keywords that don't match the ad, then take them out and stick them in a new ad group, and write a new ad that uses those specific keywords.

Create as many different ad groups as you need to, in order to make this work.

Second, *at first only allow your ads to show on Google searches alone.* Do this for the first few days or weeks until you've established that all your highest-traffic keywords are profitable. When that's settled, turn on the other sources. Google's traffic is a single, more predictable source. Display network traffic, highly unpredictable.

Q: How do I find out in advance what it will cost to be in various positions on the page?

Here are three sites you can check out. They are frequently inaccurate, but no more so than Google's Traffic Estimator:

- www.SpyFu.com
- www.KeyCompete.com
- www.iSpionage.com

Q: Should I really have thousands of keywords in my ad groups?

You want as many *relevant* keywords as humanly possible. The more good keywords the merrier—*if* they're turning out a good CTR.

And that only happens if they're in *small, tightly clustered* groups that match each ad's message well. Thousands of keywords in your whole account, yes. Thousands of keywords in individual ad groups, no.

Q: How many keywords should I have in my Display Network (GDN) ad groups?

The short answer: the fewer the better. That way Google has more leeway to find themes and therefore appropriate pages for your ads.

Q: What do single keywords in quotes " " represent?

When used in the same list along with single keywords without delimiters, these represent correct spellings and normal usage of the term in a phrase or sentence. The term without delimiters then catches misspellings and any other odd, glitchy variation on the keyword. If you include these in your keyword list, you'll find they each get searches.

Q: What does "Bid is below first page bid estimate of $x.xx" mean?

It means either (1) Google is showing you only on page 2 or 3 or lower of search results, and not the first page, or more likely (2) they're showing you only a tiny percentage of the time.

Sometimes it means you're just not bidding enough. Most of the time it's because your Quality Score is low. If your ad group isn't already set to display Quality Score, just mouse over the magnifying glass next to the keyword in question and it will tell you what your Quality Score is for that search term.

If your Quality Score is low, your first priority is to repair that before you try raising your bid.

Q: What can I do for keywords where Google says, "Bid is below first page bid estimate of $x.xx"?

Two options: 1) Bid what Google asks, or 2) tweak the copy of your Google ad and/or the content of your webpage, to convince Google's computers that your ad and website are relevant, thereby improving your Quality Score.

There are numerous ways to approach Quality Score. Among them are: Post more pages with keyword-rich content throughout your site and put links to those pages from your landing page, and then to provide more engaging/involving content on your landing page (surveys, audios, videos) to keep people there and interested longer.

Q: What should I bid for clicks on Google's Display Network (GDN)?

Start by bidding 25 percent of what you'd bid on Google search. If your max CPC for a valuable keyword in a search-only campaign is $2.00, then for the same keyword on the Display Network, bid $0.50.

Q: What is Quality Score, and what is it based on?

Google will never openly share the exact formula that it uses to determine your Quality Score and minimum bid price. But here's what we've repeatedly found to matter most:

· Your CTR
· The match between your keyword and your ad
· How that keyword has always performed across Google historically
· The amount and quality of keyword-relevant content on your landing page
· The amount and quality of keyword-relevant content on your whole website
· How quickly visitors hit the back button after visiting your site
· How quickly visitors leave and go elsewhere after visiting your site.

As far as your specific rank on the page, the primary factors are 1) your bid price, and 2) your CTR.

Q: What's the best way to find the right keywords for my product?

Do your free keyword research first using *Google's keyword tool*.

You can use Google's traffic estimator to find out what maximum bids are. Use its keyword tool to get search volume data and traffic/position/cost/competition estimates on all four keyword matching options (i.e., broad, phrase, exact, and negative). See Chapters 1, 8, and 14 for more details, screenshots, and tips.

Watch your competition:

- How many advertisers are there? The number could be anywhere from one or two to several hundred. If there are fewer than eight or ten bidders, you could get the bottom position on page 1 for as little as $0.01.
- Figure out which competitors are serious direct marketers. Pay special attention to everything they do
- *Tip:* Pay attention to Google advertisers who split test their ads—when you do a search on a keyword that you're researching, click the "search" button multiple times, and you'll see that some ads change while others stay the same. The advertisers who split test are almost *always* the sharpest pencils in the box.
- Go to Bing and find out what advertisers are doing there.
- Get keywords from dictionary/thesaurus sites such as www.LexFN.com and from printed sources on your topic, such as glossaries and indexes.

Q: What do I do when healthy, active keywords are still deathly expensive?

The top bidders in any established market on Google are going negative on the initial sale because they make it up later with a robust back end that includes cross-sells, upsells, and ongoing paid subscriptions. They may staff their phones with skilled salespeople. They may have a robust follow-up system.

Can you do any of these things, too? The first baby step in this direction is to capture contact information and then market to those contacts aggressively, maximizing the value of every visitor you get.

Also, can you:

- Get the top bidders in your market to become affiliates of your site?
- Make a joint-venture offer to your competitors, playing like the little bank branch inside the giant supermarket?
- Offer your competitors who send traffic to you a pay-per-action deal (per-click or per-download) to help them monetize some of their traffic and subsidize their $10.00 per click?
- Buy exit traffic from competitors' sites?

Q: Does Google disable/deactivate ad groups, campaigns, or keywords?

As of this writing, none of the above. It used to, though. Now Google just shows your keywords a paltry fraction of the time if the Quality Score is low.

It does *disapprove* ads that don't meet its editorial guidelines. (And if you violate its policies repeatedly, it'll shut down your whole account and ban you from Google entirely.)

But follow Google's policies and fully implement our advice, and these problems will take care of themselves.

Q: What does adding a "+" plus sign do to my keywords?

This is called "modified broad match." It gives you more control over what Google does with your broad-match keywords and what searches you do and don't show up on.

It's relevant only with multiword phrases. In your keyword list, simply add a "+" plus sign directly in front of one (or both) of the words in any broad-match phrase. That then "anchors" that particular word, limiting Google to only the closest variations on that word while letting Google get creative with the other words in the phrase.

THE PEEL & STICK METHOD

Q: What is "Peel & Stick," and when do I use it?

This can increase the CTR of your individual keywords. Very simply: *Move an underperforming keyword into a new ad group, and write an ad whose message matches it perfectly.*

For Peel & Stick to improve a keyword's CTR, though, the keyword has to meet two conditions:

1. It gets a significant number of searches.
2. It doesn't already match the ad perfectly, or it isn't used in the ad.

If the keyword doesn't meet both of these conditions, don't waste your time. *Tip: Don't delete the keyword from the old ad group. Just pause it.*

Q: Google doesn't have a Peel & Stick feature. Do I have to do this manually?

Sorry, "Peel & Stick" is our term. Google doesn't do it automatically. Pause the keyword and its closest variations in your old list, click on "Create a new ad group," and put in the new set of keywords with a new ad.

GETTING A BETTER CLICK-THROUGH RATE

Q: What do you consider to be a good CTR?

Broadly speaking, any time you're above 1 percent you're doing something right. Any time you're significantly below that, it means something needs attention.

However, this all depends on the market first, the keyword second. Keywords where people are looking for you by name will always have a high CTR. Keywords where you've got to introduce new ideas or educate people, much lower.

Regardless, *every tenth of a point of improvement you get by strengthening your copy brings you more visitors.*

On search, 3 percent is what I would consider to be a pretty respectable message-to-market match.

We've achieved CTRs of 10 percent or better when the text in the ad is a precise match to a *question* that the user types into a search engine. For example:

Ethernet Basics Guide
www.xyzcompany.com
Simple Tutorial on Ethernet, TCP/IP
5 Page Paper, Free Instant Download

. . . and note the phrase in the keyword list that got the highest CTR by far:

Keyword	Clicks	Impressions	CTR
what is ethernet	5,314	32,481	16.3%

This 16.3 percent is a dang high CTR. And it wasn't hard to achieve at all.

This suggests a strategy: What *ultra-specific questions* can you answer for your audience? Using those questions as keyword phrases can earn you excellent CTRs.

Q: How exactly do I split test ads?

Write an ad. Stick it up in your ad group. Now look for "Create New Ad" down in your Ad Variations tab, and click "Text ad." Write a second one—still following the advice we give, but as different as possible from the first. Submit it, and you're set to go.

Google will automatically alternate the two and show you the impressions, clicks, and click-through rate for each one.

Split test as many ads at a time as you want. I personally prefer just two at a time, so each one can get results faster.

What should you test for? The best click-through rate, for starters. But if you can set up Google's conversion tracking in your account, then wait longer and find which ad has a higher conversion rate or lower cost-per-conversion.

Q: How many impressions or clicks do I need before I declare a winner?

Rule of thumb: Get 30 *clicks* (not impressions) on each ad before declaring a winner and deleting the loser. But to be more sure, use the tool at www.SplitTester.com.

Q: Do you recommend clicking on your own Google ad a few times when you first post it, in order to start it off with a high click-through rate?

If you want to become a legitimate marketer, no. Google has its own built-in Click-Fraud-B.S.-Detector that tells the system when a person is trying to inflate a site's CTR with extra clicks.

The goal is to find out what works. Let the live market tell you what does and doesn't fly, and adjust your products and message to give people what they want.

Q: What's the best way to manage my daily, weekly, and monthly AdWords costs? Is there a difference between overall costs of advertising in the UK vs. the U.S. or other countries?

The two ways to control costs are: 1) adjust your daily budget, realizing that the daily amounts are very crude approximations, and 2) adjust your maximum bids.

There are differences among each country you advertise in. In most cases the traffic is most expensive in the U.S. *There are many keyword bargains to be found in other countries.*

With that in mind, if you sell all over the world, you might want to have U.S./Canadian campaigns separate from the rest of the world because otherwise you'll likely pay more than you need to for non-U.S. Google ads.

Tip: When setting bids on the Display Network, start at 25 percent of your regular Google search bids.

BETTER LANDING PAGES

Q: I want to collect opt-ins on my landing page. What's a good structure?

What has worked best for most of our students is 100 to 300 words of copy, half of which is typically bullets.

Google wants to see keyword-rich content on your landing page *and* on the rest of your site. So provide links for folks to get around to other pages. For a clean, simple example of all of this, see www.CosmicFingerprints.com. This brief, minimum-hype, straight-to-the-point approach seems to work very well. The best I've seen in the hottest, narrowest niches is over 50 percent, while 10 to 25 percent is very typical.

Q: What's the advantage of sending someone to an opt-in page vs. sending them directly to a sales letter?

Test it in your market. Google may give a higher Quality Score to an info or article page than either an opt-in page or full sales letter. Nonetheless, if you do attempt a straight sales letter, it may be hard to get a one-time impulse sale. Opt-ins can generate sales for you weeks, months, even years after the fact. Whereas 1 to 2 percent is often considered a good response to a sales letter, opt-in rates are usually ten times that.

Rule of thumb: If your product costs more than $50.00, run a multistep sales process. The more expensive your product is, the more steps you'll need.

Q: I have a simple e-commerce site. Are opt-ins of any use to me?

They won't be your bread and butter, but the bigger the mailing list you build, the more you can create trust and affinity over time. Then you sell to people later on.

Sign up and keep in touch with the people who buy from you. That's a given. But even to nonbuyers, offer a discount, a downloadable guide on how to do more with your product, a newsletter, a series of tips by email—anything relevant that gives them a reason to give you contact information. That's how you build a back end.

Q: Should I have three different websites selling the same product, all bidding on the same keywords and advertising from different Google accounts?

Google will shut down your accounts and ban you if you do this.

Now if you have different businesses selling different versions of a product, designed for different markets, you can open separate accounts, put bids for both on the same keywords, and get different slices of the same traffic. For example, bid on "flowers," and have one website that sells fresh-cut roses and another site that sells gift baskets. The ads won't cannibalize each other.

But they must be completely separate businesses running from separate websites on separate servers, selling completely different valid products. Otherwise, Google has ways to sniff out that you're simply double-serving, and you could get banned from Google for life. No joke.

GETTING YOUR CUSTOMER TO TALK TO YOU

Q: I want to survey my visitors. What tools do you recommend?

Check out Glenn Livingston's powerful and time-tested tools for this at www.LivingstonReport.com.

To manage simple surveys, we always recommend www.SurveyMonkey.com. For more involved multiquestion surveys with on-your-site data management, see www.WillMaster.com/master/survey/.

Q: How do I survey people without making them angry or losing sales?

Run surveys like a split test. Using Hypertracker or a testing interface of your choice, set it up so that only one out of three, five, or ten clicks get sent to your survey form. And of course always offer people a relevant item or service of genuine value for taking your survey.

Q: Is live chat a good investment for my site?

It's not for everyone. It's highly inefficient at selling small-dollar, small-margin products.

But if you sell high-dollar products or services that require convincing or explaining, then you should try it. Whether you actively engage people while they're on your site or are simply there if they need questions answered, it's a valuable way to get feedback from people, which you turn around and use to improve your sales process.

Learn the potential of this approach, get access to free audios and videos that help you humanize and personalize your sales approach, quickly identify buyers, and fine-tune your website at www.AriChatwise.com. Also, sign up for a two-week free trial of Live Person software at http://solutions.LivePerson.com/free-trial/.

TESTING AND CONVERTING YOUR TRAFFIC

Q: Do you recommend using Google's Conversion Tracker?

Yes, absolutely. It's far from flawless, but it lets you track conversion all the way down to individual keywords. I recommend it *plus* one or several other third-party conversion tools, such as Hypertracker.

Q: What tool do you recommend for split testing landing pages?

Hypertracker (www.hypertracker.net) is a powerful tool for doing split testing of multiple kinds—sales, opt-ins, landing page click throughs, and more. In fact, we've put together a free tutorial that shows all the basics you need in order to set up and track landing pages, opt-ins, sales, and more. It's at http://video.hypertracker.net.

Google's Website Optimizer is also a good tool for doing A/B split testing.

You can also use integrated services such as 1Shopping Cart (www.1ShoppingCart.com). This is a full shopping cart service that lets you manage split tests, run autoresponders, recruit and pay affiliates, and more.

Q: What do I do when I see that some of my keywords are converting to sales and some aren't?

Use Google's Conversion Tracker and you'll see this. Some keywords give you a cost-per-conversion of $1.00; others as much as $500.00.

There are always two directions you can go: Grow conversions and sales on your keywords or cut your spending on them. Both are valid. I recommend you do the former first. Do Peel & Stick on a keyword, send it to a landing page of its own, and do what you can to get it to sell. If that doesn't work, cut its bid price or pause it.

And remember: *High positions get more impulse traffic; low bid positions get less traffic but searchers who've done their homework.* Sometimes the solution is to just be at position 8 instead of position 2, or to be on page 2 instead of page 1.

Q: Do you recommend Google's Website Optimizer?

Yes. Any tool that makes it easier for you to test and improve conversions, we're fans of.

USING SPECIAL TOOLS

Q: How trustworthy is Google's Traffic Estimator? When I used this feature, Google predicted that the positions for my keywords would all be in the 1–6 range. However, the actual positions Google gave me, when my ads started showing, were all over the place—from 1 to 45. Is there something wrong?

The "Traffic Estimator" can be wildly inaccurate. You'll have to base your bids on past traffic and actual recorded campaign statistics, not on Google's estimates.

Q: Google never says anything about its Dynamic Keyword Insertion feature (DKI) that uses squiggly brackets { } and automatically inserts keywords into your ad. What is it?

This tool is useful if you have huge lists of nearly identical keywords and you don't want to write hundreds of ads.

Suppose your keyword list includes the following terms:

>   adaptors
>   power adaptors
>   transformers
>   power supplies
>   power supply

Then you would write up an ad like this:

> <u>{KeyWord:Adaptors} to Order</u>
> www.xyz.com
> Quality Workmanship, Low Price
> Free Shipping for $250 Orders or More

This way each term in the keyword list above shows up in your headline when someone searches on it. The ad will say "Transformers to Order" or "Power Supplies to Order," etc.

If people typed in keyword phrases that included the above keywords but were more than 25 characters total, Google would just default and show the phrase "Adaptors to Order" in the headline.

Q: If I'm in the U.S. and want to see how my Google ads look on searches from other countries, how can I do that?

Several ways. First (and easiest), try Google's free Ad Preview Tool, available at https://adwords.google.com/select/AdTargetingPreviewTool. Just enter your search terms and choose the geographic location from the dropdown menus on the right. Google will show you both paid and organic listings for that location—useful for virtually any spot on the globe.

Or you can manipulate your address bar to see results instantly. Go to Google, and search for the keywords. For example, if you search for "Linux Firewall" after the results appear, the URL in your search bar says: http://www.google.com/search?sourceid=navclient&ie=UTF-8&oe=UTF-8&q=linux+firewall. You can see the search results for other countries by copying the string back into your browser and adding some characters at the end.

For the US you add &gl=us: www.google.com/search?sourceid=navclient&ie=UTF-8&oe=UTF-8&q=linux+firewall&gl=us. For the UK change it to &gl=uk: www.google.com/search?sourceid=navclient&ie=UTF-8&oe=UTF-8&q=linux+firewall&gl=uk.

For Australia: &gl=au
For Germany: &gl=de
For Canada: &gl=ca
Etc.

The abbreviation corresponds to the domains for those countries—Ireland is .i.e., France is .fr, China is .cn, Korea is .kr, etc.

Q: When is Ad Scheduling useful?

You may discover that your best clicks come in between 4 and 6 p.m. Or at breakfast time. Or early morning and late night. You may also discover, for example, that your worst clicks always come in between 10 a.m. and noon. Or on Mondays.

So use Ad Scheduling to turn off the traffic when it's bad, and turn it on when it's good. This process is a smart way to budget your dollars and pinpoint when and where you'll get the highest visitor value.

Find Ad Scheduling in the "Settings" tab under "Advanced settings."

WHERE AND WHEN TO SHOW YOUR ADS

Q: How do I get my ads into the "preferred listings"—those ultra-high-visibility sponsored positions on the top left of Google's search results?

Google usually shows two or three. These positions go to the bidders who have been around the longest, have the highest CTRs, and pay the most money. Note that Google's Bid Simulator gives an estimate of how much you would have to pay to get impressions in those top spots, under "Estimated top impressions."

Q: I have two ads in my ad group, but Google doesn't show them evenly. One of them shows 85 percent of the time, and the other only about 15 percent. Why is this?

Click on the "Settings" tab, and under "Ad delivery: Ad rotation, frequency capping," select "Rotate: Show ads more evenly." Google should now show your ads roughly equally. It's never exactly 50/50.

Your other option is "Optimize." With this, if you have more than one ad in each ad group, Google will automatically display the better-performing one more often. It wants you (and it) to benefit from the ad that's getting the better CTR.

I prefer to disable this feature because it will take longer to get complete data if the ads aren't showing evenly.

Q: I've set it to show ads evenly, but my ads still don't get shown evenly. Sometimes it's 90 to 10 percent or worse. What's wrong?

Your ads will never be shown exactly 50/50; sometimes they'll be shown 55–45 percent or thereabouts.

However, if you disable Optimized Ad Serving and your ads are still showing at wildly different percentages—e.g., one is showing at 60-65 percent or more—then your ads may be awaiting approval by a Google editor before they get put into syndication. All ads require editorial approval before going on Search Partners or the Display Network.

For any federally regulated subjects and markets—health and medicine, adult content, etc.—editors have to approve your ads before they'll show even on Google, not to mention Google's Search Partners or Display Network sites.

So when you put up a new ad to run against your old one, it may take a week or more before your new ad starts to show on the Search Network and gets served as frequently as your older ad.

Also, be sure that both ads were active and showing for the time frame that you selected. Otherwise, change the time frame.

Q: If I delete an underperforming ad and write a new one, how can I compare the performance of the two together? Do I have to reset or resubmit the old one so that it shows their performance for the same time period?

Keep a running log for your Google campaigns, in a Word document or Excel file, and record changes you make to your ads and the exact date that you made the change.

That way you can go back into your Google account, set the date to when you submitted the new ad, and compare your performance just for the time period that both ads have been running together.

Q: With Google AdWords is there a "sweet spot" for my ad to be in—first, third, fourth, or sixth position on a page?

This is something we talk about in more careful detail in our AdWords Blackbelt course, at www.AdWordsBlackbelt.com. A quick summary:

In the majority of markets, people get the best ROI both away from the very top *and* away from the bottom of the page. That happens between positions 4 and 7.

The higher you are on a page, the more likely you are to get clicked on. You also get tire kickers and looky-loos. Especially in position 1. And the very last position on a page may get easily ignored as well.

It ultimately depends on your market. In some markets you'll want to be in top position as a means to become dominant. In other markets you'd just be throwing money away.

Q: I hear the Display Network (formerly content network) is lousy traffic. Should I advertise on it?

The Display Network wouldn't be so massive if it were lousy for everyone. It depends on the market, what you're selling, and what sites your ads are showing on. If it's possible to interest people in your product even if they weren't actively looking for it just now, the Display Network may work well for you.

Set up a separate campaign that's Display-Network-only. Test and see with small dollar amounts and short keyword lists if you can make the clicks profitable. A powerful tool for getting the most out of the Display Network is Google's placement report, which you can run from the "Reports" section of your account. It helps you identify and filter out the sites that bring you crappy traffic.

Q: Should I advertise on Yahoo/Bing or other PPC engines?

Short answer: Anyplace you can get profitable traffic is good. Only issue: There's a smaller volume of traffic, and these are different markets with different audiences.

More importantly, our view has long been that if six months to a year from now 100 percent of your business is coming to you via Google AdWords, then we've failed to do our job. Take every advantage possible of non-AdWords and non-Google traffic sources. They'll be different audiences with different response rates and conversion rates. But it's traffic. So chase it down.

WORKING IN SPECIALIZED MARKETS

Q: Does network marketing or MLM work on Google?

The days of MLM succeeding on Google are past.

There is still a glimmer of possibility that network marketing can work on Google, *if* you do in-depth keyword research, use your own 100 percent original noncookie-cutter site with many pages of unique, useful content, and don't bid against people in your own organization.

The worst examples I saw back in the day were businesses that recruited people by telling them there was an infinite amount of traffic on Google. Go bid on "make money online" and "home based business" and the like, they claimed, bring traffic to your clone site, and sign up more people to do the exact same thing.

Traffic on Google is not infinite. For each keyword there are 11 slots on page 1, 11 on page 2, and so on. Those keywords can be expensive. If you don't have a unique site with something unique and different to sell, then any people you recruit simply become your direct competitors.

If you happen to be part of a network that provides a physical product, however, and there's little or no presence on Google yet, then you can simply sell the product and get recruits later on, as long as they don't plan on competing with you directly online.

Find ways to introduce your own product or information that you can give away or sell, thus differentiating you from people who sell for the same company as you. Create a report or guide that you can offer for $10 to $50 and make enough to offset your traffic costs. You may find that you enjoy selling these books even more than selling the product itself.

Q: How do I do affiliate marketing on Google?

Google is doing everything in its power to kill thin affiliates. For example:

· Google only lets one advertiser send traffic to any given site for any one keyword
· Google will find and "slap" sites with buried affiliate links, disabling ads from showing
· Google punishes "thin sites" with only a few pages of content that then send links on to other sites.

We wish we had better news, but this is the state of Google advertising now.

Q: We sell pricey machines that range from $35,000 to $250,000. How do I market a high-dollar item like this effectively on Google?

The core principles that apply to low-dollar, high-traffic B2C markets *do* also apply to high-dollar, low-traffic, suit-and-tie B2B markets. The important thing is: (1) know whether Google is the right tool for finding your customer and (2) talk to your customers the same way they talk to each other and themselves.

Google is the ultimate quick-fix, get-it-now search engine. In this industry your ideal customer may not be as likely to search on Google for you. You may need to go looking in other venues.

A website for capital equipment is going to be an information-driven lead generation and opt-in site, not an e-commerce site. A workable short-term objective is to trade your application and problem-solving information for prospect contact information. Offer quality reports, content-rich white papers, and troubleshooting guides that help the customers solve genuine problems. I have devoted an entire course to this subject, including a free email course which you can get at www.perrymarshall.com/whitepapers.

After you have collected contact information, you plug these people into a highly targeted, content-rich autoresponder. Use direct mail and telephone contacts. Earn their trust by publishing quality information on a regular basis and "drip irrigating" them with follow-up mailings, your newsletter, opportunities to attend seminars, and more.

You can test and use all of the tools that are common to online marketers—autoresponders, multiple websites, search engine optimization, testing and tracking, streaming audio and video, Flash, live chat, and nearly every other tool used by mainstream marketers even if you're in a highly specialized technical discipline. The only difference is how the copy is written.

Q: My niche is specialized, and I have found very few keywords that draw more than a few thousand requests per month. Is this still a good venue for me?

You *can* get worthwhile results on keywords that get just a few searches a month. I call them "nano-niches." Still, there are often a lot more customers in offline markets—trade shows, print media, direct mail, radio, TV, etc. Sometimes it's less expensive to mail out postcards than to buy clicks.

I know one very successful internet marketer and self-publisher doing over $1 million per year, who generates most of his traffic by advertising in magazines.

For information products (i.e., books, e-books) as opposed to physical products, traffic that comes through search engines is often lower quality than traffic that comes from offline sources.

GOOGLE'S REGULAR SEARCH ENGINE

Q: Does using Google AdWords improve your ranking on Google's regular organic search engine listings?

Google maintains a complete editorial barrier between paid listings and free ones. (At least it says it does.) In any case, you can have a Google AdWords target page that *only* AdWords visitors are taken to, which is not accessible any other way. It may not show up in Google's free listings—unless you submit it or link to it from other pages in your site.

This barrier between the AdWords and organic sides is so complete, in fact, that it's possible for your landing pages to be at the top of organic search listings for all your best keywords and for Google to slap those same keywords in your AdWords accounts with stern warnings about landing page quality violations.

In such extreme cases, however, contacting Google's customer support will usually get a human editor to review your case and reinstate your keywords, if in fact your site is of good quality.

HOW TO BECOME AN AFFILIATE

Q: Do you have an affiliate program?

Yes, we do! You can join us and promote a variety of products for different businesses and industries, including my course on Facebook (www.PerryMarshall.com/firestorm), my 80/20 Productivity Express (www.PerryMarshall.com/productivity), and others.

You can sign up for our affiliate program by visiting www.PerryMarshall.com/affiliates/.

Chapter 31

Signature Victories

The measure of the moment
In a difference of degree
Just one little victory
A spirit breaking free
One little victory
The greatest act can be
One little victory

—*One Little Victory* by Neil Peart

■ ■ ■

The best daily ritual I picked up last year was writing one little victory, no matter how tiny, in my little black moleskin notebook. Every day. Even if you only have enough energy in the morning to write one sentence, remember something *positive* and write it. It's the 60-second habit that can change your life. A tiny hinge that swings big doors.

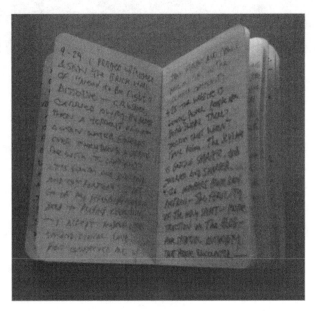

If I've learned anything from writing copy, it's that every single person lives in some certain kind of story. Stories are actually *the* thing that defines any community or culture, even more so than the language those stories are told in.

You might be surprised to find out how different people's stories can be. In Chapter 17, I told you about using Facebook and social media to profile customer stories.

We ran some ads for a coffee product. Here are the favorite movies for the people who clicked on the coffee ads:

1. *Notebook*
2. *Dirty Dancing*
3. *Juno*
4. *Fight Club*
5. *Princess Bride*

We also ran ads for an astronomy website. Here are the favorite movies for people who clicked on the astronomy ads:

1. *Star Wars*
2. *Fight Club*
3. *Lord of the Rings*
4. *Dark Knight*
5. *Gladiator*

You'll notice that the only movie in common is *Fight Club*. (I'm not sure why.) Except for that one, all the coffee lovers' movies are chick flicks and all the astronomy lovers' movies are combat films.

This shows you that coffee fans and astronomy fans live in *entirely different stories.* Up-and-coming Ninja Marketers will give this some more thought. There's an insight in what I just told you that's worth about 50X what you paid for this book.

Hint: If you know what story your customers live in, you can sell to them with ease.

I don't know exactly what story you live in, though I know for most of my customers, *Lord of the Rings* is probably closer to the sweet spot than *Princess Bride*. But there is one thing I know for certain: *You want to make your story BETTER.*

Stories run deep. If you want to change the story you've been in to the story you want to be in, it's best to just assume it's going to take everything you've got. If there's a resource that is capable of improving your story, you should avail yourself of it.

Examples of stories that people live in:

It's a good thing I showed up and fixed everything because otherwise those people would've screwed everything up.

Every time we're about to sit down to a romantic dinner, he gets an emergency call on his cell phone and has to go to the ER.

I'm always on the outside looking in.

Politicians are constantly taking advantage of us, and it just gets worse all the time.

The world is going to hell in a hand basket.

Every time I look for a parking space, someone pulls out and the space opens up for me.

Whenever things are looking completely impossible, some opportunity opens up and things work out in the end.

Whenever I'm on the cusp of a huge victory, something bad happens and snatches my Big Win away, and I go home terribly disappointed.

I never allow myself to be in a position where I can be vulnerable. I am 100-percent self-reliant.

I never allow myself to be in a position where I have to depend on myself. I rely on [him] [her] to keep me on track.

Even in the darkest journey, I fear no evil.

I always learn the hard way.

I'm teachable, and I always learn from other people's experience.

When I'm pressing against hard challenges, things might seem hopeless for months, sometimes years. But eventually I achieve a breakthrough, and things suddenly, dramatically improve.

All this stuff is self-talk. It's über-powerful. The difference between losers and champions is, losers believe they have no control over their lives. They've acquired *learned helplessness.* Winners have acquired the belief that they have some ability to affect outcomes, no matter how indirect their actions.

Self-talk is reinforcing, and people stay stuck in whatever self-talk they've been embracing. Telling yourself your own sad story may be comforting, but it keeps you in prison.

Sixty seconds of positive reflection every day changes your self-talk one sentence at a time, one day at a time. If you eat one bowl of ice cream, it makes no difference in your life. If you eat a bowl of ice cream every single night before you go to bed, you gain 25 pounds in 10 years. If you jump on a trampoline for five minutes every single day, you're still in good shape at age 70.

And if you focus on what's good about your story every single day, you build a reservoir of positive pattern recognition. That's the micro-pattern, 60 seconds to change your life. Let's talk about the Macro.

MEGA-VICTORIES

I did something the other day that I'd like you to do, too. I made a list of about a dozen **signature victories** in my own life, events that were tremendously positive. Allow me to share just one.

Signature Victory: Spent four years in the trenches at a startup company, worked my buns off, company got sold for $18 million. Cashed in my stock options, left the company, started a business.

This one move wiped out our debt in one fell swoop with money to spare. Gave us our first Christmas where we could buy whatever we wanted to buy for each other. Didn't make us "rich" by any means, but it was the first giant gulp of financial oxygen. Felt *r-e-a-l* good.

I still think about that a lot. I've had much bigger victories since then, but that was a *signature victory*—one of those defining moments in life that has so much flavor and impact that it shapes the way you think about everything after.

The time leading up to it was extremely turbulent, and there was always a feeling of *careening* nearly out of control. Yet deep down I had this quiet sense of inner calm, that it would turn out OK in the end.

When all the pieces came together, I had an overwhelming sensation of being set free. Now I can finally do what I really want to do in my life. I can pursue my own purposes instead of somebody else's. *Perry, you've been waiting for this chance. Ball and chain just cut off your leg. On your marks . . . get set . . . THE PISTOL FIRES and a new race has begun. Go man, go, go, go.*

No matter what happens to me, I have that Signature Victory under my belt. Nothing that happens tomorrow can take it away from me. Nothing that happens to you tomorrow can take your Signature Victories away from you.

Focus on them. Relish them. Savor them. Even the small ones.

I don't know where you are in your journey. Maybe you're like me and you started your business 10 years ago. You're reading this book to add some advertising mojo to an already-running business. Maybe you work at a job, and this book is your reading assignment.

Maybe your entire brand-new business hinges on how good your Google campaigns work.

Wherever you are in your story, I believe what you do is important because without marketers, nobody knows about all the great products and services that smart people are constantly developing. I believe you can make your story bigger and better.

Carpe Diem—Seize the Day!

—Perry Marshall

About the Authors

Perry Marshall

Perry Marshall is an author, speaker, and consultant in Chicago. He is known as "The Wizard of Google AdWords" and is the world's leading consultant on Google's advertising system. Google advertisers who use his methods generate well over a billion clicks per month (conservative estimate).

His company, Perry S. Marshall & Associates, consults both online and brick-and-mortar companies on generating sales leads, web traffic, and maximizing advertising results.

Prior to his consulting career, he helped grow a tech company in Chicago from $200,000 to $4 million sales in four years, and the firm was sold to a public company for $18 million.

Like direct marketing pioneer Claude Hopkins, Perry has both an engineering degree and a love for persuasive copywriting. He's published hundreds of articles on sales, marketing, and technology, and his works include *The Definitive Guide to Google*

AdWords (ebook), *The Ultimate Guide to Google AdWords* (Entrepreneur Press, 2006, 2010, 2012), *The Ultimate Guide to Facebook Advertising* (Entrepreneur Press, 2011), *Guerrilla Marketing for Hi-Tech Sales People*, and a technical book, *Industrial Ethernet* (ISA, 2nd Edition).

He's spoken at conferences around the world and consulted in over 200 industries, from computer hardware and software to high-end consulting, from health and fitness to corporate finance.

Bryan Todd

Bryan Todd is a writer and web traffic specialist in Lincoln Nebraska. He's worked in both Europe and Asia and has spent most of his career teaching—from foreign language and world history to advanced testing methods for the internet. He has worked with clients in dozens of industries from health care and book publishing to manufacturing and computer software.

Index

A

ad groups. *See also* campaigns
  creating, 22–23
  defining, 29–30
  even showing of ads in, 331
  organizing, 30, 33–34
  peel & stick in, 37–38
  split testing of, 217
ad headlines
  keywords in, 22, 37, 42, 62–64. *See also*
    keywords
  sources for, 58–59
  targeting with, 39, 59
  visitor retention and, 208
Ad Rank, 130–131
Ad Scheduling, 330
advertising copy. *See also* campaigns

creativity in, 297–298
focused ads, 68–69
headlines in. *See* headlines
inflammatory words in, 67
for niche customers, 69, 334
for remarketing, 271
research for, 61–62
stating benefits in, 64–65
successful, 67–68
testing, 70. *See also* split testing
text in, 64–67
unique selling proposition (USP) in, 190
URLs in, 23, 66, 218
vernacular for, 62
writing basics, 225–230
advertising with non-AdWords sources,
  332–333

AdWords and organic search, 335
AdWords consulting, 288–289
AdWords Editor, 300
affiliate marketing, 333
affiliates, 13, 141–147, 237, 335
America's Second Harvest, 241–242
anchor text, 251
article marketing, 254
artificial link structures, 248–249, 252
attrition, 237–240, 241–242
audiences, 121–123, 167, 261, 265–267
authoritative sites, 249
AWeber email marketing software, 14

B

banner ads, 109–117, 217–218
bans, Google, 149–153, 323–324
barriers to entry, 293
before and after clicks, 284
benefits, 64–65
bidding
    for clicks on Google's Display Network
        (GDN), 322
    cost-per-action (CPA), 79
    cost-per-click (CPC), 24, 269, 293
    cost-per-conversion, 107
    cost-per-thousand-impressions (CPM),
        269
    default bids, 24
    80/20 rule in, 79
    maximum bids, 326
    Quality Score and, 321
    on remarketing campaigns, 268–270
    strategies for, 77–81
    targeting and, 216–217
Big Ass Fans, 187–189
Blink (Gladwell), 174
bootstrapping, 292–293
braces ({ }), 329–330
brackets ([ ]), 56
brand building, 153
broad-matched keywords, 55
Brumlik, Julie, 240–241
budgeting, 21–22, 217, 326

bull's-eye keywords, 16

C

campaigns. *See also* advertising copy
    ad groups in. *See* ad groups
    defined, 29
    optimizing, 34
    organizing, 27–32, 39, 320
    peel and stick strategy in, 35–38, 324
    refining, 24–25
    segregating, 217
    setting up, 20–24
    split testing in. *See* split testing
Carlton, John, 221–222
click-through rate (CTR)
    filtering, 69
    fraudulent, 326
    improving, 324–325
    page position and, 79
    split-testing and, 83–88
combinations, 261, 266–267
competition, 237–238, 286–287
consulting, 288–289
conversion
    avoiding Google bans and, 148
    cost-per-conversion, 107
    email marketing and, 193–194
    Google's Conversion Optimizer (GCO),
        311–313
    remarketing indicators, 261–264
    value per visitor (VPV) and, 205–211
Conversion Optimizer, 311–313
Conversion Tracker, 73–77, 328
conversion tracking
    benefits of, 76
    bidding strategies and, 77–79
    example of, 77
    Google's Conversion Tracker, 73–77, 328
    reasons for, 71–73
    remarketing indicators for, 262–264
    setting up, 73–76
    tools for, 328–329
    value of, 80–81
copywriting. *See also* campaigns

creativity in, 297–298
focused ads, 68–69
headlines in. *See* headlines
inflammatory words in, 67
for niche customers, 69, 334
for remarketing, 271
research for, 61–62
stating benefits in, 64–65
successful, 67–68
testing, 70. *See also* split testing
text in, 64–67
unique selling proposition (USP) in, 190
URLs in, 23, 66, 218
vernacular for, 62
writing basics, 225–230
cost-per-action (CPA), 79
cost-per-click (CPC), 24, 269, 293
cost-per-conversion, 107
cost-per-thousand-impressions (CPM), 269
curly brackets ({ }), 329–330
Custom Geo Targeting, 214–216
customer reviews, 277, 278–280
customers
    hyper-responsive, 289
    ideal, 16–17
    satisfying all, 296–297

D
daily budgets, 21–22, 217, 326
day parting, 217
default bids, 24
destination URLs, 23
direct conversions, 262
direct mail, 202
direct traffic, 265
Display Ad Builder, 114–116
display ads, 109–117, 217–218
Display Network
    automatic placements on, 101–103
    benefits of, 95–96
    finding new customers with, 107–108
    Jet Stream on, 103–104
    managed placements on, 104–106
    managing network campaigns, 99

search vs., 97
targeting traffic on, 100–101
targeting with, 216, 218
themes in, 99–100
topic targeting on, 106–107
traffic quality on, 332
turning on/off, 97–98
display URLs, 23, 66, 218
domain names, 13, 265
Dynamic Keyword Insertion (DKI) feature, 329–330

E
e-commerce platforms, 14
e-commerce sites, 327
Ehrenreich, Barbara, 189–190
elevator speeches, 186–187, 226–228
email marketing
    conversion and, 193–194
    email system for, 14
    opt-ins, 202
    personality in, 194–196, 203
    software for, 14
    success tips for, 196–202
event name selection, 174–176
exact-matched keywords, 56

F
Facebook, 157–159, 165–170
Fanalytix, 168–171
Ford, Harrison, 237
frequency capping, 218

G
gaming the system, 149–153
geographic targeting, 20, 214–216, 307, 312
glossaries, 53
Goldilocks principle, 66
Google
    advertising history of, 141–144
    dark side of, 139, 142–144, 146–148
    impact of, 139
Google Analytics, 264–265, 313
Google bans, 149–153, 323–324
Google Cash (Carpenter), 141–142

Google maps, 281
Google Place Pages
   customer reviews on, 277, 278–280
   finding your page, 275–276
   Google maps and, 281
   negative reviews on, 278–279
   optimizing, 276–277
   star ratings on, 277
Google Places, 124–127
Google reps, 290
Google suspensions, 132, 146–147
Google's AdWords Editor, 300
Google's Conversion Optimizer (GCO), 311–313
Google's Conversion Tracker, 73–77, 328
Google's Display Ad Builder, 114–116
Google's Display Network (GDN)
   automatic placements on, 101–103
   benefits of, 95–96
   finding new customers with, 107–108
   Jet Stream on, 103–104
   managed placements on, 104–106
   managing network campaigns, 99
   search vs., 97
   targeting traffic on, 100–101
   targeting with, 216, 218
   themes in, 99–100
   topic targeting on, 106–107
   traffic quality on, 332
   turning on/off, 97–98
Google's search box, 55
Google's Traffic Estimator, 329
Google's Website Optimizer, 209, 328–329
grandma factor, 132–133, 145, 291

H
Handshake tool, 168–171
headlines
   keywords in, 22, 37, 42, 62–64. *See also* keywords
   sources for, 58–59
   targeting with, 39, 59
   visitor retention and, 208
high-dollar items, 334

Hopkins, Claude, 26
HVLS Fan Company, 187
hyped sites, 291
hyper-responsive customers, 289
Hypertracker, 209

I
ideal customers, 16–17
image ads, 109–117, 217–218
impression share, 287–288
inbound links
   controlling, 256–257
   keywords in, 246
   linkbait for, 256
   reciprocal links and, 255–256
   selecting, 248–252
   sources of, 252–255
indexes, 53
indicators, remarketing, 261–265
inflammatory words in ads, 67
infomercials, 177, 295–296
InfusionSoft, 14
internet business success, 144–145, 148
internet marketing tools, 13–14

J
Jabas, Dave, 273, 281
Jet Stream, 103–104

K
keyword center, 16
keyword lists, 45–48
keyword tool, 43–44
keywords
   in ad groups, 30, 321
   in anchor text, 251
   automatic insertion of, 329–330
   bidding on, 24
   in brackets ([ ]), 56
   brand names as, 51
   bull's-eye, 16
   developing, 45–50
   effective use of, 320–321
   expanding, 50–55
   expensive, 323

frequency of, 42
in inbound links, 246
initial, 23–24
irrelevant, 31–32
killer, 57–58
matching options for, 55–57, 324
negative, 31, 44–45
for niche markets, 69, 334
organizing, 30
plus signs (+) preceding, 56–57, 324
psychology of, 49–50
in quotation marks, 56, 321
researching, 16–19, 45–50, 322–323
sources for, 51–54
split testing and, 240–241
synonyms for, 51
targeting with, 216
worth of, 19

L
landing pages
    opt-ins on, 326
    for remarketing, 271
    split testing and, 328
    value per visitor (VPV) and, 208
language targeting, 216
learned helplessness, 339
LexFN.com, 51
link dilution, 250
linkbait, 256
links
    cautions about, 252
    inbound. *See* inbound links
    reciprocal, 255–256
    SEO and, 246
    sources of, 252–255
little victories, 337–340
live chat, 328
local advertising
    Google Places and, 124–127
    for mobile devices, 127–128
    reaching audiences with, 121–123
    search and, 119–121
    testing, 124

local business, 273–275
local search, 119, 257
losers, 325, 339

M
maps, Google, 281
market vulnerability, 292–293
marketability testing, 173–176, 178–181
marketing high-dollar items, 334
matching keyword options, 55–57, 324
mega-victories, 340
mentors, 315
messages, advertising, 271
mobile devices, 127–128
modified broad-matched keywords, 56–57, 324
multi-level marketing (MLM), 333

N
nano-niches, 334
natural link structures, 248–249, 252
negative keywords, 31, 44–45
negative reviews, 278–279
network marketing, 333
network settings, 21
new advertisers, 293–294
new visitors, 264
niche markets, 69, 334
Nickeled and Dimed: On (Not) Getting By in America (Ehrenreich), 189–190
nofollow tags, 251

O
offers, 208
one little victory, 337–340
one sentence principle, 166
1ShoppingCart.com, 14
online business success, 144–145, 148
online marketing tools, 13–14
opt-ins
    on e-commerce sites, 327
    in email marketing, 202
    on landing pages, 326
    sales letters vs., 326–327
    visitor value and, 208

organic search
    AdWords and, 335
      optimization for. *See* search engine optimization (SEO)
      pay per click (PPC) and, 243–244
Outliers (Gladwell), 283

P

page position, 77–79, 130–131, 321, 332, 335
path length, 263
peel and stick, 35–38, 324
perfect customers, 16–17
performance comparisons, 332
persistence, 237–240, 241–242
personality in advertising, 187–189, 194–196, 203, 295
persuasiveness in selling, 228–230
phrase-matched keywords, 56
Place Pages
    customer reviews on, 277, 278–280
    finding your page, 275–276
    Google maps and, 281
    negative reviews on, 278–279
    optimizing, 276–277
    star ratings on, 277
Places, 124–127
Planet Ocean, 245, 247, 252, 255, 257, 258
plus signs (+) preceding keywords, 56–57, 324
powerful keywords, 57–58. *See also* keywords
precision targeting, 213–219
pre-fab content, 146
preferred listings, 331
press releases, 254
previewing ads, 330
price-per-click, 24, 269, 294
privacy policies, 261
problem solutions, 284–286
product development, 176–177
profits, 234–236, 238–240
prospects, ideal, 16–17
psychology of keywords, 49–50

Q

Quality Scores (QS), 131–136, 321–322
quotation marks, 56, 321

R

ranking, 77–79, 130–131, 321, 332, 335
reciprocal links, 255–256
relevance, 129–131, 136–137, 201
remarketing
    advertising copy for, 271
    audiences for, 265–268, 270
    creating campaigns for, 268–271
    defined, 259–261
    landing pages for, 271
    performance indicators for, 261–265
    targeting and, 218
    terminology, 261
results, 225–226
retargeting. *See* remarketing
returning visitors, 264
review sites, 147
right-angle targeting, 163–166, 167–171
run-of-the-site links, 250

S

sales letters, 209–210, 326–327
sales messages, 229–230
sales pages, 208
salesmanship, 222–225
Scientific Advertising (Hopkins), 26
search box, 55
search engine optimization (SEO)
    basics steps for, 244–245
    getting started with, 245–246
    inbound links and. *See* inbound links
    keyword placement for, 247
    keyword selection for, 246–247
    linkbait and, 256
    local search and, 119, 257
    reciprocal links and, 255–256
    strategies for, 257–258
search process, 10–13

search strategies
    for local search, 119, 257
    for organic search. *See* organic search
"See search terms" feature, 53, 216
segmenting time, 267
self-talk, 339–340
shopping carts, 14
signature victories, 340
Site Strength Indicator (SSI) tool, 252, 255
social media
    making money with, 155–159, 161
    market research with, 159–161
    one sentence principle and, 166
    right-angle targeting with, 163–166, 167–171
    understanding audience with, 167
split testing
    ad groups, 217
    affiliates and, 237
    basics of, 32–34, 325
    improving profits with, 234–236, 238–240
    increasing click-through rate (CTR) with, 83–88
    keywords and, 240–241
    landing pages, 328
    power of, 233–234
    setting up, 85–86
    tool for, 86–87
    value per visitor (VPV) and, 207–209
    web pages, 209, 328–329
SplitTester.com, 86–87
squiggly brackets ({ }), 329–330
star ratings, 277
starting out with AdWords, 293–294, 314–315
staying power, 237–240, 241–242
stories, 338–341
suspensions, Google, 132, 146–147
synonyms, keyword, 51

T
targeting
    with headlines, 39, 59

precision, 213–219
testimonials, 254
testing. *See also* split testing
    local advertising, 124
    marketability, 173–176, 178–181
    value of, 88–94
text ads, 217
thesaurus tools, 51–52
time lag, 263–264
Traffic Estimator, 19, 329
trusted sites, 250

U
UnFair Advantage Search Engine Book (Planet Ocean), 245, 247
unique selling proposition (USP)
    advertising copy and, 190
    conveying, 186–187
    defined, 183–184
    in Google ads, 187
    identifying, 184–185
    as life skill, 189–190
    personality in, 187–189
    refining, 191
URLs, 23, 66, 218

V
value per visitor (VPV), 205–211. *See also* conversion
venture capital, 292–293
victories, 337–341
view-through conversions, 262–263
viral marketing, 256
visitors. *See also* conversion
    increasing, 265
    new vs. returning, 264
    surveying, 327–328
    value per visitor (VPV), 205–211
Visual Thesaurus, 52

W
web directories, 253
web pages, 209, 328–329
Website Optimizer, 209, 328–329

websites
    multiple, 327
    performance tracking, 264–265
    platforms for, 13
winners, 325, 339
word-of-mouth marketing, 277
Wordtracker, 47–48
Wright Brothers, 90–92
writing ads, 225–230. *See also* advertising
    copy

Here's Where You Get Your $85+ Worth of Tools and Bonus Information, Just for Purchasing This Book!

www.perrymarshall.com/supplement

Register now and you'll instantly get password access to a membership area with updates to the book. It also includes:

→ Access to Fanalytix™ software, which gives you incredibly insightful analysis of your customers, based on their Facebook profiles—this can be incredibly useful for writing ads and targeting keywords on Google

→ A "swipe file" of winning Google AdWords ads that generated hundreds of thousands to millions of clicks online—with copy ideas you can apply to your own ads

→ Guide to Google's Conversion Optimizer—make your web pages get continuously better, for free

→ A special guide to "Personality Marketing"—why it sells better than the corporate approach, and how to pull it off with style

→ $100 Credit for GoldStar Feedback software—ideal for getting consistent star-ratings and customer testimonials

→ If you're new online, you need a handful of things to be in business:

- A domain name
- A website with web pages
- An email broadcast/autoresponder service
- A shopping cart service
- A product to sell
- A Google AdWords account

The online supplement has links to dozens of resources for getting these things done, plus additional tutorials and MP3 files.

→ The entire book *Scientific Advertising* by Claude Hopkins in PDF—if you liked our "Uncle Claude Sez" sections at the end of the chapters, you'll find this 1918 classic extremely informative

→ MP3 seminars on marketing and publicity that you can load into your iPod and listen while you exercise, drive, or work around the house

→ The full contents of the interview with copywriting legend John Carlton (Chapter 23 only had room for a slice of the total conversation!)

→ An assortment of FREE keyword research tools with insightful discussion about how to use them for maximum effectiveness

→ A roundup of paid keyword research tools, with reviews of their pros and cons

→ A special report on using your AdWords skills to get clients. I have students in a half dozen countries who make six figure incomes as marketing consultants—find out how! (There's a lot of money in this business—IF you play your cards right)

→ And finally, you'll get timely email updates from Perry Marshall about Google's ever-changing system

Go to www.perrymarshall.com/supplement